WORKING WITH LLCs & FLPs

A Practitioner's Guide to Limited Liability Companies and Family Limited Partnerships

SECOND EDITION

THOMAS F. COMMITO, J.D., LL.M., CLU, CHFC

The
NATIONAL
UNDERWRITER
Company

THE NATIONAL UNDERWRITER CO. • PO BOX 14367 • CINCINNATI, OH 45250-0367
800-543-0874 • WWW.NUCO.COM

ISBN 0-87218-270-3

This publication is designed to provide accurate and authoritative information in regard to the subject matter covered. It is sold with the understanding that the publisher is not engaged in rendering legal, accounting or other professional service. If legal advice or other expert assistance is required, the services of a competent professional person should be sought. — **From a Declaration of Principles jointly adapted by a Committee of The American Bar Association and a Committee of Publishers and Associations.**

Second Edition

Printed in the United States of America

DEDICATION

To my father, Ado Commito, who has been an educator his entire life.

PREFACE AND ACKNOWLEDGEMENTS

This second edition has been expanded to include the law of Family Limited Partnerships and Family Limited Liability Companies. Thus, the material on estate planning has been significantly expanded since the first edition. Likewise, the position of LLCs has dramatically changed. At the writing of the first edition they were new and somewhat "strange." As of this edition they have become a business entity of choice in many situations. Likewise, the creativity of estate planners has expanded their application greatly.

This first edition of this book grew out of a series of lectures presented to the Estate Planning Track of the American Society of CLU & ChFC. I would like to thank all of the insurance and financial planning professionals who provided feedback on that presentation, as well as their observations and comments on the first edition.

I would also like to thank Ed Berube when he headed up CIGNA's Life insurance marketing efforts and Wes Thompson who heads up Lincoln Financial Distributors as President & CEO for all the support they provided for both the first and second editions.

The staff of the National Underwriter Company were extremely helpful and considerate during the writing and editing of this book.

Finally, the love of my wife, Jean, as well as my daughters, Kristin, Sarah, and Maura, provided the support without which this book would not have been written.

ABOUT THE AUTHOR

Thomas F. Commito is Vice President, Business & Industry Development, Lincoln Life Distributors of the Lincoln Financial Group. He is a graduate of Cornell University. He received his law degree (J.D.) from Boston College Law School and an advanced degree in law and taxation (LL.M.) from Boston University Law School. He also holds the CLU and ChFC designations.

He is licensed to practice law in Massachusetts and Vermont. In 1996, he was actively involved in the development and passage of the Vermont Limited Liability Company Act.

A well known industry speaker, he has been a featured speaker at numerous annual meetings of AALU, NALU (currently NAIFA) and the American Society National Conferences (currently Society of Financial Services Professionals), as well as MDRT. He has also been the Chairman and Moderator for numerous video teleconferences of the American Society of CLU & ChFC (currently Society of Financial Services Professionals).

Tom currently serves on the Closely Held Business Committee and also the Personal Service Organization Committee for the Section of Taxation of the American Bar Association; the Insurance Industry Committee for the Section of Antitrust of the American Bar Association; the Estate and Business Planning Committee of the AALU and the Charitable Planning Subcommittee of the AALU.

He is the author of over 50 articles on insurance and taxation. His material has appeared in the *Journal of the American Society of CLU & ChFC*, *Life Association News*, *Life Insurance Selling*, *The National Underwriter*, *Broker's World*, *Financial Planning*, *Estate & Financial Planners Quarterly*, as well as *Senior Golf*, *Dental Practice & Finance* and *Family Business*. Tom currently serves as an Assistant Editor for the *Journal of the American Society of CLU & ChFC*.

TABLE OF CONTENTS

Chapter 1

INTRODUCTION

This new, second edition updates the first volume that dealt with Limited Liability Companies and expands its contents to include Limited Partnerships, specifically Family Limited Partnerships. The reason for this is that the two subjects – Limited Liability Companies and Limited Partnerships – are so closely related that coverage in a single volume makes a great deal of sense. The second reason, and one that will be emphasized a number of times, is that the LLC is really a "super" form of the limited partnership. In a limited partnership there must be at least one general partner. That individual has personal liability – meaning that their personal assets are subject to creditor attachement – if the partnership does not have enough assets to satisfy the claim. In an LLC, the equivalent of the general partner, called the member manager, does not incur any personal liability. It is this enhancement which makes the LLC both so popular and also so similar to the limited partnerships.

Limited Partnership law is fairly old. The original act, the Uniform Limited Partnership Act, was drafted in 1916. It has been adopted by most states, though each state has generally made some customizations. In 1976, the National Conference of Commissioners on Uniform State Laws adopted the first revision of the Uniform Limited Partnership Act. The 1976 Act is known as the Revised Uniform Limited Partnership Act or "RULPA." The 1976 Act was intended to modernize the prior uniform law while retaining the special character of limited partnerships as compared with corporations. Among the goals of the Act is the maintenance of a degree of flexibility in defining the relations among the partners that is not available in the corporate form. A hallmark of limited partnership law is the relative uniformity among the states. This is to be contrasted with LLC's where little uniformity between state law exists. It is also important to note that the drafters of the Uniform Limited Partnership Act are currently proposing changes known as "Re-RULPA" which would bring the law of Limited Partnerships and Limited Liability Companies as virtually the same. For this reason, we will focus more on LLC law than on Limited Partnership law. For our purposes, we will assume that Limited Partnership state law is similar to LLC law. For taxation purposes, there should be no difference between LLC and Limited Partnership law.

The limited liability company (LLC) is the first major development in the law of business organizations since the rise of the corporation in the late nineteenth century. There has been tremendous growth in state enabling statutes in the 1990s. Only a mere handful of enabling statutes existed in 1990, whereas all states now have enabling legislation. Concomitant with state enabling legislation has been the corresponding increase in the number of businesses utilizing this form. Obviously, a critical question is – why has this growth occurred? Another way of phrasing the same question is – why are these entities so attractive?

First and foremost, as the name implies, a limited liability company provides limited liability to all of its members. In this respect it resembles a corporation. In most situations, if the corporation is sued, the assets of its individual owners (the stockholders) are insulated from attachment by corporate creditors. This is true whether the liability occurs as a result of a business dealing (contract) or as a result of an injury (tort). Second, the vast majority of LLCs operate like a partnership. This characteristic has two advantages. First, the partnership form offers extreme flexibility in operation. The owners can tailor the LLC as they see fit. Second, the partnership form can offer taxation advantages, most notably the idea that there is only a single level or "tier" of taxation. Viewed comprehensively, there is no other form of business entity that offers so many positive attributes.

A BRIEF HISTORY

The LLC form of doing business has been around for many years. The basic structure of this type of business entity is to allow business owners to formulate a business as they see fit through a valid contract. Surrounding this structure is the state statutorily providing insulation of the owner's personal assets as being beyond the scope of business creditors. This arrangement has been known for many years in such "civil law" countries as Brazil[1] and Germany.[2] Interestingly, there are a number of precursors to LLCs in the United States. In the late nineteenth century, Pennsylvania, Michigan and a few other states permitted "partnership associations" where the owners were not held personally liable for the obligations of the business. The Internal Revenue Service (IRS) has classified these partnership associations at different times as a partnership[3] and as an association taxable as a corporation.[4] In 1977, after the IRS issued its ruling classifying a partnership association as a partnership, Wyoming adopted the first statute creating an LLC.[5] However, at that time the tax status of this entity was extremely murky.

In late 1980, the IRS issued a proposed regulation[6] that basically held that no entity could be classified as a partnership if all of its owners had limited liability.[7] This proposed regulation met with a number of negative comments. Finally, in late 1982, the IRS announced that it was withdrawing the proposed regulation and would commence a study to examine the whole issue of taxation of partnership associations.[8] Shortly thereafter, Florida became the second state to adopt LLC legislation, essentially using the Wyoming statute as a model.[9] Finally, after six years of study the IRS issued an announcement to the effect that the status of a limited liability company, in and of itself, would not prevent it from being classified as a partnership.[10] This was soon followed by a revenue ruling that held a Wyoming LLC to be classified as a partnership. The rise of the LLC as a viable concept can be traced to the date that Revenue Ruling 88-76 was published.[11] This was followed by a number of private letter rulings that reinforced the concept that an LLC could be taxed as a partnership.[12] As a result of these positive developments, publicity for LLCs increased.[13] Correspondingly, four additional states adopted LLC legislation in 1991. This increased to eleven more in 1992 and eighteen more in 1993.

Finally, in the year 2000 all 50 states have enabling legislation. As states continued to adopt enabling legislation, the IRS had the opportunity to review a number of the various state statutes. This was done in a series of both published and private rulings. These rulings, which were generally most favorable, spurred other states to adopt statutes, which in turn led to more favorable IRS rulings. In January, 1995 the IRS issued Revenue Procedure 95-10 in order to eliminate the volume of ruling requests.[14] This pronouncement was designed to be the "Bible" for establishing the rules whereby everyone would understand what would be needed to establish an LLC that would be taxed either as a partnership or a C corporation. Finally, the IRS issued check-the-box regulations which greatly simply the process.[15]

APPLICABLE LAW

One of the few difficulties in working with LLCs is the fact that there is no "uniform" law governing them. To prevent confusion in many commercial areas, the National Conference of Commissioners on Uniform State Laws (NCCUSL) has proposed uniform laws that the states have adopted. For example, as discussed earlier both limited and general partnerships are governed by the uniform laws, which have been adopted in all United States jurisdictions. This ensures uniformity in legal principles that a person must learn and that apply everywhere. While there may be minor differences from state to state, on the whole, once a person learns the uniform law, he can effectively work in any state that has adopted that law. In this respect, there is no need to learn the differences of each state law.

The LLC area has grown so rapidly that in order not to be "left out" the states adopted statutes that were all different. Indeed, most states adopted statutes before the NCCUSL even had an opportunity to prepare a draft proposal of a uniform law. The net result is that no two LLC statutes are exactly the same. Those interested in LLCs must study and understand the enabling statute for their particular state. Further compounding the issue is that some states have sought to gain competitive advantage over other states in the hope of increasing revenues from filing fees when an LLC is formed. This has resulted in some states modifying their LLC statutes even though the statute may have been on the books for only a few years. While it is possible to discuss major aspects of LLC formation and operation, it is impossible to cover every state statute's nuance. Again, the individual must study the statute for each particular state.

This is not to say that a uniform LLC law will not occur. In 1992, a subcommittee of the Business Law Section of the American Bar Association completed a prototype statute. This prototype formed the basis for subsequent LLC legislation in Louisiana, Arkansas, Maine and Indiana. Likewise, the NCCUSL has also promulgated a uniform law. This law is the basis for the recently enacted legislation in Vermont.

FUNDAMENTAL CHARACTERISTICS

While each item discussed in this section will be discussed in much greater detail later in this book, it is important to point them out at this juncture so that one may understand the appeal of LLCs. A widely accepted definition of an LLC is that it is "a non-corporate business that provides its members with limited liability and allows them to participate actively in the entity's management."[16] This definition has three key elements, namely: "non-corporate elements," "limited liability," and "active participation."

Non-Corporate Elements. The LLC is *not* a corporation. It is wrong to refer to an LLC as a limited liability *corporation*. There are two key elements that distinguish an LLC from a corporation. The first distinction occurs in the areas of capital and finance. Most states impose rigorous requirements on capitalization of corporations. The capital interest must be displayed in the form of a stock certificate. These rules further require that dividends must be paid only out of corporate surplus. None of these rules apply to LLCs. Ownership interests, the disbursement of funds, capital structure and most other financial items are governed by a *contract* among the LLC owners. These provisions are not imposed by state law. This allows great flexibility in creating an LLC. It is this flexibility (and freedom from state-imposed rules and regulations) which has made LLCs appealing to entrepreneurial businesses. Likewise, there is usually less paper-work and filings required in order to form an LLC. For example, corporations generally must file by-laws with the appropriate state agency, but there is no similar requirement for an LLC.

The second non-corporate element is probably the most important as far as all of the tax reasons for forming an LLC as opposed to another business entity. The LLC is not treated as a separate tax-paying entity. The LLC will generally be treated as a partnership for federal tax purposes. As such, it will file only an "informational" return.[17] The income subject to tax will all "pass through" to the individual members. Thus, there is only one level or tier of taxation, which occurs at the owners' level.

Limited Liability: Corporations have historically been the only business organization to provide total limited liability for all of its owners. What this means is that if a corporation is sued, whether it be in contract or tort, the personal assets of the owners are immune from attachment by whomever holds a judgment against the corporation. The LLC replicates this concept. All other business organizations generally have at least one individual who is personally liable for the debts and obligations of the business.

Active Participation: LLCs may operate like a partnership, in that all members may participate in the operation of the LLC. The members can do so without losing their limited liability status. In a limited partnership, there is a trade-off between limited liability and participation. If one participates, he loses limited liability. If one wants limited liability, he must not participate in the management of the limited partnership. An LLC member may have both limited liability and participation. On the other hand, an LLC may be structured similarly to a corporation, in that management is vested in the hands of a "board" similar to a corporation's Board of Directors. This allows some members to not participate in the operational control of the LLC. One of the strengths of an LLC is that this choice is purely optional. The members who form the LLC can choose the structure that suits them best.

FAMILY LIMITED PARTNERSHIP (FLP)

A Family Limited Partnership is a most interesting vehicle. They were originally designed in the 1950's to allow for the splitting of income. At that time, income could be split among family members. Over time, this issue became less important because of a general lowering of income tax rates for all. In addition, Congress passed a provision known as the "Kiddie Tax." This provision applies only to interest and dividend income of a child under age 14. As a result, even a gift, either directly or in a partnership, of the assets that produced the income will not effectively shift the income to the child. It will be taxed at the parent's rates.[18] This provision, along with the lower rates has made the FLP no longer an income tax planning entity.

Just as the FLP was fading from view for income tax planning purposes, it became transformed into an estate planning vehicle. The reason for this is the availability of "discounts." If an individual gives a piece of property to another, it is taxed for estate or gift tax purposes at "fair market value." However, if the property is first put into an FLP and then gifts are made of the units of the partnership the property is "discounted" for federal tax purposes, since the partnership interest will have restrictions, which reduce the property's value. The utilization of an FLP and discounts is fully covered in Chapter 12.

TERMS

Like in all other human endeavors, there is a set of special terms that apply to LLCs. Fortunately, the number of special terms is small. Below is a list of some of the most important applicable terms.

Member: an owner of an LLC interest; similar to a shareholder in a corporation.

Member-Manager: a member-manager is analogous to a corporate shareholder who is on the Board of Directors. This term implies an owner (member) who also sets policy similar to that of a corporate director (manager). Generally, owners in an LLC are classified as either members or member-managers. A member is a "passive" owner, while a member-manager is an "active" owner. An LLC may be composed of all members, all member-managers, or some members and some member-managers.

Bulletproof: an LLC statute that forces the LLC to be taxed as a partnership. Early statutes, such as the original Wyoming statute, were bulletproof. If the LLC complies with the statute it will be taxed as a partnership for federal tax purposes.

Flexible: the vast majority of modern statutes are flexible in nature. This means that under the state statute the LLC may be taxed either as a corporation or a partnership for federal tax purposes. Usually, there is little to be gained in being taxed as a corporation. If one wants to be taxed as a corporation, he should just form a corporation. Under flexible statutes, care must be utilized in order to make sure the LLC is taxed as a partnership. This is generally a tightrope balancing act. One generally wants the most flexibility and the most ease in running the business, but still wants to be classified as a partnership.

Conversion: generally, this is when a partnership elects LLC status. Most states allow the partnership to simply file a document requesting LLC status. It is usually not necessary to start "from scratch" and file all the documents as a new, start-up LLC. Terminology here is confusing. Some states call the converted partnership a limited liability partnership or LLP. Some call the partnership a revised limited liability partnership or RLLP. Still others call it simply an LLC, just like a new, start-up LLC.

Limited Liability Partnership: approximately 37 states now have limited liability partnership statutes. In general, these states have taken the Uniform Limited Partnership Act (ULPA) and included limited liability for all partners.[19] In many respects this results in an entity similar to early LLCs in that the entity must be classified as a partnership because of inflexible operating rules and little opportunity for the owners to create operating rules outside those dictated by statute. As such, this legislation is useful for a partnership that wants to convert from an entity where one or more partners have unlimited liability. Rather than having to completely redo all the paperwork, these states allow the partnership to convert to an LLC-type organization. Since under these conversion statutes the entity is still technically a partnership, it is called an LLP or limited liability partnership. In general, one forming a new entity will prefer the flexibility of being an LLC and will usually not choose to form an LLP over an LLC.

Limited Liability Vehicle: a number of people are using this term as an umbrella to cover the various terminologies used in different states. It encompasses LLCs, LLPs, RLLPs, Professional LLCs, etc. The tax treatment of all of these entities is virtually the same and they all work in essentially the same manner. The term limited liability vehicle is a good term since it includes all of the sub-terms set out above and eliminates trying to keep track of all the different terms used in various jurisdictions.

Professional LLC: a number of states have special rules for professionals such as accountants, lawyers, or insurance agents who wish to form an LLC. Some states simply call this professional organization an LLC. Other states call it a PLLC or professional limited liability company, while a few others call it a professional limited liability partnership or PLLP. Other states have no special rules for professional organizations and they are simply covered under the "regular" LLC statute. In any case, a professional LLC operates just like a regular LLC. Special rules and the question of liability are discussed in further detail in Chapter 9.

Default Statute: the modern approach to state statutes is to allow the members of an LLC to create their own operating rules and structure through an operating agreement. If they fail to cover a particular point (either intentionally or unintentionally) then the statute comes into play and provides the missing piece or pieces. The statute's provisions become operative only if the contract among the members of the LLC does not cover an item that is covered by the default provisions of the governing statute.

FOOTNOTE REFERENCES

1. See Let. Rul. 8003072, which discusses a "limited" organization under Brazilian law.
2. See Let. Rul. 8221136, which discusses a German LLC.
3. Let. Rul. 7505290310A.
4. Let. Rul. 7102100370A.
5. W.S.A. §§17-15-101 to -143.
6. Former Prop. Reg. §301.7701-2.
7. Apparently the IRS was concerned more about "close" corporations, and making sure that they would be taxed as corporations. See Letter Ruling 7921084, which held that a close corporation could never be classified as a partnership.
8. IR-82-145 (12/16/82).
9. F.S.A. §§608.401 to 608.514.
10. Announcement 88-76, 1988-18 IRB 44.
11. 1988-2 CB 360.
12. Among these rulings are Let. Ruls. 9119029, 9030013, 9029019, 9010027, 8937010.
13. See for example, Tannenbaum, J.A. "States Are Sanctioning New Form of Business," *The Wall Street Journal*, July 17, 1992 at page B1.
14. 1995-1 CB 501. The Revenue Procedure was actually made public on December 28, 1994 under 26 C.F.R. 601.201.
15. The regulations are discussed extensively in Chapter 2.
16. Keatinge, R.R., et al, "The Limited Liability Company: A Study of the Emerging Entity," *Business Lawyer*, Volume 47, Number 2 (Feb., 1992) at page 384.
17. Usually IRS Form 1065. Information from this form is disbursed to each individual member of the LLC. This is done through giving each member a Schedule K-1. In all aspects this is analogous to a partnership.
18. IRC Sec. 1(g).
19. See Louisiana (LSA-RS §9:3431, et seq.); Texas (Texas R.U.L.P.A. at T.R.C.S.A. Art. 6132b-3.08(1)); District of Columbia (D.C. Code §41-151.1 et seq.).

Chapter 2

FEDERAL INCOME TAXATION: CLASSIFICATION ISSUES

INTRODUCTION

As was discussed previously, an LLC may be taxed either as a corporation or a partnership. Likewise, even though a partnership is a partnership for state law purposes, it also may be classified as a corporation or partnership for taxation purposes. In virtually all situations the choice will be to tax the LLC and the Limited Partnership as a partnership. Not only does a partnership offer more flexibility, it also allows for only one level of taxation. Prior to 1986, a corporation could distribute appreciated property to its shareholders and avoid paying capital gains tax at the corporate level.[1] The Tax Reform Act of 1986 eliminated this exception so that in virtually all situations involving corporate distributions there is a double tax. The corporation first pays tax on income when it is received. Then, when the proceeds are distributed to the shareholders there is a second tax, which is paid by the shareholders. Generally, the corporation does not get a deduction when it distributes proceeds to the shareholders.[2] Thus, there are two complete taxes – one at the corporate level and another at the shareholder level. A partnership, on the other hand, is not a taxable entity. It is merely a "passthrough" where all of the tax effects at the partnership level are reflected in the personal tax returns of the partners.[3] This can result in substantial tax savings, as demonstrated in the following example.

Example: Acme Corporation has a piece of capital gains property that has a basis of $0. The corporation sells this property for $1,000 and distributes the net proceeds, after tax, to Irv Investor, a shareholder. Assuming that both Acme and Irv are in the top marginal brackets respectively, what is the net proceeds after tax left in Irv's hands?

Corporate Tax:

Amount Realized:	$1000
Basis	0
Taxable Gain:	$1000
Tax @ 35%	350
Net to ACME	$ 650

Personal Tax to Irv:

Amount Distributed	$650.00
Tax @ 39.6%	257.40
Net to Irv:	$392.60

Effective Tax Rate — Corporate and Personal = 60.74%

Now let us assume everything is the same, except that Acme is a partnership:

Amount Realized:	$1000
Basis:	0
Gain:	$1000
Tax @ 28%[4]	280
Net to Irv	$ 720

Effective Tax Rate — 28%
Tax Savings — $327.40 (32.74%)

Besides being a much easier calculation, the single tier of taxation represented by the partnership results in a very substantial tax savings. The amount retained through the partnership tax treatment is almost double the tax treatment that occurs because of the double taxation occurring through the corporation.

HISTORICAL BACKGROUND

The classification of business entities for taxation purposes has a long, and somewhat complicated history. For many years, it was among the most complicated problems facing a person who wished to create an LLC or an FLP. Fortunately, new regulations, known as the "Check-the-Box" regulations have ameliorated the problem. A brief overview of the prior structure and format of business classification may be useful. The Internal Revenue Code contains a plethora of different taxation schemes for different types of business entities.[5] The most important and most common entity classification problem involves the difference between a partnership and a corporation. Obviously, corporations are taxed as corporations under the Internal Revenue Code. For this purpose, the Supreme Court basically established the rules for classification purposes. It said that a corporation is a legally formed entity under state corporate law organized to carry out a legal business.[6] However, business organizations that are not legally incorporated may be taxed as an "association." An association is an organization whose attributes require that it be taxed as a corporation rather than another type of organization such as a trust or a partnership. In *Morrissey v. Commissioner*, the Supreme Court held that a trust could be classified as an association and hence taxable as a corporation.[7] The key to this treatment was that the trust possessed the attributes of a corporation. The tests of *Morrissey* were later modified and enhanced in a series of regulations. These regulations once were critical to the assessment of whether an organization will be taxed as a partnership or a corporation.[8]

These former regulations identified six characteristics that are normally found in corporations. These are:[9]

- associates;
- an objective to carry on a business;
- continuity of life;
- centralized management;
- limited liability;
- free transferability of interests.

The meaning of each of these characteristics was the subject of much case law and IRS rulings and regulations.

As LLC statutes sprang up in the states, the IRS began addressing the question of whether an LLC could be taxed as a corporation or a partnership on a state by state basis in revenue rulings. Then the IRS issued Revenue Procedure 1995-10, 1995-1 CB 501, creating safe harbor rules for having an LLC taxed as a partnership. Finally, the IRS issued the "check-the-box" regulations, which essentially allow an individual to simply choose the method of taxation desired, whether as a partnership or a corporation.

"CHECK-THE-BOX" REGULATIONS

There were many problems with regards to classification under prior law. Fortunately, the former system was discontinued and a new system instituted that is much more efficient. On March 29, 1995, the IRS announced that it was considering a simple and radical alternative to the former classification test system.[10] This new approach would allow individuals to simply choose which form of taxation they desire, regardless of the criteria involved. Under this approach, all unincorporated businesses would be taxed as partnerships, unless they "check-the-box" to be taxed as a corporation on an IRS form. On May 13, 1996, the IRS issued new regulations outlining this check-the-box concept.[11] These regulations met with almost unanimous approval, and were finalized for entities created on or after January 1, 1997.[12] The structure of the new regulations is in essence a flow diagram. By a process of elimination, one is able to reach the point of electing a certain organization classification.

Under the explanation section of the new regulations, it is pointed out that "many states have revised their statutes to provide that partnerships and other unincorporated organizations may possess characteristics that traditionally have been associated with corporations, thereby narrowing considerably the traditional distinctions between corporations and partnerships, under local law."[13]

The explanation then points out that this blurring of traditional classification issues has resulted in the need for more and more sophisticated legal assistance to obtain the desired taxation result. As stated in the new regulations, "small business organizations may lack the resources and expertise to achieve the tax classification they want under current classification regulations."[14]

To alleviate these problems, the new regulations state "[i]n light of these developments, Treasury and the IRS believe that it is appropriate to replace the increasingly formalistic rules under the current regulations with a much simpler approach that generally is elective."[15]

Under the regulatory framework, it is important to determine if the organization is an "entity" as defined in the new regulations. Under the new regulations, "certain joint undertakings" are considered to be entities.[16] The new regulations go on to further expand this concept. The new regulations point out that "[a] joint venture or other contractual arrangement may create a separate entity for federal tax purposes, if the participants carry on a trade, business, financial operation, or venture and divide the profits therefrom."[17] It is important to contrast this with the former regulation. The former regulation made no mention of a "contractual arrangement" as potentially creating an entity. Presumably this was meant to specifically include LLCs, even if they were not joint ventures. Since an LLC would be created pursuant to a contractual arrangement (i.e., the operating agreement), the net effect is that this provision would clearly apply to LLCs, as well as expand the original definition.

The former regulations listed a series of organizations (such as a "pool") through which a "business, financial operation or venture" is carried on.[18] The new regulations obviously omit the examples in the former regulations. The new regulations also add "trade" to the basic definition, again signaling an expansive view of organizations that may qualify as entities. The new regulations also point out that in order to be considered an entity for federal tax purposes, those engaging in a "joint undertaking" must "divide the profits" therefrom.[19] This clause did not exist in the former version of the regulations, though it was clearly indicated as being a factor in the examples that accompanied the former regulations. These examples are carried over from the former regulations to the new regulations. In one example, two or more property owners who dig a ditch to drain surface water from their properties are not considered to be an entity for federal tax purposes.[20] Presumably, while the digging of a ditch is a joint venture, since there is no direct profit motive, the activity does not reach the level of being an entity.

Under the new regulations, once an entity exists, it is germane to determine if it is a business entity or some other kind of entity. Under the new regulations, all entities are business entities unless they are trusts.[21] Under the regulation, the key is whether or not the beneficiaries of the trust are completely passive. The regulation states that "[g]enerally speaking, an arrangement will be treated as a trust under the Internal Revenue Code if it can be shown that the purpose of the arrangement is to vest in trustees responsibility for the protection and conservation of property for beneficiaries who cannot share in the discharge of this responsibility and, therefore, are not associates in a joint enterprise for the conduct of business for profit."[22] In addition, the purpose of the trust must involve an emphasis on conservation of property as opposed to generating income or profits.

If the entity is not a trust, as defined by the regulations, then it is a business entity. Once in the realm of business entities, it is important to determine if the entity is one that will automatically be classified as a corporation. Under the new regulations, a corporation includes any business that is organized under a federal, state, or federally recognized Indian tribal law, that refers to the entity as a corporation.[23] In other words, if the entity is a corporation under state, federal or Indian tribal law, it must be treated as a corporation for federal taxation purposes. The new regulations' explanation points out that this includes national banking associations, along with such federal entities as the Student Loan Marketing Association. Another entity that must be classified as a corporation is a joint-stock company.[24] Again, this type of organization is the creature of a state enabling act and possesses such corporate attributes as a board of directors and shares of stock represented by certificates.

Insurance companies must be taxed as corporations under the new regulations.[25] For this purpose, an insurance company is defined as an entity that is taxable as such under Chapter 1, Subchapter L of the Internal Revenue Code. Likewise, state chartered banks must be taxed as corporations. The actual language of the new regulations shows an interesting interrelationship among various federal statutes. The new regulations provide that a state chartered bank must be characterized as a corporation if any of its deposits are insured by the Federal Deposit Insurance Corporation (FDIC).[26] The reason for this requirement is that in order to be eligible for federal deposit insurance, the bank must be a corporation under the banking statutes.[27]

Thus, the new regulations close the loop and provide that such a bank must be classified as a corporation. Another stated reason for this treatment is comparability. Since federally chartered banks must be corporations, this simply brings parity among banks by mandating similar rules to state chartered banks.

The new regulations also classify entities that are wholly owned by the state or any subdivision of the state as corporations.[28] Organizations wholly owned by the state that are not part of the basic functions of the state must be examined under Code section 115 and must be recognized as separate entities. Regardless of the fact that the income may or may not be taxable under Code section 115, the entity must be a corporation in all circumstances. An example of an entity falling under this provision would be a municipal utility such as an electric company or water company. The definition of a corporation for tax purposes also includes a cross reference provision that states if any other section of the Internal Revenue Code mandates that an entity be classified as a corporation then it will be classified as such under the new regulations.[29] Finally, the new regulations contain a laundry list of foreign entities that will be taxed in the United States as corporations.[30] The organizations listed are all entities that have limited liability under the laws of their respective countries.

If a business entity does not fall into any of the above categories, then it may be treated as a partnership. In essence, the partnership form of taxation becomes the default provision. In other words, if one does nothing, one will be taxed as a partnership. This default provision is described in the explanation to the new regulations as follows: "The new regulations are designed to provide most eligible entities with the classification they would choose without requiring them to file an election. Thus, the new regulations provide default classification rules that aim to match expectations. An eligible entity that wants the default classification need not file an election."

Under these default rules, if the business does not fit into any other category and it possesses at least two or more members, then it will be treated as a partnership.[31] If there is only a single member to the entity, then it will be treated as a sole proprietorship for taxation purposes.[32]

In the alternative, an organization that would be classified as a partnership or as a sole proprietorship may elect to be taxed as a corporation. The entities that may file such an election are referred to as "eligible entities."[33] Again, this applies to an entity that would normally be a partnership and has two or more members, or a sole proprietorship that has a single member. The only choice under the election scenario is for either of these organizations to elect corporate taxation. The new regulations provide that the election is to be filed on Form 8832.[34] The form would be filed at the IRS service center where the entity would normally file its income tax return. The information requested on the form includes be the name, address, taxpayer identification number, the chosen classification, whether this choice is a change from an existing classification, and whether the entity is a foreign or domestic entity.

One issue that arose after the IRS published the original notice of the check-the-box concept was whether all members of the entity would be required to sign the election. In other words, would unanimous consent be required in order to elect corporate taxation? The new regulations provide two alternatives in this regard. First, the election may be accomplished if all members of an "electing eligible entity" indicate that they wish the entity to be taxed as a corporation.[35] The second methodology is simply to have any authorized officer, manager, or owner make the election.[36] In any case, the new regulations specify that the entity provide an employer identification number (EIN) on the election form. If an entity does not have an EIN at the time of filing, it must have at least simultaneously applied for an EIN through the filing of an appropriate SS-4.

With regard to the election, the new regulations basically provide that it cannot be changed for five years (60 months).[37] This 60-month limitation applies only to a change in classification. Thus, if a new eligible entity files an initial election that is not a "change," then the 60-month limitation does not apply. Similarly, if the business from an electing eligible entity is transferred to another entity, the 60-month limitation does not apply. Likewise, an existing entity that changes its classification when the new regulations become final is deemed not to make a change, and the election is deemed to be the same as if it were a new business electing an initial classification. In other words, it will be free to change again within 60 months.

Figure 2.01 is a "flow chart" that illustrates the steps in entity classification under the new check-the-box regulations.

Figure 2.01

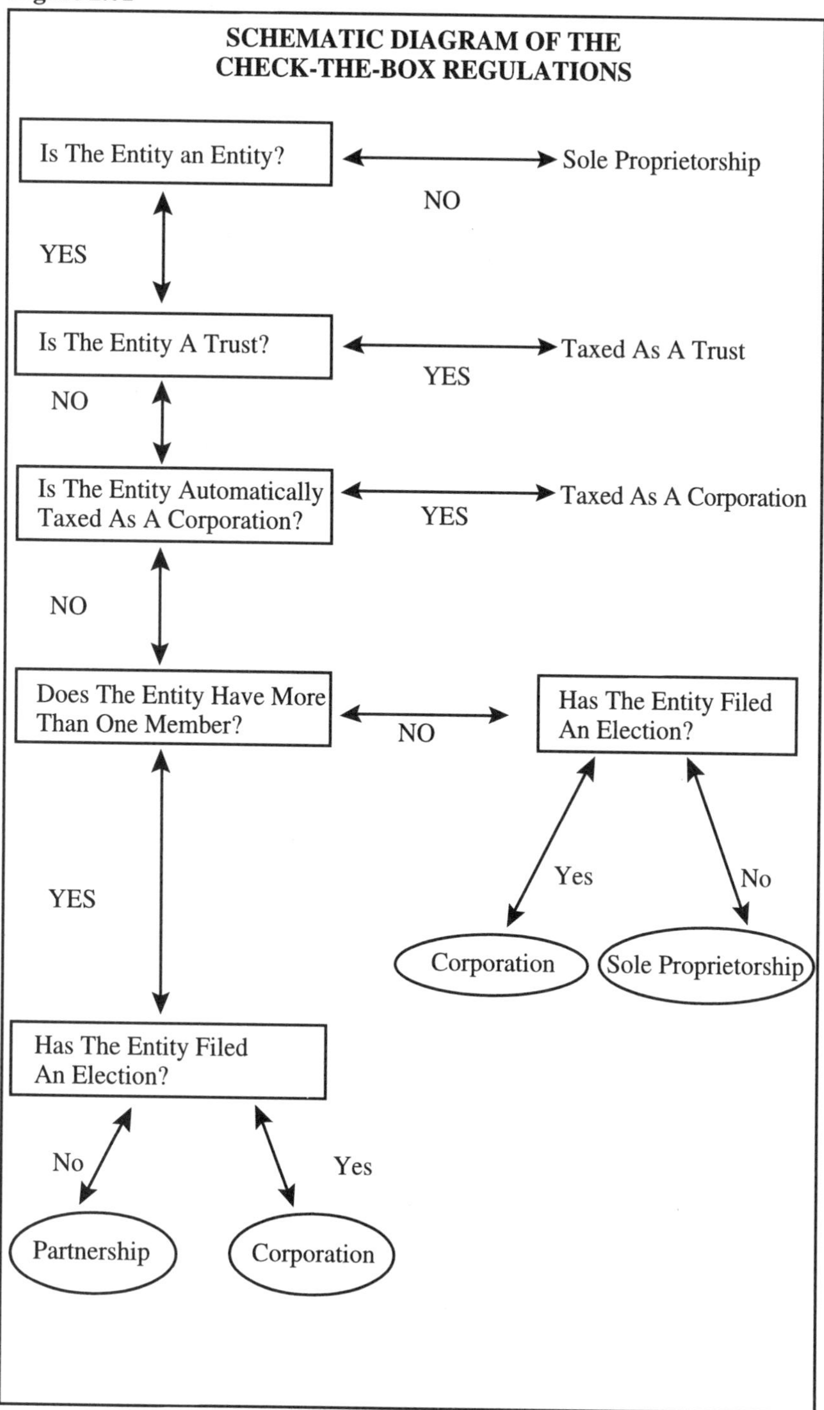
SCHEMATIC DIAGRAM OF THE
CHECK-THE-BOX REGULATIONS
Is The Entity an Entity?
Sole Proprietorship
NO
YES
Is The Entity A Trust?
Taxed As A Trust
YES
NO
Is The Entity Automatically Taxed As A Corporation?
Taxed As A Corporation
YES
NO
Does The Entity Have More Than One Member?
NO
Has The Entity Filed An Election?
Yes
No
Corporation
Sole Proprietorship
YES
Has The Entity Filed An Election?
No
Yes
Partnership
Corporation

The Impact of the New Regulations

The new regulations have succeeded in their goals. One of the prime concerns under the former regulations was that the IRS was continually flooded with ruling requests on the issue of classification. Because of the simplicity and effectiveness of the new regulations this has ceased and there are virtually no ruliungs which need to be issued on the classification issue. The idea of making it easier to form an LLC or FLP has been accomplished.

An Exciting Concept: Single Member LLCs Under the New Regulations

As was discussed above, an on-going concern has been the issue of single member LLCs. The newer state statutes permit single member LLCs, but the IRS has never classified such an organization as a partnership. The new classification regulations have an interesting and effective solution to this problem.

Under the new regulations "single owner organizations" are afforded their own special rules.[38] Under these rules, a single member organization may elect to be taxed as a corporation. On the other hand, the single member organization may elect not to be taxed as an "entity."[39] In such a case, the LLC would be taxed as a sole proprietorship. This is a positive result. Most of the sole proprietorship rules will be similar to the partnership rules. There will be a single level of taxation and the basis rules will be very similar.

The LLC would be valid under state law. Thus, the sole member will have the limited liability afforded the LLC form of organization. On the other hand, there will be only one tier of taxation. Thus, while not classified as a partnership, the organization will be valid, will achieve limited liability, and will achieve a single level of taxation and flexibility. Thus, in a round about way, the new regulations should open the door for single member LLCs. Thus, a single member LLC, where permitted by the local law, becomes a most effective organization. Limited Liability accrues to the owner of the LLC. On the other hand, it is taxed as a sole proprietorship. This means that the owner can still file a Schedule C for purposes of Form 1040. Schedule C is much more simple than filing a partnership or corporate return.

Another area of interest relates to the assignment of income problem that sometimes affects financial planners and commission based sellers of financial products. A number of financial service companies, particularly thosed regulated by the Securities and Exchange commission, pay commissions only to an individual. They are prohibited from paying an "entity" unless the "entity" is licensed as a broker dealer. On the other hand, the individual broker or planner will usually have a business entity. This entity is useful to the planner because it affords the opportunity to provide the planner with fringe benefits. The tactic that would appear to solve the problem would be to simply endorse the commission check over to the business entity. The problem with this is the case of *Helvering v. Eubank*.[40] In this case an agent tried to assign his renewal commissions to a corporation. The Supreme Court held that this constituted "assignment of income"

The Court established the following rule in the companion case of *Helvering v. Horst*.[41]

> The power to dispose of income is the equivalent of ownership of it. The exercise of that power to procure the payment of income to another is the enjoyment and hence the realization of the income by him who exercises it. We have had no difficulty in applying that proposition where the assignment preceded the rendition of the services, [cite omitted] for it was recognized ... that in such a case the rendition of the service by the assignor was the means by which the income was controlled by the donor and of making his assignment effective. But it is the assignment by which the disposition of income is controlled when the service precedes the assignment and in both cases it is the exercise of the power of disposition of the interest or compensation with the resulting payment to the donee which is the enjoyment by the donor of income derived from them.

Thus, the income earned is taxed to the earner, and in essence cannot be assigned. This is not an issue that has been relegated to history. Periodically, the issue reappears in the court system. For example, in the case of *Hagy v. U.S.*,[42] an agent for Massachusetts Mutual attempted to assign commissions to his corporation. The Court rejected this approach on the following four grounds:

> First, Hagy had no employment contract with the Hagy Agency. The Hagy Agency could not force Hagy to sell for Massachusetts Mutual or for any other company. It simply had the purported right to receive any commission income Hagy received from Massachusetts Mutual.
>
> Second, there was no contract between Massachusetts Mutual and the Hagy Agency. To the contrary, Massachusetts Mutual refused to contract with the Hagy Agency.
>
> Third, although the Hagy Agency was organized, according to its articles of incorporation, to sell "all lines of insurance," Hagy earned and deposited in his personal account commissions from companies other than Massachusetts Mutual. Although he deposited all of the commissions from Massachusetts Mutual in the Hagy Agency's account, he was free to devote his time to selling in his discretion either Massachusetts Mutual policies or the policies of the other companies. If his arrangement was recognized for tax purposes, Hagy easily could manipulate his personal earned income by selling more Massachusetts Mutual policies and assigning his commissions to the Hagy Agency. For that matter, Hagy could set up as many corporations as he desired, limited only by the number of insurance companies for which be sells. Then, he could deflect and dilute earned income by selling various companies' policies and assigning the commissions to his various corporations.
>
> Fourth, Hagy has demonstrated the irrelevance of his corporations to the Massachusetts Mutual business. Originally, Hagy assigned his "career contract for full-time agents" to Mountaineer. Later, he simply terminated the assignment to Mountaineer and reassigned the contract to the Hagy Agency under a written assignment identical in all respects to the original assignment to Mountaineer. Expedience, likewise, presumably would permit him to terminate the assignment to the Hagy Agency and reassign it to another

> closely held corporation. Thus, whatever theoretical legal rights and obligations that might have arisen by virtue of the assignments clearly have been subordinated to Hagy's overriding control as shareholder, officer and director.

In a more recent case, *Zaal v. Commissioner*,[43] the Tax Court also had the opportunity to examine the same issue. The Court followed the "assignment of income concept, expressing it as follows:

> An individual cannot escape tax on income to which he is entitled by "turning his back" upon that income. If he has received the income or had a right to receive the income, he is taxable thereon.

Thus, "assignment of income" doctrine apparently blocks the strategy of assigning the income to the business entity. This is where the single member LLC solves the problem. Under the new regulations, a single member LLC is "disregarded" for tax purposes.[44] If the LLC is disregarded, then it cannot be an assignee of income. The net effect is that the assignment of income doctrine will be totally inapplicable. Yet the money will reside in the LLC. As such, it will be afforded protection from creditors. In addition, it will be available for fringe benefits. Thus, a single member LLC uniquely solves this problem.

Given the importance of these new regulations, they are reproduced in their entirety in Appendix E.

FOOTNOTE REFERENCES

1. This exception was established in the case of *General Utilities & Operating Co. v. Helvering*, 296 U.S. 200 (1935). The principles of the case were codified in the 1954 Internal Revenue Code, particularly in Sections 311 and 336 of that Code. Starting in 1962, virtually every tax act eroded some part of the doctrine. Finally, in 1985 a complete repeal was proposed in the Tax Reform Bill of 1985. This bill was never enacted, but was carried over into 1986 where it became part of the Tax Reform Act of 1986, P.L. 99-514.
2. It would generally be characterized as a dividend under Code section 316(a) and would not be deductible since it is a distribution of property.
3. Code section 701 states in its entirety "A partnership as such shall not be subject to the income tax imposed by this chapter. Persons carrying on business as partners shall be liable for income tax only in their separate or individual capacities."
4. The maximum individual tax rate on capital gains is 28%. See IRC Sec. 1(h).
5. Among the different types of entities are: sole proprietorship; joint venture; partnership; trust; association (corporation); S corporation; real estate investment trust

(REIT); regulated investment company (RIC); real estate mortgage investment conduit (REMIC); domestic international sales corporation (DISC); controlled foreign corporation (CFC); foreign sales corporation (FSC); an insurance company; a bank; a credit union; a tax exempt entity; a cooperative. This list is meant to be demonstrative and is not inclusive of all the different types of entities available.

6. *Moline Properties v. Comm.*, 319 U.S. 436 (1943).
7. 296 U.S. 344 (1935).
8. The regulations were former Regs. §§301.7701-2 and 301.7701-3. These regulations were sometimes referred to as the *Morrissey* regulations.
9. All are discussed in former Reg. §301.7701-2.
10. Notice 95-14, 1995-1 CB 297.
11. 61 Fed. Reg. 21989 (May 13, 1996).
12. TD 8697 (12/17/96).
13. Regs. §§301.7701-1 through 301.7701-3 (introduction and explanation of provisions).
14. Regs. §§301.7701-1 through 301.7701-3 (introduction and explanation of provisions).
15. Regs. §§301.7701-1 through 301.7701-3 (introduction and explanation of provisions).
16. Reg. §301.7701-1(a)(2).
17. Reg. §301.7701-1(a)(2).
18. Reg. §301.7701-3(a).
19. Reg. §301.7701-1(a)(2).
20. Reg. §301.7701-1(a)(2) and Reg. §301.7701-3(a).
21. Reg. §301.7701-2(a).
22. Reg. §301.7701-4(a).
23. Reg. §301.7701-2(b)(1).
24. Reg. §301.7701-2(b)(3).
25. Reg. §301.7701-2(b)(4).
26. Reg. §301.7701-2(b)(5).
27. 12 U.S.C. 1813(a)(2)
28. Reg. §301.7701-2(b)(6).
29. Reg. §301.7701-2(b)(7).
30. Reg. §301.7701-2(b)(8).
31. Reg. §301.7701-3(b)(1)(i).
32. Reg. §301.7701-3(b)(1)(ii).
33. Reg. §301.7701-3(a).
34. Reg. §301.7701-3(c).
35. Reg. §301.7701-3(c)(2)(i)(A).
36. Reg. §301.7701-3(c)(2)(i)(B).
37. Reg. §301.7701-3(c)(1)(v).
38. Reg. §301.7701-1(a)(4).
39. Reg. §301.7701-3(a).
40. 311 US 122 (1940).
41. 311 US 111 (1940).
42. 91-2 USTC ¶50,461 (WD VA, 1991).
43. TC Memo 1998-222.
44. Reg. §301.7701-3(b)(1)(ii).

Chapter 3

FEDERAL TAX ISSUES: OPERATING THE LLC OR FLP

OVERVIEW

As described in Chapter 2, most LLCs or FLPs will be taxed as partnerships. This chapter examines the consequences of such classification. It will focus on the many positive features that occur as a result of partnership taxation. It is not, however, meant to be a treatise on partnership taxation. For that, readers are directed to any number of fine works that comprehensively cover all aspects of partnership taxation.

The basic system of partnership taxation is that of being a "passthrough" entity. This system of taxation that is the foundation of passthrough tax treatment under Subchapter K for partnerships works, in general, in this way: Partners are required to report their share of the partnership's income and loss (determined by reference to the operating agreement). To ensure that earnings are not taxed twice, each partner's basis is adjusted to reflect undistributed profits. And if a partner sells his interest in the partnership, the partnership's bases in its assets are adjusted so that gains implicitly taxed to the partners will not be taxed again to the partnership. Partnership income is taxed at the earlier of when profit is realized at the partner or partnership level, and then basis is adjusted to prevent the same gain from being taxed when the funds are actually distributed to the partner.

The complex elements of this system of taxation include:

- Determining each investor's share of the entity's income and loss

- Making the necessary basis adjustments so that all income (and loss) is taxed once and only once.

To accomplish these goals, the rules of partnership taxation must require that basis rules work together with recognition rules to ensure that income is taxed only one time. Rules are also introduced to prevent what are potential abuses and schemes. Among the goals of these various rules is the intent to prevent such abuses as the conversion of ordinary income into capital gain, the conversion of capital loss into ordinary deduction, the acceleration of deductions and the deferral of income, and the shifting of income among taxpayers.

Partnerships are passthrough entities and therefore not subject to direct taxation. Instead, the partners must report and assume liability for their share of the partnership's gain or loss.[1] Avoiding an "entity" level tax ensures that income flowing into a partnership is taxed only once. As such, partnership taxation involves essentially a two-step process. First, a partnership must compute its taxable income as if it were an individual, but with certain adjustments for being a partnership.[2] Although partnerships are not directly subject to tax liability, this step is necessary to analyze the taxable activities in which a partnership entity is involved in order to determine the tax liabilities of the entity's partners. After the partnership's taxable income is computed, the income is allocated among the various partners for inclusion in their individual tax returns. This step is usually determined as part of the operating agreement. It is important to note that the amount that each partner must include in his individual tax return (known as the partner's "distributive share") may not equal the amount the partner actually receives. For example, a partnership agreement might provide that no funds are to be distributed to any partner during the first three years of the partnership, without the approval of the general partner or partners. Even though there will be no distributions during these years, as the partnership earns (or loses) income, the partners must include (or deduct) the amount on their individual tax returns.

There are two ways to allocate partnership income among the partners. Either a designated percentage of each item of the partnership's gross income, deduction, credit, and loss can be allocated to each partner, or a percentage of the partnership's net income, can be allocated to each partner. In fact, the Internal Revenue Code actually uses both of these methods. Some taxation items pass through to the partners as individual items and others are combined into one net figure. Generally, most items are netted. However, there are important exceptions. For example, charitable contributions are passed through on a gross basis and not on a net basis. The reason for this is that under Code section 170(b)(1)(A), such a contribution generally is deductible up to 50 percent of a taxpayer's adjusted gross income. As a result, the extent to which the partnership's contribution is deductible cannot be ascertained without knowing each partner's adjusted gross income as well as all other charitable contributions made by (or allocable to) each partner. Because the status of the partnership's contribution is dependent upon a nonpartnership tax item appearing on a partner's individual tax return, the charitable contribution is not combined with other taxable partnership items. Instead, the contribution amount is allocated as a "separately stated" item among the partners.

Once each partner's share of the partnership's income, deductions, credits, and loss is allocated, certain basis adjustments are necessary to ensure that "double taxation" of partnership income does not occur. The following sections discuss these adjustments as they relate to four basic transactions in the life of a partnership:

- Formation
- Recognition of gain (or loss)
- Current (or "non –liquidating" distributions
- Liquidating distributions (liquidation of the partnership and/or sales of partnership interests).

FORMATION

Under Code section 721(a), a contribution of property to an LLC or FLP classified as a partnership is a "nonrecognition" event. By nonrecognition event, it is meant that any gain (or loss) inherent in the property is not taxed. A key advantage to partnership taxation is that it is easier to qualify for nonrecognition treatment of property contributed to a partnership, as opposed to a corporation. This section is much simpler than Code section 351, which governs nonrecognition in the corporate setting. Code section 351 requires that the transferors be in control after the property is transferred.

Property may include many various items. It is important to note that trade secrets and business processes may constitute property.[3]

In the estate planning context, property may also be transferred to an LLC OR FLP formed for purposes similar to a family limited partnership (FLP). More will be discussed on this topic in Chapter 10, which deals with estate planning considerations. Here, it is important to realize that transfers to investment companies lose the tax-free transfer exemption under Code section 721(b). Such transfers become taxable upon the transfer into the LLC OR FLP. An investment company is one that has more than 80% of its assets in marketable stocks, mutual funds or REITs.[4] In order to be an investment company, the transfer must also be an attempt to diversify the portfolio of the transferors. Diversification occurs when "two or more persons transfer non-identical assets."[5] The IRS utilizes a broad definition of non-identical assets. In one revenue ruling, the transfer of cash and stock in a single corporation was held to be a diversification attempt.[6]

Of great importance in many start-up LLCs or FLPs is the contribution of services in exchange for an interest in the LLC or FLP. If the transfer of services is for an immediate interest in the capital of the LLC or FLP, then the transfer is taxable.[7] However, the IRS has held that the transfer will be tax-free if the exchange for services will result in the receipt of an interest in *future appreciation* or *future profits*. This exception that the transfer of services for future profits will not be a taxable exchange, will be disregarded in three circumstances: (1) if the profits result from a substantially certain and predictable income stream from items such as interest bearing securities; or (2) if the LLC or FLP member disposes of the interest exchanged for services within two years of the transfer; or (3) if the profits interest is that of a limited partner in a publicly traded partnership. If any of these occur, the transfer will be taxable.[8]

Another exception to the rule that transfers to an LLC or FLP will be tax-free occurs when the transfer is deemed to be a disguised sale. If within two years from the transfer of property a member receives cash or other consideration, the transfer is presumed to be a disguised sale of property where the LLC or FLP is a mere conduit. This presumption may be rebutted if the member is able to demonstrate that the "facts and circumstances clearly indicate" that the transfers were not part of a sale.[9]

If contributed property is subsequently sold, the contributing member will generally be taxed on the gain from the sale.[10] If the property is not sold, but is distributed to another member within seven years from the date of contribution, then the original contributing member will report the gain inherent in the property.[11]

The basic basis rules for a member are contained in a number of Internal Revenue Code provisions. The initial starting point for basis is equal to cash and the adjusted basis of property contributed (as described above).[12] Basis is then increased by the income of the LLC or FLP attributable to the member.[13] An LLC or FLP may make tax-free distributions up to a member's basis. The reason for this rule is that the member has already paid the tax on any income and hence there is no further tax on distribution.[14] When distributions are in fact made, they, of course, reduce basis.[15]

Debt serves to complicate this picture somewhat. A member's basis will include his share of the debt of an LLC or FLP.[16] The analogy is that an increase in a member's share of LLC or FLP debt is the same as a cash contribution. Likewise, if a member's share of debt is reduced, this is treated the same as a cash distribution.[17] Critical here is whether the debt is recourse or nonrecourse debt. Recourse debt is defined as debt where the member may be held personally liable.[18] A member's share of recourse debt is equal to the amount of debt for which he bears the economic loss.[19] A member will bear the economic loss if he is required to make payments on the debt upon liquidation of the LLC or FLP without a right of reimbursement from other members.[20] Nonrecourse debt is debt where no member is personally liable.[21]

The general principle of debt, and the underlying theme, is that debt is shared by all members of the LLC or FLP. If a member contributes property that is subject to recourse liability and the member retains the liability, then the basis of the member's interest in the LLC or FLP is increased by the liability. In this situation, the debt is not shared and hence serves to increase the basis of the member who retained the obligation. The result is the same if the LLC or FLP is the debtor and the recourse liability accrues to a single member. If on the other hand, a member contributes property with a recourse obligation to him and either the LLC or FLP relieves him of the obligation, or another member relieves him of the obligation, the transferor may have taxable gain. For example, suppose member A contributes property with a basis of $50 and with $100 of recourse debt. Assume member B assumes the recourse obligation. In this case, A is assumed to have received $100 through the relinquishment of the debt. Since the $100 exceeds his or her basis by $50, the member will be deemed to have $50 in gain.[22]

In the more likely scenario, debt of an LLC or FLP will be nonrecourse debt since the debtor is the LLC or FLP and all members of the LLC or FLP will have limited liability. This means that no member will be individually liable for the debt. In general, nonrecourse liabilities are deemed to be shared by members in a percentage equal to each member's share of profits or losses.[23] To the extent that a member contributes property with nonrecourse debt and is relieved of a percentage of that debt through the sharing rules, the member may have a reduction in basis or even potential gain. However, a special rule allocates the debt to the contributing partner in an amount at least equal to the difference between the basis in the property and the debt.[24] This special rule will result in a basis reduction, as opposed to gain treatment for many contributions of nonrecourse liabilities. For example, suppose a member contributes property with a basis of $50, which is encumbered by nonrecourse debt of $100. Assume this member is entitled to 40% of the profits and losses. Under the special rule, the member's share of the debt is equal to the difference between the debt amount and basis, or $100 minus $50 equals $50. In addition, the member is allocated 40% of the rest of the debt. Forty percent times $50 of the rest of the unallocated debt equals $20. The total debt allocated to the member is equal to $50 plus $20 or $70. Since the member has had his amount of debt reduced from $100 to $70, one must account for the $30 difference. It is applied first to reduce the member's basis. The member's basis is reduced by $30, so it now becomes $20 ($50 minus $30). Since the debt has been allocated and the member still has a positive basis, there is no income taxed to him on the transfer.[25]

PASS THROUGH OF INCOME AND EXPENSES

The basic rule for taxation of an LLC or FLP that qualifies for partnership taxation treatment is that the LLC or FLP will be disregarded as a separate taxable entity.[26] Instead, each member is taxed on his distributive share of partnership income, expense, gain, loss or credit.[27] The character of an item constituting a distributive share is classified as the same type for taxation purposes in the member's tax return as it would have been characterized had it been taxed at the LLC or FLP level.[28] Thus, a capital gain at the LLC or FLP level is taxed as a capital gain at the member level.

A limited liability company may elect either the cash or accrual method of accounting and it may choose a different method from that of its members.[29] Whatever method of accounting is used must accurately reflect income. If it does not, then the IRS is authorized to recompute the income.[30] Likewise, an LLC or FLP is required to generally have the same taxable year as its members.[31] This rule, instituted as part of the Tax Reform Act of 1986, is designed to prevent a spread of income, that is, an LLC or FLP receiving income in one year, but allowing the individual members to report it in a later year. In most situations, this requires the LLC or FLP to be on a calendar year basis, since most individual members will be on that basis as well.

In general, it will be advantageous for the LLC or FLP to use the cash method of accounting. Consider an LLC or FLP that is on the accrual method of accounting and assume that the LLC or FLP and the individual members are on a calendar year basis, that is, both the LLC or FLP and the members' tax year ends on December 31. Assume the LLC or FLP accrues an item of income on December 31, which is not collected until July 1 of the next year. Since the LLC or FLP must accrue the item on the December 31 close, the individual members must also report the item on the December 31 close, even though they are on the cash method and the item is not collected until the next tax year. If the LLC or FLP were on the cash method, then the members would have until December 31 of the next tax year to report the item – thereby achieving a deferral for taxation purposes of one additional year.[32] While the cash method will generally be advantageous to the LLC or FLP, there are some restrictions on its use. If the LLC or FLP has a member that is a C corporation or a tax shelter, then the cash method of accounting is denied.[33] This should be relatively rare for an LLC or FLP, since there is limited liability for all. The use of a C corporation is much more prevalent in a partnership where the C corporation is the general partner. Such a structure predates the LLC or FLP as a means to achieve limited liability for all in the partnership context. The LLC or FLP eliminates the need for this device, as well as avoids the imposition of the accrual method of accounting. In a recent private letter ruling, the IRS held that the tax shelter prohibition included a situation where more than 35% of an entity's losses could be allocated to members who did not "actively participate" in the business or enterprise.[34] While this ruling dealt with a limited partnership, it would seem to apply to an LLC or FLP, especially where the LLC or FLP is being utilized for purposes of estate planning such as a family LLC or FLP that is holding investment assets. Such a situation may warrant an operating agreement that limits the allocation of losses to "passive" members.

ALLOCATIONS

Of great importance to LLC or FLP planning is the ability to allocate taxable items among various members through the operating agreement. In general, state LLC, FLP, and LLP statutes allow complete freedom in the hands of members to allocate profits, losses, income, expenses and credits as the members see fit. The IRS will follow these allocations provided that they have "substantial economic effect." This test is designed to ensure that the allocation bears a strong correlation to the economic activities of the LLC or FLP. In other words, the economic realities and the tax treatment should be relatively synchronized.

The IRS will find that an allocation has substantial economic effect if three conditions are met:[35]

- Capital accounts must be maintained for each member and allocation of taxable events be reflected in these capital accounts;
- LLC or FLP assets must be distributed to members upon liquidation of the LLC or FLP on the basis of these capital accounts; and
- Any member with a deficit in his capital account must be required to contribute additional capital to make up this deficit.

The third provision, the deficit make-up rule, is the most troublesome for LLCs or FLPs. The reason for this is that if an operating agreement provides for a deficit reduction in the manner prescribed by the regulation, the net effect is that the LLC or FLP members will lose limited liability. The member will be required to "make-up" any liabilities of the LLC or FLP in excess of the assets of the LLC or FLP. Thus, limited liability is effectively lost. Fortunately, an alternative rule in the regulations allows for the operating agreement to forego this deficit make-up provision.[36] Under the alternate rule, any deficit must be made up through a "qualified income offset." A qualified income offset is created by a special allocation from the LLC or FLP to the member of income and gain, as quickly as possible, to eliminate the deficit in the capital account of that particular member.

In addition, special rules allow a member's capital account to become negative if the deficit is attributable either to nonrecourse debt owned by the LLC OR FLP or if the proceeds of nonrecourse debt placed on properties of the LLC OR FLP are subsequently distributed to the members. These special rules are called minimum gain chargebacks and require that allocations of income be used to offset the deductions or distributions previously allowed the members when the amount of nonrecourse debt is either reduced or guaranteed by a member with more than a 10% interest.[37]

The above discussion of special allocations is meant to provide some familiarity with the concepts. It is not meant to be exhaustive. It is important to note that if tax items and debt items are allocated in proportion to capital accounts, there will not be any "special allocations" and hence these complicated rules would not apply.

CURRENT DISTRIBUTIONS

Generally, non-liquidating distributions (sometimes referred to as current distributions) are non-taxable to the distributee partner. Where property (other than cash) is distributed, the partner's basis in the distributed property is the same as the partnership's adjusted basis in the property immediately before the distribution.[38] However, the basis of the property to the partner cannot be more than the adjusted basis of his partnership interest, reduced by any money received in the same transaction.[39] A non-liquidating distribution also reduces a partner's adjusted basis in the partnership (but not below zero) by the amount of the adjusted basis of distributed property.[40]

Thus, when a member receives a distribution of property, including cash, neither the LLC or FLP nor the member will report gain.[41] This is the critical rule that prevents the double taxation inherent in a C corporation when it distributes property or cash.[42] There are two exceptions to this rule. First, if the distribution is a disproportionate one in that not all members receive it and if there is no corresponding adjustment in the distributee's ownership in the LLC or FLP and if simultaneously the LLC or FLP has ordinary income, then the distribution may be classified as a disproportionate distribution and therefore taxable.[43] Second, if the distribution occurs within two years of the member having contributed appreciated property to the LLC or FLP, it may be classified as a disguised sale unless "the facts and circumstances clearly establish that the transfers do not constitute a sale."[44]

A number of additional special rules exist in this context. Marketable securities are generally treated the same as cash.[45] Gain will be recognized if a member receives marketable securities in excess of his basis. Gain will also be recognized if a member receives a distribution of property within seven years of contributing appreciated property on a tax-free basis.[46] Finally, if appreciated property is distributed to a member and the property was contributed to the LLC or FLP by another member on a tax-free basis within seven years of the distribution, the contributing member will also have to report gain.[47]

LIQUIDATION DISTRIBUTIONS

A liquidating distribution is conceptually a sale of the partnership interest back to the partnership (and through it to the other partners). Despite this, a liquidating distribution is taxed more like a current distribution than a sale. Thus, gain or loss generally is not recognized on a liquidating distribution even if the value of the property received by the terminating partner exceeds her outside basis. Rather, any gain or loss realized on the liquidating distribution is deferred, and it is built into the basis of the property distributed. This represents a key advantage to partnership taxation versus corporate taxation. In the corporate situation, it is normal for the corporation to have capital gains on the property and then when the property is distributed to the shareholder, the shareholder must report the full fair market value as an ordinary income dividend. Gain or loss is computed by comparing the amount realized by the selling partner with his or her adjusted basis. The character of that gain or loss as ordinary or capital will turn on the character of the assets held by the partnership. The selling partner's distributive share of the partnership's unrealized cash-basis items accruing prior to the sale is also computed and allocated to him or her.[48]

An LLC or FLP will terminate for tax purposes if no part of the business continues, or if there is a sale or exchange of more than 50% of the total capital and profits interests within a 12-month timeframe.[49] The effect of such a termination is to close the tax year with regard to all LLC or FLP members.[50] If the termination arises as the result of a sale or exchange, the consequence is a complete liquidation of the LLC or FLP followed by a transfer of assets to a new LLC or FLP. If there is a merger of two or more LLCs or FLPs, there is also a termination and new formation. The surviving LLC or FLP in such a situation is deemed to be the old LLC or FLP that had as its members those members that own more than 50% in the new entity.[51] If the new LLC or FLP does not meet the 50% rule, then all of the old LLC or FLPs are deemed to terminate and the newly formed LLC or FLP is just that – a completely new LLC or FLP.

In any case, a termination for LLC or FLP tax purposes generally is not a taxation event of major consequence. While a C corporation when liquidated may carry out massive amounts of gain, an LLC or FLP taxed as a partnership will generally not create a sizable taxable event for all members, unless the complete distribution carries out a "bunching" of income into one taxable year. This does not occur in the usual situation where all of the LLC or FLP members and the LLC or FLP have the same taxable years.[52] The reason that a termination and liquidation is a minor event for an LLC or FLP taxed as a partnership is that the member has already been taxed on the income of the LLC or FLP and a distribution to such a member does not create an additional taxable event. In general, when property is distributed from the LLC or FLP on a non-liquidation basis, no income is recognized by the member and the member's basis is the same as the property had within the LLC or FLP. The distributee member's basis cannot exceed the basis he has in the LLC or FLP.[53] Where property is distributed in liquidation of the member's interest, the basis in the distributed property will be equal to the member's basis in the LLC or FLP.[54] The significance of the fact that termination is not a major tax concern will be discussed in greater detail in Chapter 9 entitled *Mergers and Conversions*.

SOME SPECIAL TAX CONCERNS

Passive Activity Loss Rules

A potential problem occurs with the passive activity loss rules. In general, these rules prohibit taxpayers from using net losses from passive activities to reduce other types of taxable income.[55] This is how tax shelters were formerly structured. The losses from these shelters could be utilized to reduce income from other sources, including salary and compensation. The purpose of these rules was to shut-down such tax shelters and they have been remarkably effective in this regard. In the case of LLC or FLPs taxed as partnerships, the rules are applied at the individual member level and not at the entity or LLC or FLP level.

The rules are applied by separating a member's income into three "baskets." The three baskets are: (1) passive income (2) portfolio income and (3) active income. In general, passive income is generated whenever a taxpayer receives income from a trade or business in which the taxpayer does not materially participate.[56] Passive losses cannot be utilized to offset income from either a portfolio source or an active source. Instead, passive losses can be used against passive income and they can be stored up and utilized against any form of income where the taxpayer disposes of his entire interest in the passive activity.[57] Portfolio income is actually a passive-type of income that is given the classification of portfolio as opposed to passive. The reason for this is that portfolio income is usually generated in activities that create positive income even taking expenses into account. As such, in the tax shelter "heyday" period, passive losses were utilized to offset portfolio income, since portfolio income was usually positive.[58] Thus, portfolio income is essentially treated the same as active income. The list of portfolio income is purely a creature of statute and regulation. Included in this list are interest, dividends, annuities and royalties.[59]

In determining whether income or loss is passive or active, one must analyze the various activities of an endeavor. In this analysis, the taxpayer must examine which of these activities is passive. In general, a passive activity is one in which the taxpayer does not "materially participate."[60] Material participation is defined as active involvement in the operations of a business, and this active involvement occurs on a "regular,...continuous, and...substantial" basis.[61] The IRS has generated two sets of regulations to assess whether or not partners are deemed to have material participation in the business activities of the partnership. Since an LLC or FLP is more likely to be taxed as a partnership, it would seem that these regulations will be applicable. Under the regulations, general partners may qualify for material participation by meeting any one of seven different safe-harbor tests.[62] Unfortunately, it appears that these tests can never be met in the LLC or FLP situation. A second set of tests apply to limited partners. A limited partner for these purposes is defined as a holder who is not personally responsible for an entity's debts, even if the entity is not technically a limited partnership under state law.[63] Because of the limited liability nature of the LLC or FLP, it would appear under these regulations that the material participation test would therefore have to be met under the limited partner safe harbor in the regulations. This regulation provides for a three-fold test to determine material participation. The test is met if any one of the three criteria are met.

The three tests are:

- The individual participates in the activity for more than 500 hours during the year;[64] or

- The individual materially participated in the activity for any five tax years during the preceding ten tax years;[65] or

- The activity is a personal service activity.[66]

For purposes of the third test, a personal service activity is further defined as the performance of services either in "the fields of health, law, engineering, architecture, accounting, actuarial science, performing arts, or consulting." or the performance of personal services in "any other trade or business in which capital is not a material income-producing factor."[67]

While the above test would seem to be the result generated by the regulations, it would seem that the more generous seven test scenario would be applicable since this is the scenario that would apply to S corporation shareholders. In this context, it would seem that the analogy of an LLC or FLP member better fits the S shareholder than it does a limited partner. This inequity is particularly striking in an LLC or FLP member who participates for more than 100 hours, but less than 500 hours. In such a twilight area, the LLC or FLP member will fall under the traditional passive loss limitations described above.

In general, rental real estate activities are automatically deemed to be passive.[68] However, an exception to this rule has been added that allows taxpayers who are actively involved in real estate management to deduct up to $25,000 of rental real estate losses against active and portfolio income annually. This deduction is not available to a limited partner.[69] The question then becomes whether or not an LLC or FLP member is deemed to be a limited partner. It would seem reasonable for this purpose that a member will not be deemed a limited partner. The rule described above categorizing a member of an LLC or FLP as a limited partner is used only for purposes of assessing which material participation test is to be utilized. It is not in itself an across the board definition. As such, it would appear that the generic or business law definition of limited partner should apply in the real estate exception area. Thus, for these purposes, it can be argued that a member is not a limited partner and the exception should be available to all appropriate LLC or FLP members.

At Risk Rules

The ability of an LLC or FLP member to deduct expenses and losses is limited by the "at risk" rules.[70] These rules are designed to prevent a taxpayer from deducting expenses and losses in excess of the economic risk that the taxpayer has in the activity. A member is considered at risk for the amount of money and appreciated property that he contributed to the LLC or FLP. In addition, if the member is personally liable for any debt owed by the LLC or FLP, this is deemed to increase his amount at risk.[71] Furthermore, if the debt of the LLC or FLP is qualified nonrecourse financing, the member will be treated as being at risk even though the debt is the LLC or FLP's nonrecourse debt. In general, qualified nonrecourse financing is debt borrowed from a lender whose business is lending money, the proceeds of which are used to purchase and hold real estate.[72] As is evident, these rules should allow ample planning opportunities in the LLC or FLP context to maximize the amount at risk.

Transfers of Property in Satisfaction of Debt

The transfer of property to an LLC or FLP in satisfaction of debt can pose its own set of taxation problems. Chief among these problems is the cancellation of debt income inherent in the rules of Code section 108. A critical distinction is drawn between recourse and nonrecourse financing. If property is transferred to an LLC or FLP, generally the debt issued will be nonrecourse debt. As such, the full amount of any gain will be taxable, since none of the nonrecognition provisions of Code section 108 will apply.[73]

Self Employment Income

In general, income to limited partners is exempt from self-employment tax.[74] While there is appeal in not having to pay any of the self-employment taxes (such as FICA and FUTA), the downside may be the denial of access to a qualified retirement plan because the partner would have no earnings for this purpose.[75] The question then is whether or not an LLC or FLP member is deemed to be a limited partner, or will the IRS recognize the fact that many LLC or FLP members are significantly more involved in entity activities than the usual limited partner. In response, the IRS has issued proposed regulations that explicitly state that an LLC or FLP member's income would be fully subject to self-employment taxes and concomitantly also qualify for earnings.[76] There is an exception to this rule. A member's income would not be subject to self-employment taxes under these proposed regulations if: (1) the member is not a manager; and (2) the LLC or FLP could have been formed as a limited partnership under the applicable state limited partnership law; and (3) the member in question could have qualified as a limited partner. A member would have to meet all three tests in order to be exempt.

Partnership Audit Issues

Code section 6221 allows a facilitation of audits of partnerships by allowing the audit to occur at the partnership level, as opposed to going after each individual partner. It would seem that these rules would also apply to an LLC or FLP, although this is by no means clear. In general, for these rules to apply there must be at least 10 partners. An exception exempts partnerships (or LLC or FLPs) that have 10 or fewer partners that are all natural persons.[77] Every partnership or LLC or FLP that falls under the purview of the statute must have a "tax matters partner." The statute defines a tax matters partner as one who is a general partner.[78] Thus, at least superficially it would appear that no member in an LLC or FLP could qualify. On the other hand, it would seem that any member of an LLC or FLP who actively participates in the LLC or FLP should be able to qualify as a tax matters partner. It remains to be seen if the IRS will establish definitive rules in creating a tax matters partner in the LLC or FLP context.

FOOTNOTE REFERENCES

1. IRC Sec. 701.
2. IRC Sec. 703.
3. Rev. Rul. 71-564, 1971-2 CB 179.
4. Reg. §1.351-1(c).
5. Reg. §1.351-1(c)(5).
6. Rev. Rul. 87-9, 1987-1 CB 133.
7. Reg. §1.721-1(b)(1).

8. Rev. Proc. 93-27, 1993-2 CB 343.
9. Reg. §1.707-3(c)(1).
10. Reg. §1.704-3(b)(1).
11. IRC Sec. 704(c)(1)(B).
12. IRC Sec. 722.
13. IRC Sec. 705(a)(1).
14. IRC Sec. 731(a)(1).
15. IRC Sec. 705(a)(2).
16. IRC Sec. 752(a).
17. IRC Sec. 752(b).
18. Reg. §1.752-1(a)(1).
19. Reg. §1.752-2(a).
20. Reg. §1.752-2(b)(1).
21. Reg. §1.752-1(a)(2).
22. IRC Sec. 752(b).
23. Reg. §1.752-3(a)(3).
24. Reg. §1.752-3(a)(2) cross references IRC Secs. 704(b) and 704(c).
25. This example is meant to be a simplified version of the detailed example contained in Revenue Ruling 95-41, 1995-1 CB 132.
26. IRC Sec. 701.
27. IRC Sec. 702(a).
28. IRC Sec. 702(b).
29. Reg. §1.703-1(b)(1).
30. IRC Sec. 446.
31. IRC Sec. 706(b).
32. See *Wilson v. Comm.*, TC Memo 1964-71.
33. IRC Sec. 448(a).
34. Let. Rul. 9535036.
35. Reg. §1.704-1(b)(2)(ii)(b).
36. Reg. §1.704-1(b)(2)(ii)(d).
37. Reg. §1.704-2(f).
38. IRC Sec. 732(a)(1).
39. IRC Sec. 732(a)(2).
40. IRC Sec. 733.
41. IRC Sec. 731(a).
42. Contrast this provision with Code sections 311 and 301, which create a taxable event both at the C corporation level and at the shareholder level.
43. IRC Sec. 751(b).
44. Reg. §1.707-3(c)(1).
45. IRC Sec. 731(c).
46. IRC Sec. 737(a).
47. IRC Sec. 704(c)(1)(B).
48. IRC Sec. 706(d)(2).
49. IRC Sec. 708(b)(1).
50. Reg. §1.708-1(b).
51. IRC Sec. 708(b)(2).
52. See Kemp, K.N., 718 T.M., "Dispositions of Partnership Interests; Termination of a Partnership," at page A-50.
53. IRC Sec. 732(a).
54. IRC Sec. 732(b).
55. IRC Sec. 469.
56. IRC Sec. 469(c).

57. IRC Sec. 469(g).
58. See Senate Report to Tax Reform Act of 1986.
59. IRC Sec. 469(e)(1)(A), Reg. §1.469-2T(c)(3).
60. IRC Sec. 469(c).
61. IRC Sec. 469(h).
62. Reg. §1.469-5T(a).
63. Reg. §1.469-5T(e)(3).
64. Reg. §1.469-5T-(a)(1).
65. Reg. §1.469-5T(a)(5).
66. Reg. §1.469-5T(a)(6).
67. Reg. §1.469-5T(d).
68. IRC Sec. 469(c)(2).
69. IRC Sec. 469(i).
70. IRC Sec. 465.
71. IRC Sec. 465(b).
72. IRC Sec. 465(b)(6).
73. See Reg. §1.1001-2(c), Ex. 8.
74. IRC Sec. 1402(a)(13).
75. See IRC Sec. 401(c).
76. Prop. Reg. §1.1402(a)-18(b).
77. IRC Sec. 6231(a)(1). A husband and wife are treated as one person for purposes of these rules.
78. IRC Sec. 6231(a)(7).

Chapter 4

COMPARISON OF LLCs AND OTHER BUSINESS FORMS

INTRODUCTION

In many instances, it is easier to frame both the positive and negative issues surrounding LLCs by comparing them with various entities. When all is said and done, usually an LLC will have more favorable attributes, in toto, than other forms of business entities. This reflects the hybrid nature of an LLC, which is a hybrid designed to inculcate the best, positive features of other business organizations. See Appendix F for a chart comparing the various business entities.

LLCs VERSUS CORPORATIONS

Formation

Both LLCs and corporations are formed through the filing of documents with an agency of the state. In most states this agency is the Secretary of State. There is a relatively small filing charge. Many states have the same fee for both corporations and LLCs. Others, like Massachusetts, charge more for LLC filings. The current filing costs in Massachusetts are $200 for a corporation and $500 for an LLC. For corporate formation in many states, one is required to submit articles of organization and a copy of the corporate by-laws to the appropriate state agency. Usually LLC formation is much easier. Most states simply require the filing of a document similar to the corporate articles of organization. Indeed, in many states this LLC filing document is also called articles of organization, though other states may use various names, such as a certificate of organization.[1] The LLC advantage here is that only this one document is filed. In the corporation context, the actual operational provisions of the corporation, the by-laws, must also be filed with the state. The actual operating agreement of an LLC is not filed with the state.

The operating agreement remains a contract among the members of the LLC. The operating agreement should be in writing and obviously drafted by competent counsel. However, there is no standard form of what should be in an operating agreement. Most modern LLC statutes are of a type labeled default statutes. In the structure of default statutes, the members are free to modify any statutory provision, except for a few that are "locked in" by law. If an item is not covered in the operating agreement, then the state statute fills in the blanks. One can therefore have a simple agreement where most provisions will be governed by the state statute, or a complex agreement where the statutory provisions are modified, or something in between.

In general, formation of an LLC is easier than corporate formation particularly where appreciated property is going to be contributed to the new entity. Both corporations and partnerships have non-recognition provisions mandating that a transfer of appreciated property will not be deemed to be a sale, thus avoiding triggering gain.[2] Normally an LLC will fall under the partnership rules. These rules are easier than the corporate rules, since the corporate rules have a "control" test, which the partnership rules do not. Under the control test,[3] control means the retention by the transferors of at least 80% of the voting power of all classes of stock and 80% of the total number of shares.[4] No such control exists in the LLC context so it is a much easier provision to work with in order to avoid gain.

Capital Structure

A corporation's capital structure is based on the desires of the owners. A corporation may have any capital structure, which is represented by shares of stock in different classes and series. In general, all shares in a class or series must receive the same treatment. One may discriminate in rights *between* classes of stock, but one cannot discriminate in rights *within* classes of stock.[5] In addition, the total number of authorized shares and the terms of the respective classes must generally be disclosed in the corporate articles of organization.[6] Limited liability companies, on the other hand, have no similar rules for either disclosure or non-discrimination. It is this flexibility that gives LLCs great appeal. An LLC does not issue shares of stock, but simply records member contributions in a business document or record. In part, this is done so that the interests in an LLC are not as freely transferable as corporate stock. As has been previously discussed, free transferability must be avoided so that partnership taxation rules will apply.

Both LLC members and corporate shareholders are liable for contributions to the business to which they agree, but which in reality they fail to make. In corporations this generally falls under corporate law, while in LLCs this is generally a matter of the terms of the contract forming the LLC – the operating agreement. In general, the shareholders of a corporation are not directly liable to creditors for failure to make the requisite contribution.[7] However, many LLC statutes specifically hold that members are directly liable to creditors of the LLC if they fail to make the requisite and legally binding contribution. Furthermore, a compromise at the corporate level will serve to modify the shareholder's obligation, while it would appear that a compromise at the LLC level does not affect a creditor's rights. In many LLC statutes, the LLC is simply not a party to the obligation of contribution because the statute sets up the relationship directly between the creditor and the LLC member. In some states reliance by creditors is a requisite element of any legal action, while in others reliance by the creditor is not a factor.[8]

Great flexibility in a corporation or an LLC may occur in capital structure. However, neither in the corporate world nor the LLC world is this right unfettered for taxation purposes. Under Code section 385, the IRS has been given the power to promulgate regulations to recharacterize items of equity and debt in the corporate context. However, in a series of fits and starts, the IRS has never been able to finalize any regulations on this IRC section. The IRS, however, has been successful in a "facts and circumstances" series of cases to recharacterize debt as really being an equity interest.[9] It appears that the IRS will continue to be able to challenge items of debt as being equity in the future on such a case by case basis.

In the LLC context, the challenge is that the equity structure and the income/expenses structure must have "substantial economic effect."[10] While there is great flexibility under these rules, allocations must still meet this test. A failure to meet the test will result in allocations based on the members' ownership interests in the LLC.

Organizational Structure

A corporation must have a board of directors elected by the shareholders and responsible for their interests. While not statutorily required, most corporations have requirements that members of the board of directors must themselves be shareholders.

An LLC can be totally flexible in this regard. The LLC may resemble a partnership in that all members participate in the management of the LLC. On the other hand, the LLC may have a centralized form of management with managers. In the LLC context, the term managers is equivalent to the directors on a board of directors, as opposed to corporate managers who generally have some administrative capacities in an employment framework. These managers may or may not be members of the LLC. One may limit managers to those who are also members in the operating agreement. In the phraseology of LLCs, such individuals are usually referred to as member-managers.

The duties of LLC managers to members is consistent with the principles of fiduciary duties established for corporations. The basic duties of loyalty and care apply to both corporations and LLCs. In general, corporate statutes provide only a limited ability to reimburse officers and directors for breaches of fiduciary duties.[11] Given the strong policy of allowing the members to contract their own rights in LLCs, either the statute, the operating agreement or both may allow for comprehensive indemnification of members, managers or employees.[12] This makes sense, since LLCs generally tend to be smaller companies than corporations. The opportunity for breaches of fiduciary duty will also be less since members will generally be involved in management decision-making. Since it seems that less protection would be needed in this area for LLCs as opposed to corporations, it also seems logical that indemnification opportunities would be greater.

Ownership Structure

A corporation may have one owner (or shareholder) or numerous owners. One of the hot topics in the area of LLCs is whether or not there may be a single owner or single member LLC. Some states specifically allow for a single member LLC.[13] Other states specifically require at least two owners.[14] In states that mandate two members, it is apparently possible to circumvent the statute by the use of a nominal or straw member. Other than that, there are no limitations on ownership structure.

Limited Liability

In general, both owners of corporations and LLCs have limited liability. In the corporate context, there is the doctrine known as "piercing the corporate veil." This doctrine does impose liabilities for the individual wrongs of shareholders where the wrong is committed in the corporate name. The doctrine is purely a common law construction. Among the reasons cited to allow a "piercing" are when the legal entity is used to "defeat public convenience, justify wrong, protect fraud, or defend crime."[15] Usually the courts use a facts and circumstances test to pierce and even then the doctrine is used only in the most egregious of circumstances.[16]

In the LLC context, Colorado has notably provided a provision in its LLC statute that brings the common law corporate doctrine of piercing into the LLC arena.[17] However, even with such a statute, or a public policy of wanting to utilize the piercing concepts in the LLC context, it would seem that an LLC would offer substantially more protection than a corporation in this regard. One of the main reasons that piercing is allowed in the corporate context is when there is a wanton disregard for corporate formalities. The theory essentially is that if an owner disregards the corporate rules, then the public should also be allowed to disregard the rule of limited liability. There are numerous corporate rules to this effect. For example, a corporation is generally required to hold meetings, write by-laws, file reports and issue shares.[18] In the LLC context, there are substantially fewer formalities to follow. Since there are substantially fewer formalities, this means there are substantially fewer opportunities to pierce the corporate veil. In general, most statutes simply require the filing of articles of organization and the appointment of a registered agent therein.[19]

Entity Characterization

Both corporations and LLCs are deemed to be separate legal entities. This is true even though the LLC is not treated as an entity for taxation purposes. Since it is an entity, an LLC, like a corporation, may bring suit in its own name.[20] Just like a corporation, the LLC may have its own name provided that the name is not deceptive.[21] Just as a corporation uses an indicia to indicate it is a corporation, the LLC uses an indicia to indicate its status. Corporate indicia generally include such items as Inc., Incorporated or Ltd. Limited liability company indicia may be L.L.C. or LLC. Likewise, if the LLC is an LLP or RLLP, those indicia may be used.

Shareholders of a corporation and members of an LLC may sue on behalf of the corporation or LLC. These suits are known in the corporate world as shareholder derivative suits. This allows minority shareholders, or shareholders who are not directors, to bring suits where the majority, for whatever reason, chooses not to do so. It also serves the function of being a "watchdog" check on the unfettered discretion of majority owners. Many state statutes allow for derivative suits in the LLC context to be brought by an LLC member.[22]

Taxation

There is a major difference between LLCs and corporations in the area of taxation. The corporation is an entity for taxation purposes and has to file a return in its own name and pay its own tax. The LLC is a passthrough entity where the tax occurs at the individual member level. The passthrough method is generally advantageous since one tax to pay is generally better than having two taxes to pay – one at the corporate and the other at the shareholder or employee level. Some corporations try to mimic this approach by distributing all of the corporate income and hence trying to obtain deductions eliminating all corporate income. This will work so long as the compensation paid is deemed to be reasonable.[23] To the extent that the payment is not reasonable, it will be considered a non-deductible dividend.

Distributions

A corporation is under no compulsion to make a distribution as a dividend. Dividends are completely discretionary. The only usual requirement is that they must be made out of surplus and not when the corporation is insolvent. Absent a provision in the operating agreement to the contrary, profits in an LLC may be allocated on a per capita basis,[24] or on a basis of the value of contributed capital.[25] Given this discrepancy in default treatment, it is therefore best to spell out the methodology in the operating agreement. The key difference here is that distributions are more precisely based in an LLC. In a corporation, dividend distributions occur in proportion to the amount of stock issued. However, the board of directors has discretion in issuing stock for adequate consideration and this determination is conclusive.[26]

Thus, the distribution in the corporate context may be less precise in proportion to all distributions, as opposed to the more precise nature of LLC distributions.

Withdrawals

In general, there is no right to withdrawal by a shareholder in a corporation. The withdrawal is accomplished by selling the corporate interest. However, such unlimited opportunity to sell one's interest cannot be afforded an LLC member because to do so would result in the corporate attribute of free transferability. The LLC alternative, in the absence of a provision in the operating agreement to the contrary, is to allow a withdrawal right. Most LLC statutes give the member this withdrawal right along with the concomitant ability to receive the fair market value of one's interest upon withdrawal.[27] Thus, the withdrawal right generally is something that a shareholder does not possess. However, the operating agreement may modify or even eliminate this right.

Termination

A corporation cannot be terminated through any inadvertent activity. It takes a conscious effort and requisite document filings to terminate a corporation. Limited liability companies, on the other hand, must have termination provisions that act automatically in order to prevent the corporate attribute of continuity of life. Termination must occur upon death, disability or other disassociation of a member. Also, termination may occur after the expiration of a period of time, or upon the happening of a contingency event.[28] Neither of these concepts are found in the corporate context. Consent and judicial orders may also terminate an LLC. These are concepts that have no direct corresponding feature in the corporate context. It is important to note that a termination does not necessarily mean the business must cease. The survivors, upon a majority vote, may agree to form a successor LLC. Of course, the non-agreeing members must be bought out in such a contingency.

LLCs VERSUS S CORPORATIONS

S Corporation as a Corporation

In general, most of the distinctions described above also apply to S corporations versus LLCs. The reason for this is that S corporations must be valid corporations under state law before they file the special S election.[29] Thus, the key differences between S corporations and LLCs lie in the taxation areas. Many individuals assume that the taxation issues are essentially the same since both S corporations and LLCs (taxed as a partnerships) are passthrough entities. There are however, substantial differences that are discussed below.

Formation

One of the critical differences between LLCs and S corporations involves the rather restrictive rules that limit the formation of S corporations. Among these restrictive rules are the following:

- An S corporation is limited to 75 shareholders.[30] Shareholders must generally be individuals.[31]
- Trust ownership is limited to a limited number of trusts such as qualified subchapter S trusts and grantor trusts.[32]
- Non-resident aliens cannot be shareholders.[33]
- An S corporation cannot have more than one class of stock.[34]
- An S corporation cannot be a financial institution, insurance company, DISC, or have elected the Code section 936 tax credit.[35]

None of these restrictive rules apply to LLCs. It is important to note that one may lose S status through an inadvertent termination. Likewise, the paperwork to create an S corporation is even greater than a regular C corporation. The reason for this is that an S corporation must first be formed as a corporation under state law. In addition, the election of S status must be filed with the IRS. There are a number of technical rules regarding this election. It is filed on IRS Form 2553 and must be made during the first two and one-half months of the taxable year. All shareholders must unanimously agree to the initial election. New shareholders must accept the election unless they acquire more than 50% of the stock, then they can force a revocation of the election.[36]

Capital Structure

An S corporation can have only one class of stock. This class of stock must be common stock, which means that all shareholders have equal voting and distribution rights.[37] This means that if a shareholder owns 10 shares out of 100 outstanding of S corporate stock, the shareholder must receive 10% of the income and 10% of the proceeds upon liquidation. There is no exception to this rule. Contrast this with an LLC taxed as a partnership, where special allocations may be made. The relative flexibility of the special allocation rules allow for creative structures involving capital and income.

Taxation

Generally, both S corporations and LLCs are passthrough entities, so there is a single level of taxation, all occurring at the shareholder or member level. However, there are two situations in which an S corporation may be subject to an entity level tax. If the S corporation was an active C corporation when it made the S election, it will be subject to a tax on gains of property held by the C corporation if the property is disposed of within ten years of the S election.[38] Likewise, an S corporation is subject to a set of complex rules to force out any accumulated earnings and profits as a taxable dividend. This is done through a mechanism usually referred to as the "triple A."[39] After a C corporation with accumulated earnings and profits converts to an S corporation, income generated after the conversion is deemed to create an accumulated adjustments account or triple A. To the extent that a corporation makes total distributions less than the triple A account, the normal rules will apply. That is, the distribution will be deemed to be a tax-free distribution of basis. If a distribution exceeds the triple A amount, then the excess is deemed to be a dividend. The normal dividend rules of no deduction to the business and income to the recipient will therefore apply.[40]

The second situation where an S corporation may have an entity level tax involves an S corporation that has net passive income and accumulated earnings and profits as a C corporation. In this situation, the corporation will have to report income on the passive investment income.[41] An LLC is not subject to tax under either theory.

Basis and Deductibility of Losses

Limited liability companies and S corporations have similar treatment with regard to losses. In both instances, losses are deductible by owners to the extent of each owner's outside basis in the entity.[42] Outside basis is the basis that the owner has in the stock of the S corporation or the ownership interest in the LLC. This is opposed to inside basis, which is the basis of assets within the S corporation or LLC.

A critical difference is that liabilities and debts of the S corporation do not increase the outside basis of an S corporate shareholder, unless the shareholder makes a direct loan to the corporation.[43] For an LLC member, basis is increased by LLC debt in which the LLC member retains personal liability. This type of debt is called recourse debt. In most situations, recourse debt and its applicable rules do not apply. The reason for this is that because of limited liability, no member of the LLC will have recourse liability. In these situations, the debt is construed as nonrecourse debt. In nonrecourse debt, members are allocated basis in an amount equal to their percentage of the profits multiplied by the amount of recourse debt.[44] Thus, for both recourse and nonrecourse situations, there will be an allocation of debt to increase the member's basis. With an S corporation, there would be no increase in basis. This rule holds true for either recourse or nonrecourse debt situations. This represents a substantial tax planning advantage in favor of the LLC.

Another basis advantage occurs in favor of LLCs as a result of Code section 754. The basis structure of Section 754 is to allow a step-up in basis at a member's death of the inside basis of LLC assets in an amount not to exceed the decedent LLC member's outside basis. In other words, the basis of assets in an LLC is stepped up for a decedent member. When the property is sold, the decedent member's estate or beneficiary will report gain only on the amount of gain accruing after the death of the original member. The importance of this can be demonstrated in the following example:

A is a 50% owner of an LLC. The LLC owns a piece of real estate that has a fair market value of $1,000. A's basis in the LLC is $400. Suppose that the property is sold for $1,000. A has left his interest to S.

With IRC 754 Election:

Basis	$400
IRC 754 basis after "step-up"	$500
Sale Proceeds	$1,000
Decedent's allocation of proceeds (50%)	$500
Taxable Gain	$0

Without IRC 754 Election (i.e., S Corporation):

Basis	$400
Sale Proceeds	$1,000
Decedent's allocation of proceeds (50%)	$500
Taxable Gain	$100

Employment Taxes

An S shareholder employed by the S corporation is considered an employee for employment taxation purposes. The corporation is liable therefore for both the employer and employee share of such items as FICA, including OASDI and HI taxes, as well as FUTA.[45]

In general, an LLC member is not subject to employment taxes because the member is analogous to a limited partner. Likewise, self-employment tax would also not apply.[46] The IRS has issued a proposed regulation that would make all members subject to employment taxes at both the entity and individual level, unless the member is not a manager and where the LLC could have been formed as a limited partnership and the particular member would have qualified as a limited partner.[47]

Miscellaneous

In general, the passthrough rules will apply equally to S corporations and LLCs. Likewise, the limited liability afforded to members or shareholders should be virtually the same. One of the few advantages that an S corporation has is that it can clearly be formed with only one member. Finally, it is important to note that some states do not recognize the existence of an S corporation. In such a situation, there may be state corporate tax to pay. In the LLC context, Florida is the only state that imposes a business profits tax similar to that imposed on both C and S corporations.

LLCs VERSUS GENERAL PARTNERSHIPS

Formation

Limited liability companies are formed by filing a document with a central state agency. This serves to put the world on notice that the members have limited liability and that the LLC exists. Because partnerships do not have limited liability, there is no similar need to put anyone on notice. As such, a partnership may be formed informally. Indeed, a partnership may be formed without intent to specifically form a partnership.[48]

Finance

Since partnerships do not have limited liability and partners remain personally liable for partnership debts, there is no need to have special rules for a partnership making distributions that serve to defeat the interests of creditors. In contrast, most LLC statutes have provisions that prohibit the LLC from making distributions to members when it is unable to pay its debts in the usual course of business.[49] If an LLC makes a distribution in such a situation, the individual members will have personal liability for the debt. In most statutes, the member has to have either voted for or assented to the distribution,[50] or have known that the distribution took place.[51] Furthermore, if a member is forced to pay the debt in such a situation, he is entitled to contribution from fellow members. Thus, in a wrongful distribution situation, a member has greater protection than a partner and if the member does not have knowledge of or participation in the distribution event, limited liability is retained.

A second aspect relates to default provisions. A partnership generally makes profits on a per capita basis; profits and losses are allocated equally. This is because a partner generally will contribute services in addition to capital. On the other hand, the default provisions in most LLC statutes provide for distributions based on capital contributions.[52] However, some states do follow the partnership rule and allocate on a per capita basis.[53] In any event, both partnerships and LLCs are able to cover this in either the partnership or operating agreement. There may be a difference in allocations if this is not covered in the operating agreement. In general, the partnership default will be per capita while the LLC default will be per contributions.

Withdrawals

In general, partners and LLC members may withdraw at will. However, in the absence of a provision in the partnership agreement, a partner is not entitled to goodwill upon a withdrawal.[54] In general, members of an LLC are entitled to the full amount of their interests upon withdrawal.[55] On the other hand, LLC statutes generally require a notice period before a member may withdraw. Historically, six months has been the traditional time period for notice prior to withdrawal. However, some of the newer statutes have shortened this time period to as little as 30 days.

Dissolution

Limited liability companies and partnerships both dissolve upon such events as death, disability, or bankruptcy. In general, non-withdrawing members may continue the LLC with a unanimous vote of the non-withdrawing members.[56] In the partnership context, the partnership has to be dissolved upon dissolution. A new partnership may be formulated to carry on the business, but that is exactly what it will be – an entirely new entity.[57]

Miscellaneous

In general, partnership statutes do not have provisions dealing with mergers or conversions. This generally means that if any partnership merges it must do so through a dissolution and reformation of a new partnership. Most modern LLC statutes have merger provisions, often set out in great detail. Likewise, partnership law is generally silent on foreign partnerships. Here, a foreign partnership means a partnership that operates in a different state from where it was formed. There is also a trend in the modern LLC statutes to have detailed provisions on foreign LLCs.

LLCs VERSUS LIMITED PARTNERSHIPS (INCLUDING FLPs)

Overview

In many aspects, there are more similarities between LLCs and limited partnerships than there are differences. The critical difference lies in management. Limited partnerships are managed by general partners who have unlimited personal liability.

Management

A limited partnership must have at least one general partner who manages the business and who has unlimited liability. As such, limited partners have a negligible role in management. Indeed, if limited partners are at all active in the partnership they may come under the control rule and lose their limited liability status.[58] The rule is predicated on the concept that a creditor may have relied on the actions of a limited partner. Such reliance should result in the loss of limited liability because of the reliance factor. No similar rule is needed in LLCs since it is presumed that all members have limited liability. Reliance, as such, has no place in such a framework. As such, there is no way that one can lose limited liability. This gives rise to a number of very flexible planning opportunities. Like a partnership, all members may participate in management. Like a corporation, the members may elect member-managers to act like a board of directors. There may be something in between where members may participate in some aspects of management, but not in others. All of these decisions remain business decisions. They have no tax or personal liability impact. As such, this management flexibility represents an attribute of LLCs that outshines all other business forms.

FOOTNOTE REFERENCES

1. M.G.L.A. Ch. 156C, Sec. 12 (Massachusetts).
2. Corporations: IRC Sec. 351; Partnerships: IRC Sec. 721.
3. IRC Sec. 351(a).
4. IRC Sec. 368(c).
5. Revised Model Business Corporations Act, Sec. 6.02.
6. Revised Model Business Corporations Act, Sec. 6.01.
7. Revised Model Business Corporations Act, Sec 6.22.
8. Colorado (C.R.S. §7-80-502), for example, requires reliance.
9. See, for example, *Berkowitz v. U.S.*, 411 F.2d 818 (5th Cir. 1969).
10. IRC Sec. 704(b). This section is discussed in great detail in Chapter 3.
11. Revised Model Business Corporations Act, Sec. 8.61- 8.63
12. Maine: 31 M.R.S.A. §654.
13. See for example, Delaware: 6 D.C.A. §18-201.
14. Massachusets: M.G.L. Ch. 156C, Sec. 2(5).
15. *U.S. v. Milwaukee Refrigerator Transit Co.*, 142 F. 247, 255 (E.D. WI, 1905).
16. *Prudential-Bache Securities, Inc. v. Angelastro*, 474 U.S. 935 (1985).
17. Colorado: C.R.S. §7-80-107.
18. See Revised Model Business Corporations Act, Secs. 2.05, 2.06, 5.01, 6.21 and 8.20.
19. See Delaware: 6 D.C.A. §§18-201 and 18-104.
20. Delaware: 6 D.C.A. §18-207.
21. Maine: 31 M.R.S.A. §605.7.
22. Delaware: 6 D.C.A. §§18-1001 through 18-1004.
23. IRC Sec. 162(a)(1).
24. Maine: 31 M.R.S.A. §663.
25. Delaware: 6 D.C.A §18-503.
26. Revised Model Business Corporations Act, Sec. 6.21(c).
27. Delaware: 6 D.C.A. §18-603; Maine: 31 M.R.S.A. §692.3.
28. Maine: 31 M.R.S.A. §701.
29. IRC Sec. 1361(b).
30. IRC Sec. 1361(b)(1)(A).
31. IRC Sec. 1361 (b)(1)(B). Estates and certain trusts are also permitted shareholders.
32. IRC Sec. 1361(c)(2).
33. IRC Sec. 1361(b)(1)(C).
34. IRC Sec. 1361(b)(1)(D).

35. IRC Sec. 1361(b)(2).
36. All of these rules are in Code sections 1362(a) through (d).
37. Reg. §1.1361-1(l).
38. IRC Sec. 1374.
39. IRC Sec. 1368(c).
40. IRC Sec. 301(c).
41. IRC Sec. 1375.
42. IRC Secs. 704(d) and 1366(d).
43. IRC Sec. 1367(a).
44. Reg. §1.752-3(a)(3).
45. See Rev. Rul. 74-44, 1974-1 CB 287.
46. IRC Sec. 1402(a).
47. Prop. Reg. §1.1402(a)-18.
48. Uniform Partnership Act (UPA), Secs. 6 and 7.
49. Maine: 31 M.R.S.A. §675(1)A); Delaware: 6 D.C.A. §18-607(a).
50. Maine: 31 M.R.S.A. §676.
51. Delaware: 6 D.C.A. §18-607.
52. Delaware: 6 D.C.A. §18-503.
53. Maine: 6 M.R.S.A. §663.
54. UPA, Sec. 38(2).
55. Delaware: 6 D.C.A. §18-604.
56. Maine: 31 M.R.S.A. §701.3.A.
57. UPA, Sec. 38(2).
58. Revised Uniform Limited Partnership Act (RULPA) Sec. 303.

Chapter 5

THE STATUTORY FRAMEWORK

OVERVIEW

All state LLC statutes are different. In addition, the America Bar Association (ABA) has formulated a prototype act, as has the National Conference of Commissioners on Uniform State Laws (NCCUSL). As such, it is impossible to categorize all of the similarities and differences among state statutes. Further compounding this is the fact that some states have and will continue to revise the already existing statutes.

This disparity is minimized by the fact that most are "default" statutes, which means that the LLC members may create their own operating rules. The statutory provisions become operative only if the agreement is silent on a particular issue.

In spite of this, it is possible to see some similarities, at least in terms of what issues should be addressed in a statute. This general perception of what a statute should address, even though the particulars may be different, is important in terms of giving direction to what items should be considered in the actual operation of an LLC. This chapter examines the overall structure and issues involved in the statutory framework.

GENERAL PROVISIONS

Nature of Business

Most states allow LLCs to be formed for any lawful business purpose. Rhode Island does not allow professionals to utilize the form.[1] A number of states prohibit an LLC from doing business in banking and/or insurance.[2] Two states, Iowa and Minnesota, do not allow an LLC to hold agricultural land.[3] A number of statutes simply refer to lawful purpose.[4] It would seem that in these states, an LLC does not necessarily have to have a business purpose and may be merely an investment vehicle. This would seemingly also allow an LLC to be utilized for personal planning, financial planning and estate planning.

Powers

Older statutes generally contain a laundry list of powers including the ability to sue, make contracts, conduct operations, etc. A number of newer statutes simply denote that LLCs have the powers to carry out their business and affairs.[5] Many of the newest statutes, as well as the two prototype acts, simply delete any mention or delineation of powers.

Name

In general, an LLC may use any name provided that it is not deemed to be deceptive. Most states require the use of "Limited Liability Company," "L.L.C." or "LLC" in the name.[6] Delaware allows the additional use of words such as "association," "limited," "institute" or "society."[7]

For obvious reasons, some states do not allow corporate words, such as "corporation," "incorporated" or "Inc."[8] Even in states without express prohibitions against using corporate-type words, it would seem unlikely that a secretary of state's office or other filing agency would allow the use of such words in an LLC name. Most states allow for the reservation of names. One may apply to the secretary of state's office and reserve a name for a stated time period. Probably, the most frequent maximum time period that one may reserve a name is 120 days.[9] Some states allow for an injunction or even monetary damages for the omission of the word "limited" or use of any other name in violation of the statute.[10]

FORMATION

Who May Form an LLC?

In general, one or more individual natural persons may form an LLC. Some states have a minimum age requirement, usually age 18.[11] The person who forms the LLC does not usually have to be a member of the ultimately formed LLC.[12] Other states require that two individuals are needed to form an LLC. This is because two people may be needed to form a valid LLC for taxation purposes.

Articles of Organization

The document filed with the state central filing agency is generally referred to as the articles of organization. The articles of organization are also referred to in various states as a certificate of formation.[13] The articles generally require the submission of some basic information. For example, standard items that must be included are:

- The name of the LLC.

- The name and address of a registered agent. A registered agent must be a resident of and have an office in the state where the LLC is formed. The purpose of a registered agent is to facilitate the institution of legal actions against the LLC. A legal action may be instituted against an LLC by filing legal documents with the registered agent.[14]

- A statement of whether the LLC will be managed by all of its members or by member-managers.[15]

Some states require additional information. For example, Maryland requires a statement of the purpose of the LLC.[16] Some states require the statement of maximum duration of time for the existence of an LLC. In Nevada and Colorado this time period cannot exceed 30 years. Rhode Island requires a statement as to whether the intent is to form the LLC as a corporation or partnership for taxation purposes.[17] In addition, the articles may state any other information that the organizer or organizers wish to provide so long as this is not inconsistent at law with any other provision.[18] Since the articles serve to put the world on notice, organizers usually put in additional information, particularly when it comes to whom in the LLC has the ability to enter into contracts and other business arrangements. In general, articles may be amended by filing of amendments with the state's central filing agency. There is a fee for filing the articles.

In most states, the articles of organization need not be filed by members and may be filed by an outside third party such as an attorney. Formerly, some states required the filing of details of the members' profit sharing arrangements. These provisions have either been repealed, or in the case of the newer statutes, never imposed at all.[19]

In many states, so long as there is substantial compliance with statutes concerning formation, the LLC is valid.[20] In virtually all states, once the articles are filed the LLC is deemed to be valid.[21] Some states allow for the organizers of an LLC to specify a later date than the filing date for it to become effective. In general, this delayed effective date cannot be more than 90 days from the date of filing.[22]

In general, states may require filing of any amendments to the articles of organization. Some states impose a time limit for filing amendments. In addition, some states have a statutory requirement that a member or a manager is under an obligation to correct any false information contained in the articles through the filing of an amendment thereto.[23]

THE OPERATING AGREEMENT

In most states, the filing of an operating agreement is entirely optional. If the operating agreement is filed, the state statute will govern all aspects of the LLC and usually this is not what is desired by its members. In Texas the operating agreement is referred to as regulations.[24] In Delaware and New Hampshire it is called a limited liability agreement.[25] Minnesota allows for two agreements – one is the operating agreement and the other is a member control agreement.[26] In general, the agreement is a contract among the members that governs the LLC's affairs.[27] The provisions in the operating agreement supersede any statutory provision. While most states allow the agreement to be written or oral, obvious prudence and care would dictate that the agreement be in writing.[28] Some states limit an operating agreement to being a written agreement. For example, Massachusetts permits the modification of a number of statutory default provisions only through a written operating agreement.[29] In some states there are statutory provisions that cannot be modified by an operating agreement. These non-waivable provisions include such items as fiduciary duties, ability to inspect the books and the ability of members to withdraw from the LLC.[30]

MANAGEMENT

In most states, an LLC is deemed to be operated by its members unless managers are elected. Failure to enumerate managers in the articles of organization or operating agreement will generally indicate that management resides with its members.[31] The Oklahoma statute reverses the normal presumption and provides that managers shall govern the LLC unless the members elect to vest management in themselves.[32] Colorado clearly mandates that an LLC must have managers[33] and North Dakota seems to suggest that an LLC must have managers.[34] In addition, North Dakota requires a board of governors whose function is analogous to that of corporate directors.[35]

Most statutes allow great flexibility regarding members, managers and voting. Classes of voting power, discrimination in terms of which issues require votes and the allocation of votes between members and managers are usually all permitted without restriction.[36] As a default statutory rule, most states allocate voting power on the basis of contributions. However, Delaware defaults voting power on the basis of interest in profits[37] and Maine defaults to a per capita voting rule.[38]

AUTHORITY TO BIND

If the LLC is managed by all members, then each member has the authority to bind the LLC. In essence, the member is an agent of the LLC. Maine specifically invokes agency law in this regard.[39] Other states are silent, but it is implicit that members are agents and have the power to bind.[40] The authority of members to bind the LLC may be either modified or removed entirely if specifically provided in the operating agreement or articles of organization. If an outside party to a transaction knows that a member lacks authority to bind the LLC, then he is bound by that knowledge even if he enters into an agreement in contravention of the lack of authority. In such an instance, the LLC will have no liability for the lack of authority. If the outside party does not have such knowledge and the activity is within the normal course of business of the LLC, then the LLC will be bound by the actions of the member, even though the member entering into the agreement did not have the authority to enter into the agreement. In such a case, the other members will have the recourse to sue the member for exceeding his authority.

If the LLC is managed by managers, then no member alone can bind the LLC. A member obviously can also be a manager or member-manager who has the ability to bind the LLC in his capacity as a manager. In a member-manager LLC, each manager is an agent for the LLC and can bind the LLC. The ABA prototype provides that a manager can bind the LLC in "carrying on in the usual way" the LLC's business.[41] If the operating agreement limits this authority of a manager and a third party has knowledge that the manager lacks authority to bind the LLC, then that knowledge will serve to block liability on the part of the LLC. In many states, the inclusion of this information in the articles of organization will serve to impart the requisite knowledge upon third parties. Other states take the opposite view – knowledge means actual knowledge, not presumed knowledge through any state filing.[42] If the third party does not have knowledge of the lack of authority, then the LLC will be bound. However, as in the case of a member-only LLC, the individual manager will be personally liable for any liability incurred by the LLC in this regard.

A manager or member in a member-only managed LLC may bind the LLC for acts which do not constitute a "carrying on in the usual way" under the ABA prototype. In order for the LLC to be bound in this instance, either the operating agreement or articles of organization must specifically grant authority for the manager to so act. Since the act is beyond the normal scope of authority, the liability for acting beyond the scope of authority falls upon the outside third party. As such, it is generally wise when dealing with an LLC in important transactions involving such items as loans and sales of property, to obtain a copy of the articles of organization, or operating agreement, which grants to the manager the ability to undertake any extraordinary transaction. The operating agreement becomes critical in this regard.

If it is a manager LLC or a member-only LLC, specific provisions should be provided in the agreement that clearly indicate those areas where the manager or member may act unilaterally. It can be structured that such a member or manager will need specific authority from the members to carry out certain acts. In other words, the members must vote on an act by act or specific act basis to allow a manager to bind the LLC. In these situations as well, the LLC must spell out these details either in the operating agreement, articles of organization or both. Sometimes unilateral authority is granted for some acts, but specific authority is needed for actions thereafter. For example, a manager may be unilaterally entitled to borrow money from a bank up to a stated amount, while a vote would be needed for any borrowing above that amount.

In addition to binding the LLC, members and managers may make statements that legally constitute admissions. In a member-manager LLC an admission by a manager within the scope of his authority is evidence that can legally be used against the LLC. On the other hand, if it is a member-managed LLC and the admission is by a member who is not a manager, then the admission cannot be used in any legal proceeding.[43]

DUTIES OF MEMBERS AND MANAGERS

The states vary dramatically on the question of what duties members or managers owe to each other and to the LLC. The duties that must be examined in this context are the duties owed from the member or manager to the LLC as well as the duties owed to other members or other managers. Many states require a basic fundamental duty of the member or manager to act in good faith and to undertake the affairs of the LLC with the care that an ordinary prudent person would undertake in similar circumstances.[44] This duty is somewhat ameliorated by the fact that a member or manager has no liability for acting without good faith if, in undertaking a particular action, the member or manager relied on any documentation provided to him by the LLC.[45] Other states are silent on the obligation of a member or manager to act in good faith.[46] Wisconsin follows partnership law and assesses partnership duties to an LLC member,[47] while a number of states allow the operating agreement to define the manager's duties.[48] A number of states define the duties, but then allow for their modification in the operating agreement, while others specifically provide that such enumerated duties cannot be waived or modified.[49]

Duties that cannot be modified by the operating agreement usually fall into the following categories and have the following effect:

- A member or manager is not liable to the LLC or to any member unless the act or omission constitutes gross negligence or willful misconduct.[50] In some states the standard is simple negligence, not gross negligence.[51]

- A member or manager must act with a duty of loyalty. In many states this is explicitly spelled out with a provision that a member or manager must account for any personal profit involved with the conduct of or the winding up of the LLC, unless that person has obtained the prior consent of more than 50% of the disinterested managers (if a manager), or more than 50% of the disinterested members (if a member). In Delaware, the 50% is measured on the basis of profits, not on a per capita basis.[52]

- A member or manager is permitted to enter into transactions with the LLC and to have the same status as a third person.[53]

- Members (and member-managers) have a right to inspect the books.[54]

INDEMNIFICATION

Indemnification is the ability of the members and managers to be reimbursed for any personal liability that they may incur as a result of LLC activity. In general, the provisions are liberal and follow the concepts utilized for directors in the corporate world. The operating agreement or articles of organization may require indemnification.[55] Indemnification means the LLC is required to reimburse a member for any personal liability that he may incur as a result of LLC endeavors. This indemnification right may extend to agents and employees as well as managers and members. The member or manager may be indemnified for expenses as a result of threatened litigation as well as expenses incurred as a result of actual litigation.[56] If the person to whom indemnification may apply is adjudicated criminally or civilly responsible, then indemnification must be denied as a matter of public policy.[57] The compromise or settlement of a suit is not a final adjudication so in that situation indemnification is not prohibited.[58] The operating agreement is free to set other standards. Many LLCs reserve judgment to make indemnification based on a desirability standard as opposed to a purely legal standard. An LLC may refuse to indemnify a member or manager for moral or ethical reasons even though the appropriate statute may allow indemnification in such circumstances.

Indemnification is generally not permitted when a member brings a derivative action unless the member bringing the action is ultimately unsuccessful.[59] A derivative action is when a member brings suit in the name of the LLC. Generally, the opportunity to bring suit must first be presented to the LLC or its managers. A member may bring suit in the LLC's name only if the LLC refuses to bring the action. The member will be entitled to fees from the defendant upon the successful completion of the legal action. There is obviously no need for indemnification in this situation.

Maine has a very comprehensive section on indemnification that provides if the member or manager is successful on any lawsuit where a third party has asserted personal liability to the manager or member for actions undertaken by the LLC, then the LLC *must* indemnify the member or manager. If the LLC does not so indemnify, then the member or manager has a right to bring suit against the LLC in his own name.[60]

FINANCIAL MATTERS

Contributions

Contributions are amounts of money or property used to form the company and "get it off the ground." In most states, cash, property, services, or a written promise to provide cash, property or services, are permitted forms of contributions.[61] Most states have provisions governing contributions but some, such as Kansas, have statutes that do not discuss contributions.

A few states specifically do not permit the contribution of services to be considered a capital contribution.[62] Most states require an agreement for future contributions to be in writing. A few states also apparently allow oral agreements on future contributions to be binding, since these states do not explicitly require written agreements for binding obligations of future contributions.[63]

In general, members are liable upon the agreement to make a contribution. If a member defaults on this agreement, he may be held liable for breach of contract. In most states, this obligation survives the member, meaning that even if the member becomes disabled or dies, the LLC may still bring an action against him or his estate.[64] The obligation to provide a capital contribution may be waived by vote of all LLC members. Virtually all states require that this vote to release a member from the capital contribution must be unanimous.[65] This provision is usually modifiable in the operating agreement so that the members may require less than a unanimous vote for the release of the obligation to provide a contribution.[66]

In most states, if a creditor has relied on the written obligation to provide a capital contribution, then the creditor may enforce his rights for any loss occurring due to this reliance. As is customarily the case, the respective statutes vary from state to state. Virtually all states allow the creditor to enforce these rights against the LLC. This is similar to the corporate rule that the obligation of members for contributions is a corporate level problem, not a purely individual or personal action. If a creditor is successful against the LLC, the LLC may then pursue its right against the individual member.

Under most statutes, the LLC may modify and compromise any claims of any creditors for member contributions. Consent of all members is required for such a compromise.[67] If the creditor has knowledge of the compromise on the contribution issue prior to submitting his claim, then the creditor is bound by the terms of the compromise. If the creditor perfects his claim prior to the compromise, then the compromise is without effect and the creditor may sue on the original obligation to provide a capital contribution. The compromise, however, will still be valid among the members. The net effect is that the LLC will have full liability to the creditor, but will be bound by the compromise in terms of recouping any losses from the individual member. A few states allow creditors to disregard a compromise even if they have knowledge of it. In these states, reliance is not a critical factor in assessing the validity of a compromise. The creditor still has an action even if he has knowledge of the compromise.[68]

The operating agreement may generally provide for penalties for failure of a member to provide the agreed upon capital contribution. Some statutes contain a series of possible penalties and course of action for such a failure. A common form, used in many states is as follows:

If a member fails to make the agreed upon contribution the LLC may:

- Reduce the member's interest in the LLC.
- Subordinate the defaulting member's interest to the interest of non-defaulting members.
- Force a sale of the defaulting member's interest to others to raise the capital.
- Force a forfeiture of the defaulting member's interest.
- Make a loan to the member so that he can make the contribution.

- Conduct a valuation of the member's interest followed by a redemption of that interest.[69]

Allocation of Profits and Losses

This obviously is one of the most important items covered in an operating agreement. Indeed, the flexibility inherent in such an allocation is one of the critical reasons that many planners prefer LLCs over the rigid rules of an S corporation. In an S corporation, allocations other than on a pro rata basis based on stock ownership are prohibited. As was discussed in the chapter on taxation, allocations must fall within the substantial economic effect rules. Also, care must be given that allocations do not create Chapter 14 estate tax problems. This is discussed in detail in the chapter on estate planning. However, subject to the aforementioned caveats, great creativity and great planning potential exists in the area of allocations.

Historically, absent any agreement to the contrary, there have been two basic ways of allocating profits and losses. One way follows the normal corporation model. This model bases contributions on the amount of capital contributed. In a regular corporation, the amount of capital contributed is reflected in stock. Each share of stock gets the same dividend. A dividend is a pro rata division of earnings or profits. Most states require that there must be positive earnings in order to pay out a dividend. Thus, if one contributes more capital, as reflected in more shares of stock, then one receives more profits in the form of dividends. The bottom line is that the more profits one receives, the more one has made in capital contributions. Another way of stating this is to simply say that the allocation of profits is based on capital contributions.

The partnership model on the other hand, dictates that allocations of earnings and profits should be based on a per capita model. This means that the profits are allocated based on the number of partners regardless of their capital contributions. Profits are shared by simply taking the profits and dividing them by the number of partners. For example, if there are six partners, then each receives one-sixth of the profits. The reason for this rule has been the perception in partnerships that contributions of one's efforts are more important than contributions of one's capital. In other words, historically, each member of a partnership was to have contributed mainly and principally their work efforts, and as such, the profits were simply allocated on the per capita basis.

Most states follow the corporation model in allocating LLC profits, if the operating agreement is silent. In other words, absent a provision in the operating agreement, profits will be allocated on the basis of contributions and not per capita.[70]

However, a few states do allocate on the basis of a per capita distribution, absent a provision in the operating agreement.[71] It is important to know which default provision applies in your particular state. However, it is even more important to not leave this decision up to the state statute. All states let members make this decision as part of the operating agreement. Good practice would mandate that all operating agreements address the issue even if the applicable default provision under state law is the methodology desired. The reason for this is that states are constantly revising their statutes. Leaving it up to the statute subjects this most important decision to the potential whims of a particular state legislature.

Distributions

Nothing is more important to a member of an LLC than a distribution. This is the physical transfer of either money or property to the LLC owner. It is hoped that the LLC will make money and the fruits of this profitability are distributions. Profits and losses are allocated annually, but this does not require that there be a physical distribution of these returns. That is, an LLC with substantial profits is not required to make a distribution. A distribution is the actual, physical transfer of property to the member, as opposed to a right to receive property.

Distributions should be covered, in all necessary detail, in the operating agreement. Absent a provision in the operating agreement, the state statute handles the issue of distributions. In general, there are two forms of distributions: (1) distributions upon dissolution and (2) interim distributions. Distributions on dissolution go by a number of different names. They are also known as disassociation distributions, termination distributions, winding-up distributions and distributions upon resignation. All these terms are synonyms. The key here is that the distribution is occurring because a member's interest is terminating and he is exiting the LLC. It may be a distribution affecting only a single member, or it may be that the LLC is completely terminating so that the exit distributions are for all members. In either case, the distribution occurs as an exit corollary and the states refer to this type of distribution as simply a distribution. The member, for whatever valid reason, has left the LLC. Said member has a right to receive a distribution reflecting his economic interests in the LLC. Most statutes provide that in such a situation, absent a contrary provision in the operating agreement, the exit distribution shall be based on the original capital contribution. This original contribution is then augmented or reduced by the allocation of any profits or losses attributable to this original capital contribution.[72] In a somewhat unique provision, Delaware simply provides for a distribution in an amount equal to the agreed value as determined by the LLC records, if the operating agreement is silent.[73]

Distributions other than the exit distribution are known as interim distributions. There are many different provisions among the states regarding interim distributions. All of these variations are confusing to categorize, which is all the more reason to address distributions in the operating agreement. Some states, such as Maine, Arizona, Minnesota and North Dakota, have state statutes that prohibit interim distributions *unless* the operating agreement so provides.[74] Some other states, such as Delaware, Connecticut and New Hampshire, allow for interim distributions based on contributions to the LLC to the extent that the contributions have not been returned to the distributee member.[75] Others allow for interim distributions based on the allocation of profits and losses.[76] Still others use a per capita rule, that is, distributions must be distributed equally.[77]

In virtually all states, there are limitations on when distributions can be made. A very common provision is that distributions cannot be made if the LLC is insolvent. This, of course, is analogous to the corporation rule that dividends cannot be declared unless there is a corporate surplus. A common way of expressing this concept is that the LLC is prohibited from making a distribution if the liabilities due creditors (other than those owed to LLC members) exceed the fair market value of LLC assets.[78] In addition to this provision, Maine also prohibits distributions if the LLC is unable to pay its debts to creditors as they become due in the usual course of business.[79]

If a distribution is made in contravention of this prohibition, then it is a wrongful distribution. In general, a member is personally liable for a wrongful distribution. This liability is due to the LLC and such a distribution must be legally returned to the LLC. There are generally conditions and limitations on this liability for wrongful distributions. Delaware requires that the member know that the distribution is wrongful.[80] If the member does not know that the distribution is wrongful, then he does not have to repay the distribution to the LLC.[81] Maine, which follows the ABA prototype, holds a member personally liable for a wrongful distribution only if the member voted for or assented to the distribution.[82] In addition, if a member is personally liable for a wrongful distribution, the member is entitled to a contribution from fellow members of the LLC who likewise should have had liability for a similar wrongful distribution to them.[83]

All states provide for a statute of limitations on the time period that a member can be liable for a wrongful distribution. Delaware has a limitation of three years from the date of the distribution.[84] Other states utilize a two year limitation,[85] while still others are silent in this regard.[86]

Except as provided in an operating agreement, a member is not entitled to a distribution in kind. This means receiving articles of property as opposed to cash. Likewise, the LLC cannot force a distribution in kind on a member unless the distribution in kind is a complete piece of property, not a partial or divided interest, and the piece of property represents an amount equal to what that member would have received had it been a cash distribution.

A final consideration is the concept of how distributions are to physically be paid upon the dissolution of the LLC. These distributions are also known as "winding up" distributions. There is generally an order followed in making these distributions. First, distributions are made to creditors to satisfy claims. For these purposes, a member who is also a creditor is deemed to be a creditor.[87] Next are distributions to members or former members in satisfaction of any liabilities for distributions. This provision and position in the order may be modified by the operating agreement.[88] Next, the members are entitled to a return of their capital contribution. Finally, members receive any other assets in proportion to the manner in which they would share in distributions. These last two ordering provisions, likewise, may be modified in the operating agreement.[89]

DISSOLUTION

Older LLC statutes have provisions requiring an LLC's articles of organization to set forth a duration period or maximum time for the LLC to exist. The LLC must dissolve at its time of expiration. Some states have a limit on the maximum period of duration. Colorado, Florida, Nebraska, North Dakota, Nevada and Texas all limit the maximum duration of an LLC to 30 years.

A number of the more recent statutes do not state a required maximum duration for the LLC.[90] In these states, the provision of a duration period is generally optional. It is certainly permissible to include duration in the articles of organization or operating agreement, but it is not required.[91]

Besides the expiration of a set time period of duration for the LLC, a number of other occurrences may result in dissolution. These triggering events include:

- Written consent of all members;[92]
- The happening of some event specified in the operating agreement;[93]
- Withdrawal of a member;
- Death, retirement, resignation, expulsion, bankruptcy, or dissolution of a member;[94]
- Judicial decree.

A member petitions the court for dissolution in the case of dissolution by judicial decree. The statutes vary on these provisions. Delaware has a relatively sparse provision. In Delaware, the test for a judicial dissolution is that it "is not reasonably practicable to carry on the business in conformity with a limited liability company agreement."[95] Other states have statutes with much greater detail in expressing the standards for judicial dissolution. For example, in Maine judicial dissolution may occur upon the following:

Actions Brought by a Member:[96]

- Managers are so divided that the votes required for operation of the LLC cannot be obtained;
- Members are so divided respecting management that the LLC is or will suffer irreparable injury;

- Acts of managers or those in control are fraudulent;
- The assets of the LLC are being misapplied or wasted;
- The member has a right under the operating agreement to cause a dissolution;
- The LLC has failed and has abandoned its business.

Actions Brought by a Creditor:[97]

- The LLC is insolvent;
- The LLC's liabilities exceed its assets.

Actions Brought by the LLC:[98]

- Filing of intent to dissolve and petition to have court oversee the liquidation.

Actions Brought by the Attorney General:[99]

- Liquidation of LLC affairs prior to entry of decree of dissolution.

WINDING-UP OR CONTINUING THE BUSINESS

After dissolution, the affairs of the LLC are "wound up" and the LLC ceases to exist. However, the members may agree to continue the business in the case of a dissolution event. As was discussed in the section on taxation, this area is critical. If there are no standards and the business is continued on a "too easy" basis, then the IRS may find that there is continuity of life and the LLC will be taxed as a corporation instead of a partnership. In most situations, if the LLC has the corporate attribute of continuity of life it will have a preponderance of corporate attributes and be taxed as a C corporation. To avoid this treatment, it is necessary to avoid having the attribute of continuity of life. Revenue Procedure 95-10 basically provides that a majority vote of surviving members is a sufficient enough hurdle to preclude a finding of continuity of life.[100] Under this pronouncement, if a majority of survivors agree to continue the business it will not have continuity of life. A number of states statutorily allow for a majority vote to continue the business, absent anything contrary in the operating agreement. Other states require a unanimous vote, but this may be modified to a majority vote through the operating agreement.[101] In states with bulletproof statutes, there is no opportunity to modify the statutory provision in an operating agreement. Combine this with the requirement of unanimous consent of all surviving members and continuity of life is defeated.[102]

Absent the vote to continue, the affairs of the LLC will cease. Since the LLC was formed through the articles of organization filed with a central agency of the state, many states require the filing of a similar notice on dissolution. These notice requirements generally require a statement that the LLC intends to dissolve, along with basic other information and a basic description on how the LLC's assets will be distributed upon dissolution. This notice to dissolve is generally referred to as either articles of dissolution or a certificate of cancellation.[103] Prior to filing the certificate, the LLC must discharge all of its liabilities owed to creditors and then distribute its assets as described above under the dissolution ordering rules. After this takes place, then the necessary paperwork on dissolution may be filed with the state.

The filing of a certificate of cancellation will serve to cut off the claims of unknown creditors. In Delaware, a final distribution of assets to a member may be challenged for up to three years, after which it ceases.[104] In Maine, if a notice is published in a "newspaper of general circulation in the county where the dissolved limited liability company's principal office is located," then all claimants are barred from bringing any action after five years from either the filing of the certificate of cancellation or the newspaper notice publication date, whichever is later.[105] This is an area of wide discrepancy among the states and particular statutes ought to be examined for this "cut-off" provision.

SPECIFIC STATE STATUTES

All of the states with LLC legislation have different statutes. These statutes are changing constantly. The above material represents a best effort to describe the attributes that are found in most statutes. However, this general summary material can never supplant the thorough examination of the applicable state statute. It would be next to impossible to continually update the summary material taking into account the differences inherent in all the states, compounded by constant change. While the above material discusses a number of various state provisions there is an admitted focus on two states – Delaware and Maine.

Delaware was chosen because of its position of being a leading state in attempting to convince LLCs to form pursuant to the Delaware statute. Just as Delaware seeks to encourage corporations to form under the Delaware corporate statute, Delaware also encourages LLC formation. As such, Delaware generally has a statute that is attractive to members who want to form an LLC. It generally has flexibility, as well as modern and creative provisions. Many states copy various Delaware provisions in the interest of remaining competitive in attracting LLCs and the revenue dollars that the various state filings generate. The Delaware statute is drafted on a fairly economical scale. As such, it is a very good specimen statute and is set out in Appendix C for that reason.

The footnotes reference the Maine statute since it follows the American Bar Association prototype very closely. Unfortunately, unlike various other areas of the law, such as partnerships and limited partnerships, there are no uniform laws among the various states concerning LLCs. Where a uniform law exists, say for example in the partnership area, one can reference the law, and the exact provision will apply for all or most other states. Again, no such adoption of laws in the LLC area has occurred. Part of the reason is that two different bodies have chosen to try and attempt drafting uniform laws. Both of these efforts started relatively late so that a majority of states had already adopted LLC legislation before the uniform law drafts even appeared. However, the uniform laws represent an attempt to coalesce the thinking on LLCs among various professionals throughout the United States. In this regard, the Maine statute is informative since it does follow very closely the uniform law drafted by the American Bar Association.[106] Another feature of the Maine statute is its comprehensiveness. All statutes are silent on some provision that may be part of another state's statute. Maine has very few silent provisions in comparison to other state laws.

FOOTNOTE REFERENCES

1. Rhode Island: G.L.R.I. §7-16-3.
2. Nevada: N.R.S. §86.141.
3. Iowa: I.C.A. §9H.4; Minnesota: M.S.A. §500.24.3.
4. Maine: 31 M.R.S.A. §611.
5. Georgia: G.C.A. §14-11-202.

6. Delaware: 6 D.C.A. §18-102(1).
7. *Id.* at §18-102(4).
8. Iowa: I.C.A. §490A.401.
9. Maine: 31 M.R.S.A §604; Delaware: 6 D.C.A. §18-103.
10. Wyoming: W.S. §17-15-105(b).
11. Colorado: C.R.S. §7-80-203.
12. Maine: 31 M.R.S.A. §621.
13. Delaware: 6 D.C.A. §18-201.
14. *Id.* at §18-104.
15. Maine: 31 M.R.S.A. §622.
16. Maryland: A.C.M. §4A-204(a).
17. Rhode Island: G.L.R.I. §7-16-6.
18. Iowa: I.C.A. §490A.303.
19. Wyoming had this provision initially and has since repealed it.
20. Maine: 31 M.R.S.A. §622(2).
21. *Id.*
22. Kansas: K.S.A. §17-7674.
23. Delaware: 6 D.C.A. §18-202(b).
24. Texas: 32 T.R.C.S.A. Art. 1528n, Art. 2.09.
25. New Hampshire: N.H.R.S.A. §304-C:1.VI; Delaware: 6 D.C.A. §18-101(7).
26. Minnesota: M.S.A. §322B.37.
27. Delaware: 6 D.C.A. §18-101(7).
28. *Id.*
29. Massachusetts: A.L.M. G.L. Ch.156C §§7, 8, 11, 28, and 32.
30. See Sec. 3003 of H. 346 of proposed Vermont LLC statute. This is modeled after the NCCUSL prototype.
31. Maine: 31 M.R.S.A. §622(1)(C).
32. Oklahoma: 18 O.S. §2013.
33. Colorado: C.R.S. §7-80-401.
34. North Dakota: N.D.C.C. §10-32-88.
35. *Id.* at §10-32-69.
36. Delaware: 6 D.C.A. §18-404.
37. *Id.* at §18-402.
38. Maine closely follows the A.B.A. prototype, which also has provisions for per capita default voting. See 31 M.R.S.A. §653.
39. *Id.* at §641.
40. See Delaware: 6 D.C.A. §18-301, which covers the role of members, but does not describe any particular authority that members may have.
41. See Maine: 31 M.R.S.A. §641, which replicates the prototype language.
42. Maine: 31 M.R.S.A. §752.
43. See Maine: 31 M.R.S.A. §642.
44. Maine: 31 M.R.S.A. §652(1).
45. Delaware: 6 D.C.A. §18-406.
46. Virginia has no such provision.
47. Wisconsin: W.S. §183.0402.
48. Arizona: A.R.S. §29-681.
49. Maine: 31 M.R.S.A. §652(3).
50. New Hampshire: N.H.R.S.A. §304-C:31 IV.
51. Maine: 31 M.R.S.A. §652(1).
52. Delaware: 6 D.C.A. §18-402.
53. New Hampshire: N.H.R.S.A. §304-C:8.
54. Delaware: 6 D.C.A §18-305. This right can be modified in the operating agreement.

55. Maine: 31 M.R.S.A §654.
56. *Id.* at §654(1).
57. *Id.*
58. *Id.*
59. *Id.* at §654(2). The court is free to order indemnification in a successful "derivative" suit if the court determines the member or manager should still be reasonably entitled to indemnification.
60. *Id.*
61. Delaware: 6 D.C.A. §18-501.
62. Wyoming: W.S. §17-15-115.
63. Oklahoma: 18 O.S. §2023.
64. Arizona: A.R.S. §29-702(B).
65. Wyoming: W.S. §17-15-121; Maine: 31 M.R.S.A. §662.4.
66. Maine: 31 M.R.S.A. §662(4).
67. Delaware: 6 D.C.A. §18-502(b).
68. Nevada: N.R.S.A. §86.391(3).
69. Maine: 31 M.R.S.A. §662(6); Delaware: 6 D.C.A. §18-502(c).
70. Delaware: 6 D.C.A. §18-503; Colorado: C.R.S. §§7-80-503 and -504.
71. Maine: 31 M.R.S.A. §663.
72. Oklahoma: 18 O.S. §2025.
73. Delaware: 6 D.C.A. §18-504.
74. Maine: 31 M.R.S.A. §671; Arizona: A.R.S. §29-703; North Dakota: N.D.C.C. §10-32-60; Minnesota M.S.A. §322B.51.
75. Delaware: 6 D.C.A. §§18-601, 18-607; Connecticut: G.S.C. Ch. 16, §34-158; New Hampshire: N.H.R.S.A. §304-C:39.
76. Oregon: 7 O.R.S. §63.195; Maryland: A.C.M. §4A-505(2).
77. Georgia: G.S.A. §14-11-404; Idaho: I.C. §53-629.
78. Maine: 31 M.R.S.A. §675(1)(B); Delaware: 6 D.C.A. §18-607(a).
79. Maine: 31 M.R.S.A. §675(1)(A).
80. Delaware: 6 D.C.A. §18-607(b).
81. *Id.*
82. Maine: 31 M.R.S.A. §676(1).
83. *Id.* at §676(2).
84. Delaware: 6 D.C.A. §18-607(c).
85. Maine: 31 M.R.S.A. §676(3).
86. See, New Hampshire: N.H.R.S.A. §304-C.
87. Delaware: 6 D.C.A. §18-804(a)(1).
88. Maine: 31 M.R.S.A. §705(1)(B).
89. Delaware: 6 D.C.A. §18-804(a)(3); Maine: 31 M.R.S.A. §705(1)(C)(2).
90. Maine: 31 M.R.S.A. §701(1).
91. *Id.*
92. Delaware: 6 D.C.A. §18-801(3); Maine: 31 M.R.S.A. §701(2).
93. Delaware: 6 D.C.A. §18-801(2); Maine: 31 M.R.S.A. §701(1).
94. Delaware: 6 D.C.A. §18-801(4).
95. *Id.* at §18-802.
96. Maine: 31 M.R.S.A. §702(1).
97. *Id.* at §702(2).
98. *Id.* at §702(3).
99. *Id.* at §702(4).
100. See Rev. Proc. 95-10, Sec. 5.01, 1995-1 CB 501.
101. Florida: F.S.A. §608.441.
102. Colorado: C.R.S. §7-80-801(1).

103. Maine: 31 M.R.S.A. §625.
104. Delaware: 6 D.C.A. §18-607(C).
105. Maine: 31 M.R.S.A. §707.
106. The American Bar Association document is referred to as the "prototype" in various articles.

Chapter 6

BUY SELL AGREEMENTS

OVERVIEW

Many professionals, from attorneys to financial planners to financial officers, are generally very familiar with buy sell agreements in the corporate world. However, buy sell agreements in the LLC or FLP world offer a number of different and exciting planning opportunities. Due to the flexibility of the partnership tax rules, a number of interesting and exciting choices exist.

In the context of LLCs or FLPs, it is possible to structure the arrangement similar to those in the corporate world. For example, one may do a redemption agreement wherein the LLC or FLP will redeem the interest of a departing or deceased member. The other form is the cross purchase where other members in the LLC or FLP will purchase the interest of the departing or deceased member. There are two critical advantages to a redemption form. Much of the following tax material will discuss a liquidation of a member's interest. The term "liquidation of the interest" is synonymous with the idea of a corporate redemption of stock. The two advantages relate to two planning problems that exist in the corporate redemption area. The first relates to the interaction of the redemption provisions of the Internal Revenue Code[1] and the attribution rules.[2] The redemption rules basically provide requirements with which one must comply in order to have the transaction treated as a capital transaction as opposed to a dividend.[3] These rules state that the provisions of Code section 302 must be met in order to have capital transaction treatment. Code section 302 provides that the transaction between the corporation and the shareholder must be one that is (1) not "substantially equivalent to a dividend,"[4] or (2) is "substantially disproportionate,"[5] or (3) is a complete termination of the shareholder's interest.[6] If one of these provisions is met, then the shareholder receives capital transaction treatment. In such a case, tax is assessed on the difference between basis and the amount realized upon disposition. If the transaction so qualifies, it may be taxed at advantageous capital gains rates.

The principal provision that is relied upon is the complete termination provision. Whether or not the requirements of this provision are met may be determined easily and with precision. However, complicating this provision are the attribution rules.[7] These rules provide that family members are deemed to own each other's stock for purposes of the complete termination test. Thus, if a corporation redeems all of father's stock and daughter also owns stock, the redemption is not complete since daughter owns father's stock, and more importantly, father owns daughter's stock under the attribution rules. Similar rules apply to business entities that attribute ownership to and from estates and trusts.

If the corporate distribution is deemed to be a dividend, a whole parade of tax negatives follow. The recipient pays tax on the full amount of the distribution. There is no basis in such a distribution. The full amount will be deemed ordinary income taxable at the highest rate. Of course, there is no deduction to the corporation.

None of these rules apply to an LLC or FLP taxable as a partnership.

The second reason relates to the alternative minimum tax (AMT). Particularly, in transactions involving life insurance funding, the redemption of stock in a C corporation may create an AMT problem. The insurance proceeds will increase book income and potentially trigger the adjustment wherein the alternative minimum taxable income (AMTI) is increased by 75% of the difference between adjusted current earnings and alternative minimum taxable income.[8] This serves to increase the income tax due and payable by the corporation.

This problem also does not exist for an LLC or FLP taxed as a partnership.

Thus, neither one of these problems, which pose difficulties for the unwary in the corporate world, are an issue for the redemption of an LLC or FLP taxed as a partnership. In addition, an LLC or FLP redemption can result in a number of different tax treatments, some of which may be more advantageous than others. This positive of more flexibility of design, with fewer negatives than those inherent in a corporation, give a decided advantage to the LLC or FLP in buy sell planning.

IRC SECTION 736 – THE GATEKEEPER

Code section 736 determines the tax consequences when a member's entire interest is redeemed by the LLC or FLP. The section applies to "payments made in liquidation of the interest of a retiring partner or a deceased partner."[9] Under the Internal Revenue Code, a liquidation of a partner's interest means "the termination of the interest in a single distribution or series of distributions."[10] These distributions may be made over any period of time, so long as the member's interest is completely redeemed.[11] A member is considered retired when he or she ceases to be a member under local law.[12] Thus, under either the operating agreement or, if it is not governed by the operating agreement, then under the statute, the member must have ceased being a member. If the payments are not a complete termination of the partner's interest, then the normal distribution rules of Code section 731 control. In general, distributions are deemed to first reduce basis. If the fair market value of the distribution exceeds basis, then the excess is taxable as capital gain.[13]

Code section 736 does not apply to a sale by one member to another member.[14] This means that great care should be taken in planning for payments to a withdrawing member in a two member LLC or FLP. If Section 736 treatment is desired, it should clearly be spelled out that the payments are liquidation types of payments as opposed to a normal distribution. There is no need to provide a reason to trigger Section 736 treatment. If a member ceases to be a member under either the operating agreement or statute, then Section 736 will apply.[15] It appears that Section 736 applies to distributions of both cash and property. In most situations, the payment for the interest will be in cash, which creates few problems. When the regulations were originally proposed, there was specific language to the effect that Section 736 only applied to cash payments.[16] However, the final regulations deleted this "cash only" provision. As such, it is a logical inference that Section 736 will apply to payments of both cash and property.

The section itself does not provide for operative tax rules. Rather, it is really a classification section wherein payments are categorized as being either one of two different types. Once it is determined in which category the payment falls, then the taxation is governed by other Internal Revenue Code provisions.

Under Section 736(b) payments for a member's interest in an LLC or FLP are treated as a distribution. A distribution is analogous to the capital transaction treatment applied to corporations through Code section 302. Thus, it results in capital gain treatment and then only in an amount equal to the difference between the fair market value of cash and property received and the member's basis. Once a payment is classified as a Section 736(b) payment, or as a distribution, then Section 731 is triggered to apply the appropriate tax result, along with further defining through Code sections 732, 734 and 751(b).

If the payments are not Section 736(b) payments, then they are Section 736(a) payments. Code section 736(a) payments include all of those that are not deemed to be Section 736(b) payments. In general, Section 736(a) payments are further subdivided into two categories. If the payments are predicated upon the income of the LLC or FLP, then they are considered distributive shares.[17] If the payments are determined without reference to the income of the LLC or FLP, they are deemed to be guaranteed payments.[18] If the payments are guaranteed payments, then the special rules for guaranteed payments are also invoked.[19] In no case are Section 736(a) payments ever deemed to be distributions.

The following material will discuss all of these options and their effects in detail.

IRC Section 736(b)

In general, Code section 736(b) applies to a withdrawing LLC or FLP member where the LLC or FLP is taxed as a partnership. There are two special types of property subject to the special rules described below. These are unrealized receivables and goodwill. These special rules only apply to "general partners where capital is not a material income-producing factor."[20]

The cross reference for Section 736(b) is Section 731. In other words, once the payment is deemed to be a Section 736(b) payment, it triggers the tax rules of Section 731. Code section 731 is a very straight-forward provision. Any distribution from an LLC or FLP pursuant to Section 731 is tax-free up to the member's basis in the LLC or FLP.[21] The reason for this is that the LLC or FLP is a passthrough entity and as such, the LLC or FLP member will pay tax on the LLC or FLP's income on a year by year basis.[22] Once a member pays tax on the income, the member's basis is increased by the amount of that income.[23] Thus, the member can withdraw any amount up to basis tax free. To impose a tax on such a distribution would result in double taxation. Basis is the critical factor in LLC or FLP taxation.

In general, all of the normal basis rules apply. Some important elements to note include:

- Taxable income increases basis.[24]
- Tax-free income, including life insurance proceeds, increases basis.[25]
- At death, a member's basis is stepped-up to date of death value, except for IRD items of the LLC or FLP.[26]
- Losses of the LLC or FLP decrease basis.
- Distributions decrease basis.
- An LLC or FLP recognizes no gain or loss in connection with a distribution that liquidates the member's interest.[27]

If a distribution exceeds basis, then the excess is treated as capital gain. This reflects the fact that the interest has appreciated and any such gain to the LLC or FLP is transmitted to the LLC or FLP member. Losses cannot be recognized on a current distribution. The reason for this is that the LLC or FLP is still an operating entity and as such might generate a profit in the future. Generally, the taxation rules do not allow a loss to be taken until a transaction is closed. Since the LLC or FLP would still be in an operating mode, the transaction is not closed. If the LLC or FLP is liquidated, then the transaction is deemed to be closed. As such, losses may be recognized on a liquidation distribution provided that the distribution is paid in money, inventory items or unrealized receivables.[28] The reason that losses are permitted in inventory items and unrealized receivables is that these losses will be deemed to be capital losses, which are subject to a number of restrictions. If they are not deemed to be capital loss items, then they could be distributed at their basis to a member who could then, in turn, dispose of them. This would result in less ordinary income treatment. By allowing the loss, subject to a number of limitations on its use, basis is also reduced.[29] On a subsequent disposition, all of the gain will be taxed as ordinary income. Since the loss is a capital loss, meaning it is restricted and any income is ordinary income, which is not restricted, the IRS has a built-in advantage. The odds are very good that the loss will not be useable, that basis will remain low and the disposition could create sizable ordinary income. This result is an excellent reason to examine life insurance funding of a buy sell agreement within an LLC or FLP. The insurance proceeds increase basis fully and avoid this problem. If property other than life insurance is utilized and the obligation to purchase the member's interest is made with inventory items or unrealized receivables, the estate may have a loss, which is unusable, unless for some reason there is also gain in the estate. This is a rare occurrence and usually does not happen.[30] However, there may be substantial ordinary income upon the sale of such an item.

If a liquidating LLC or FLP member is relieved of a liability, whether it is recourse or non-recourse, the member's basis is subsequently reduced. This generally does not create any problems. A member's basis is increased by a recourse loan in the amount of his liability, or in a nonrecourse loan (which is usually the case in an LLC or FLP) by a pro rata share of the liability.[31] If the liability decreases, then there should be a corresponding drop in basis. The effect is in essence a tax wash. Since the member received an increase in basis when the liability was established, there must also be a corresponding decrease in basis when it is discharged.

If the distribution is of in-kind property, neither the LLC or FLP nor the member is taxed on the gain.[32] The reason for this is that such property is distributed at its basis and the distributee member takes his basis from that of the LLC or FLP. Upon ultimate disposition of the property, the member will have to personally report all of the gain. This creates only a single level of capital gains taxation. This is a decided advantage over a C corporation, which would have two tiers of taxation – one at the corporate level and one at the shareholder level.

An exception to the rule that distributions of in-kind property are tax free occurs for distributions occurring on or after June 25, 1992. If an LLC or FLP member contributes appreciated property to an LLC or FLP and within seven years of the contribution receives a distribution, then one of two different rules may result in taxation of the gain to the member. Code section 704 requires the contributing member to recognize gain if the property is distributed to another member. The amount of gain taxable to the contributing member is allocated entirely first to the LLC or FLP. Then, the individual member is allocated gain on the basis of the terms of the operating agreement or other operative allocation provision.[33] Code section 737 covers the reverse situation when the contributing member receives property that is different from that which he or she contributed. Under Section 737, the amount of gain is limited to the lesser of actual gain in the property at the time of distribution, or the amount of gain that the property had at the time of contribution.[34]

Two items of property cannot receive Section 736(b) treatment. As discussed above, Section 736(b) allows treatment under Section 731, which basically mandates that distributions first reduce basis and after basis is zero, the excess is capital gain. This treatment leads to the potential tax device of distributing property that has inherent ordinary income and being able to convert it into capital gain property. As a result, distributions of Section 751 property are taxed as ordinary income. Since these items are taxed as ordinary income to the recipient, the LLC or FLP will receive a tax deduction for these amounts.[35] Code section 751 property is defined to include two types of property: (1) substantially appreciated inventory and (2) unrealized receivables. Substantially appreciated property is inventory that has a fair market value more than 120% greater than its adjusted basis.[36] Unrealized receivables is defined in Section 751(c) as including most ordinary income property. Specifically, unrealized receivables includes a right to receive payment for goods to be delivered and services rendered or to be rendered. Also, distribution of rights relating to recapture types of property are also included.[37] If Section 751 property is distributed, the transaction is treated as a hypothetical sale of the property to the member. The member will have ordinary income equal to the difference between the property's adjusted basis and fair market value.[38] The LLC or FLP will receive a step-up in basis equal to the amount of ordinary income taxed to the withdrawing member.[39] The critical difference between unrealized receivables and substantially appreciated inventory relates to how the LLC or FLP treats the payments. In general, payments for unrealized receivables are deductible to the LLC or FLP.[40] However, payments for substantially appreciated inventory are deemed to be a sale or exchange and hence not deductible to the LLC or FLP, even though it carries out ordinary income to the recipient.[41]

The second item of special property is goodwill. Goodwill is also treated as ordinary income, unless the operating agreement allows it to be treated as a Section 736(b) type of payment.

In conjunction with goodwill, a very important planning exception applies that introduces the ability to create very efficient buy sell agreements on a tax favored basis. Under the provisions of Section 736(b)(2)(B), items of goodwill are treated as ordinary income items *unless the operating agreement specifically provides for payments of goodwill to be treated as Section 736(b) capital gain property.* Prior to 1993, this provided great planning opportunities for the LLC or FLP to treat payments as either ordinary income or capital gains property. This would often be a critical negotiation item for the members in forming the LLC or FLP and in formulating the LLC or FLP buy sell agreement.

In 1993 Congress decided to limit this flexibility. The flexibility still exists if the withdrawing member is deemed to be a general partner and capital is not a material income-producing factor.[42] Thus, the ability to treat goodwill as an item of ordinary income is still available to a withdrawing general partner in an entity where capital is not an income-producing factor. Making this an even more attractive provision is the fact that goodwill is now deductible, generally under a 15-year amortization schedule.[43] Thus, it is possible to create a tax mismatch. Under the exception, the withdrawing member can have capital gains treatment by covering the goodwill as a capital gains producing item in the agreement. The LLC or FLP may, however, deduct the item over a 15-year period and this deduction may be utilized against ordinary income. Prior to 1993, this provision could apply to all members, but since that time the exception only applies to general partners and LLCs or FLPs where capital is not a material income-producing factor. In the alternative, the payments can be treated as ordinary income to the withdrawing member and fully deductible, in one year, to the LLC or FLP.[44] Thus, in the case of the qualifying member, the choice is a full deduction and ordinary income versus capital gain treatment and a 15-year deduction. In the death situation, with a step-up in basis, the choice becomes a deduction over 15 years and no income, versus a full deduction and full income. In the usual course of business, the better choice is the first choice – no income to the estate or beneficiaries with a deduction to the LLC or FLP over 15 years.

There are a number of further definitional provisions that must be examined to achieve this result. As must be stressed and repeated, this result only occurs to a general partner where, at the LLC level, capital is not a material income-producing factor. The first problem is that the term general partner has not been defined in the LLC context. There are no IRS pronouncements on how this term is to be utilized in the LLC context. After all, LLC are so new it is not a great surprise that there is scant information on the issue. It would seem reasonable by analogy that all members in a member-only LLC would be treated as general partners for this purpose. The idea is that general partner refers to management capabilities. Stating this another way, if a member has on-going responsibility and direct involvement with the operation of the business, the member should be equivalent to a general partner. In the case of a member-managed LLC, the manager should be directly equivalent to the general partner.

Capital is not deemed to be a material income-producing factor where substantially all the income of the business consists of "fees, commissions, or other compensation for personal services performed by an individual."[45] This is not to exclude the fact that some businesses in this category have substantial capital. For example, it is not uncommon for doctors to have extensive equipment to perform various procedures in their offices. Even if this equipment is quite expensive, it will not create an income-producing based-on-capital LLC or FLP if the equipment is incidental to the performance of services. Thus, LLCs or FLPs formed by professionals providing services can still meet the test and have great flexibility in handling goodwill originated distributions.

Two further factors are notable in this discussion that relate to the potential deductibility of goodwill under Section 197. First, in order for the LLC or FLP to avail itself of the 15-year amortization provision, the Section 754 election must be filed. This is discussed below. Second, Section 197 contains a number of anti-churning provisions. Chief among these are provisions that disallow the amortization for purchases by related parties.[46] Related parties are determined at the LLC or FLP level where each member is deemed to own a proportionate interest in the LLC or FLP.[47] A related person is defined generally as members of the same family, controlled groups of partnerships or corporations, and trusts where the grantor is also the trustee and/or beneficiary.[48]

IRC Section 736(a) Payments

Payments that do not qualify under Section 736(b) are deemed to be Section 736(a) payments. Code section 736(a) calls these payments distributive share payments and they can either be based on the income of the LLC or FLP (distributive shares)[49] or not based on the income of the LLC or FLP where they are then called guaranteed payments.[50]

Apart from the technical differences on how the end result is achieved, in general, an item that is classified as a Section 736(a) payment is fully deductible to the LLC or FLP and fully includable in income.

Ascertaining Whether a Payment is an IRC Section 736(a) or IRC Section 736(b) Payment

One of the critical factors in ascertaining whether or not a payment is a Section 736(b) or Section 736(a) payment is that the IRS will respect an allocation made between the LLC or FLP and its members. The regulations specify detailed allocation rules where an operating agreement or separate buy sell agreement is silent on the issue.[51] The regulations basically provide for the creation of a fraction. The numerator is the agreed value of the member's interest. The denominator is the total sum of all payments. The ratio is applied to all distributions. The product of applying the fraction to each payment results in that portion being treated as a Section 736(b) payment. Any excess distribution is deemed to be a Section 736(a) payment.

In most instances, the members will want to create their own allocations. Here, creative planning may create advantageous tax results, but if done incorrectly creates a tax disaster. The regulations allow members to create any allocation that they see fit, provided that the total amount of Section 736(b) payments to the withdrawing member do not exceed the total amount of the fair market value of the withdrawing member's share of property in the LLC or FLP at the time of death or withdrawal.[52] The reason that this leeway is granted is because for these purposes a member and the LLC or FLP have different interests. The member probably wants more payments characterized under Section 736(b), since there is no tax until basis is recovered, and then the tax is at capital gains rates. The LLC or FLP and other members will want Section 736(a) treatment since they will receive a deduction for the payments. Negotiating skill comes to the forefront in such a situation. While not mandatory, most people put the buy sell provisions in the operating agreement. Thus, this planning often becomes critical at the time the LLC or FLP is formed. The trade-off of the various possibilities must be discussed up front.

In addition, it is possible to treat different items separately. For example, one may specify in the operating agreement that a payment or any part of a payment is compensation for past services. The legislative history for the 1993 revisions to Section 736 makes it clear that the changes do not affect deductibility of these compensation related items. Likewise, some practitioners include an item of mutual insurance, which is similar to compensation, and use this device to create a payment or part of a payment as being ordinary income and fully deductible. As has been previously mentioned, it makes sense to carefully structure the buy sell provisions. It is possible for example, where a member is in a low income tax bracket to create more Section 736(a) payments. The fact that they are ordinary income versus capital gains is not germane under current law until one exceeds the 28% bracket. Thus, that member would not care if the payments qualified under Section 736(a) or Section 736(b), but the LLC or FLP would want the Section 736(a) treatment in order to receive the deduction. A high bracket taxpayer who is a member will want more Section 736(b) treatment. In the LLC or FLP that qualifies for its special rules, the whole nature of goodwill allocations and treatments represents a science in and of itself. The skillful planner will be able, after thinking through the process, to maximize tax planning or provide the greatest amount of LLC or FLP deduction with the least amount of taxes paid. To achieve this flexibility, the LLC or FLP needs cash to make the payments. Payments of property can create problems. As such, life insurance plays a key role in this flexibility and it is discussed below.

THE IRC SECTION 754 ELECTION

The Internal Revenue Code allows for an adjustment to basis in the case of any liquidation of a member's interest. The election is provided for in Section 754 and usually referred to as a Section 754 election. However, the operative provisions of the section are not contained in Section 754. They are contained in either Section 734 or Section 743. Code section 734 applies to lifetime liquidations and Section 743 to liquidations at death. There are different rules with different effects under each provision. The provision is optional and its purpose is to eliminate potential double taxation. The reason for this is that under the "normal" rules there is no adjustment in basis to the LLC or FLP for a distribution. The problem can be illustrated with an example of a three person LLC or FLP that has three members, each with a basis of $200,000. The LLC or FLP has $500,000 in cash and property worth $1,000,000. If one member leaves and his interest is paid with the cash, which represents one-third of the total assets, he will report $200,000 in gain. If the LLC or FLP subsequently sells the property, then each member reports $300,000 in gain, *not $200,000.* Thus, the $200,000 gain reported by the departed member has no effect on the survivors and the gain has been taxed twice.

Under Section 743(b), an LLC or FLP that distributes property upon the death of a member, where the member's interest is liquidated under Section 736(b), may adjust the basis of the LLC or FLP assets to reflect the basis that is stepped-up at death by the member's estate. The adjustment is equal to the difference between the estate tax value and the basis of the assets in the LLC or FLP. Code section 743 also applies to living buy-outs that are deemed to be sales or exchanges to third parties. In other words, this adjustment would apply to a cross purchase arrangement. The basic idea of this section is to put the transferee member, the purchaser, in the same position as if he had purchased assets as opposed to the LLC or FLP interest. In the latter situation, the basis is adjusted between the differential in basis of the member and that of the LLC or FLP assets. In the usual sense, the basis of the member will be the purchase price plus any liabilities he has assumed. It is important to note that in a living buy-out this adjustment could reduce the basis in a negative sense. If the member's basis is lower than the basis of the assets in the LLC or FLP, the LLC or FLP adjustment will be downward.

Once the basis adjustment is done, it must be allocated to the remaining LLC or FLP members.[53] There are two steps to this allocation. First, the assets of the LLC or FLP are divided into two classes – ordinary assets and capital assets.[54]

Next, the basis is allocated to individual assets in accordance with the type of property that has triggered the basis adjustment. In other words, the basis adjustment at the LLC or FLP level mirrors the type of property that triggered the adjustment. If the adjustment is triggered by an increase in basis due to capital assets, then it is the capital assets in the LLC or FLP that receive the step-up in basis.[55]

A similar rule occurs if the distribution is a liquidation distribution governed by Section 736(b). In that situation, the adjustment is by the amount of gain the member has had to report as taxable rather than the basis adjustment.[56] The only major difference with this election is that the adjustment must be spread among only capital assets.[57]

There are great debates on whether an LLC or FLP should file the election.

In general, basis adjustments under IRC Section 734(b) are much less common than adjustments under IRC Section 743(b), so the issue boils down to who profits and who loses when an IRC section 743(b) basis adjustment is generated. Because most partners anticipate that the partnership will make, rather than lose, money, most partners anticipate eventually selling their interests at a gain. Disposition of a partnership interest for more than the selling partner's outside basis results in a positive basis adjustment under IRC Section 743(b).

A positive basis adjustment under IRC Section 743(b) will benefit the purchaser of a partnership interest by allowing the purchaser to recognize less gain when the partnership sells its appreciated assets, albeit at the cost of additional gain (or less loss) upon a subsequent disposition of the partnership interest. Thus, the nominal beneficiary of the optional basis adjustment is a prospective purchaser of a partnership interest. Accordingly, the purchaser should be willing to pay more for an appreciated partnership interest if there is an election under IRC Section 754 in effect, with the value of the IRC Section 754 election being captured by the selling partner in the form of a higher sale price.

Because the selling partner will profit from the election and the other partners seemingly are unaffected by it, it might appear that IRC Section 754 elections are commonplace and non-controversial. This superficial view however may hide the truth. Because an adjustment under IRC Section 743(b) affects only the purchasing partner, each transfer of a partnership interest forces the partnership to open a new set of books reflecting the inside basis of all partnership assets as adjusted under IRC Sections 743(b) and 755. Opening and maintaining a new set of books increases the partnership's accounting costs that will be borne for the indefinite future by every partner other than the selling partner. The benefit of the IRC Section 743(b) basis adjustment flows to one partner, and its costs remain with the others.

In the case of a publicly held partnership, the costs associated with repeated sales of small partnership interests by hundreds or even thousands of partners far exceeds the benefits of the optional basis adjustments, so the partnership agreements for such partnerships invariably provide that no IRC Section 754 election will be filed. For smaller partnerships, the costs associated with IRC Section 754 election are lower, so the election might be worth its costs. But these smaller partnerships should delineate the IRC 754 election in the partnership agreement.

Once it is filed, it may be revoked only with the approval of the IRS and then only for a valid business purpose.[58] It is complex and complicated and will apply to all future transactions. As was stated above, it may sometimes result in a downward basis adjustment. With all this said and done, it can be effective where the intent is to hold onto the LLC or FLP until death. In such a situation, the deceased member receives a step-up in basis anyway under Section 1014. The survivors get to share in this step-up at no risk to themselves. When coupled with life insurance this can represent a win-win situation for all.

CROSS PURCHASE ARRANGEMENTS

A cross purchase arrangement can represent an option to transfer one's interest in an LLC or FLP. A cross purchase arrangement is a buy sell arrangement between individuals. At the time of disposition, Member A will sell to Member B and vice versa. As was discussed above, the Section 754 election is available and in many respects the tax treatment of the liquidation or cross purchase are the same. It is important to note that under Section 741, a cross purchase arrangement cannot be used to bail-out Section 751 assets. As was previously discussed, these Section 751 items are deemed to be ordinary income when distributed. To prevent members from avoiding the impact of Section 751 through a cross purchase arrangement, Section 741 mandates that a cross purchase is deemed to be an asset sale. Thus, a pro rata portion of LLC or FLP assets is deemed to be distributed and sold in the cross purchase sale. The net result is that part of the transaction will be deemed to include Section 751 assets and taxable as ordinary income. The net result is that there is no tax advantage to doing a cross purchase. In addition, there may be much less flexibility since one cannot do the allocations between Section 736(a) and Section 736(b) that make the buy sell situation in an LLC or FLP such a flexible arrangement. In other words, some of the flexibility may be lost in a cross purchase arrangement, resulting in no tax advantage.

There are other problems with a cross purchase arrangement that have to be addressed. One major problem is that multiple policies have to be used if more than a one member to one member agreement is structured. Also, if insurance is owned, it is owned personally by the prospective purchaser as an individual on the life of the prospective seller. There are no guarantees or checks to make sure the premiums are paid. In the redemption situation, all members must have access to the LLC or FLP books.[59] One can therefore readily check and make sure that the policy is still in force.

In the cross purchase arrangement, one must be careful not to trigger a free transferability scenario. It is important that there be at least a unanimous vote approving any would-be purchaser. If one member is free to enter into any cross purchase with anyone, there is at least the specter of a free transferability issue. As such, the approving vote is needed.

LIFE INSURANCE

Life insurance is an effective planning tool. The cash surrender value of a policy can be a source of cash for a living buy-out. As previously mentioned, the LLC or FLP members have great flexibility in structuring the buy-out. The buy sell arrangement can be structured so that payments are classified as Section 736(b) payments. This would result in a reduction in basis and then capital gain. The parties may elect to make some of the payment taxable by classifying the distribution, in whole or in part, as a Section 736(a) payment. In this case, the payment is deductible to the LLC or FLP and income to the estate or recipient beneficiary.[60] Having cash on hand can make these allocations significantly easier than having to distribute property. Life insurance provides this cash.

Payments for goodwill are critical here. As previously discussed, given the right facts, it is possible to have capital gains treatment to the selling member of an LLC or FLP while allowing a 15-year write-off of the purchase price to the LLC or FLP. At death, there will generally be no capital gains on the deceased member's estate because of the fact that the interest will receive a stepped-up basis. Thus, there is no income tax to the estate and a write-off to the LLC or FLP. These types of planning opportunities are few and far between. As such, it represents a planning advantage. Having cash at death to purchase the good will is a lot simpler than distributing assets. Since goodwill is a tangible asset, it in and of itself cannot be distributed. Having cash, however, can make the goodwill "real" and allow for advantageous planning.

Two issues sometimes arise with regard to life insurance owned by an LLC or FLP. Both issues relate to estate taxation. The first issue is whether or not a member has an incident of ownership over a life insurance policy owned by the LLC or FLP. The potential problem here is one of double taxation. Code section 2042 provides that if an insured has an incident of ownership in a life insurance policy the policy is includable in his estate. The potential for double taxation exists since the value of the proceeds would be included in the value of the LLC or FLP and taxed under Section 2033. Fortunately, in Revenue Ruling 83-147 the IRS held that so long as the proceeds are payable to a partnership of which the insured is a partner Section 2042 will not apply.[61] A similar result should occur in an LLC or FLP taxable as a partnership.

The second issue is taxation of the proceeds by increasing the value of the member's interest. Under Revenue Ruling 59-60, insurance proceeds on a key employee usually create a valuation wash.[62] The proceeds increase value, yet the LLC or FLP has lost a key member thereby decreasing its value. The revenue ruling says that such a situation simply restores the value to what it was before, obviating the double taxation problem.

Finally, it is important to note that life insurance proceeds increase the basis of all members of the LLC or FLP. Basis is increased in an LLC or FLP by tax-free as well as taxable items. Life insurance proceeds from whatever source increase basis. Under most situations, members may withdraw amounts equal to basis tax free. Generally, the larger the member's basis the better. Since life insurance increases basis, it is always a plus.

DRAFTING THE BUY SELL AGREEMENT

Most buy sell provisions in an LLC or FLP are not drafted as a separate document. Rather, the terms and provisions of the buy sell are incorporated into the operating agreement. This is excellent practice since it forces the members to address the issue at the formation of the LLC or FLP rather than allowing the members to procrastinate on the issue. As is the usual case, proper planning would mandate that appropriate life insurance funding for the buy sell provisions also occur at this formation period.

In the above material, much discussion occurred on the ability to treat goodwill as a capital item or Section 736(b) property. This can be accomplished simply by adding the following provision to the operating agreement:

> It is the intent of the parties hereto that payments made in liquidation of a member's interest in the Company as specified herein shall be solely in exchange for the interest of the member in the property of the Company, including the goodwill of the company, and that IRC 736(b)(1) shall apply in all such instances.

A sample operating agreement is included in Appendix D.

FOOTNOTE REFERENCES

1. IRC Sec. 302.
2. IRC Sec. 318.
3. A dividend under Code section 301 will result in the entire payment from the corporation being treated as ordinary income to the extent that the corporation has earnings and profits. At death, the step-up basis rules would not apply so that, at worst, the entire payment will be ordinary income. This is opposed to capital transaction treatment. In a capital transaction, the redeeming party generally pays capital gains tax on the amount equal to the difference between his basis and the amount of money he receives. In addition, the tax rates are lower for capital gains as opposed to ordinary income. Thus, less amount of the received money is subject to tax and at that lower rate. Under the rules of Code section 302, capital transaction treatment occurs if the transaction is not (1) substantially equivalent to a dividend, or (2) substantially disproportionate, or (3) a complete termination of the interest. The most commonly used provision is complete termination. However, complete termination will not occur under the financial attribution rules if family members or certain entities such as trusts or estates also own stock. This stock is attributed to the redeeming party.
4. IRC Sec. 302(b)(1).
5. IRC Sec. 302(b)(2).
6. IRC Sec. 302(b)(3).
7. IRC Secs. 302(c) and 318.
8. IRC Sec. 56(g)(1).
9. IRC Sec. 736(a).

10. IRC Sec. 761(d).
11. Reg. §1.761-1(d).
12. Reg. §1.736-1(a)(1)(ii).
13. IRC Sec. 731(a)(1).
14. Reg. §1.736-1(a)(1)(i).
15. Reg. §1.736-1(a)(1)(ii).
16. See 20 Fed. Reg. 5854, 5871 (8/12/55).
17. IRC Sec. 736(a)(1).
18. IRC Sec. 736(a)(2).
19. IRC Sec. 707(c).
20. IRC Sec. 736(b)(3)(A).
21. IRC Sec. 731(a)(1).
22. IRC Sec. 702.
23. IRC Sec. 705(a).
24. IRC Sec. 705(a)(1)(A).
25. IRC Sec. 705(a)(1)(B).
26. IRC Secs. 1014(a) and 1014(c).
27. IRC Sec. 731(b).
28. IRC Sec. 731(a)(2).
29. IRC Sec. 732(c)(1).
30. Code section 1014 and the "step-up" rules result in little likelihood of any taxable gain above the stepped-up basis.
31. IRC Sec. 752(a).
32. IRC Sec. 731(b).
33. IRC Sec. 704(c)(1)(B).
34. This is called net precontribution gain and is defined in Code section 737(b).
35. These types of payments are discussed fully in the next section. They are technically Code section 736(a) payments.
36. IRC Sec. 751(b).
37. IRC Sec. 751(c).
38. Reg. §1.751-1(b)(2)(iii).
39. IRC Sec. 751(a).
40. Reg. §§1.736-1(b)(2) and 1.736-1(a)(4)
41. Reg. §1.736-1(b)(4).
42. IRC Sec. 736(b)(3).
43. IRC Sec. 197.
44. See *Foxman v. Comm.*, 352 F.2d 466 (3rd Cir. 1965) and *Pickett v. Comm.*, TC Memo 1965-196.
45. 1993 RRA Conference Report at p. 179. See also present and prior law. Present: IRC Secs. 401(c)(2) and 911(d). Prior: IRC Sec. 1348(b)(1).
46. IRC Sec. 197(f)(9)(A).
47. IRC Sec. 197(f)(9)(E).
48. Code section 197(f)(9)(C)(i) essentially applies the rules of Code sections 41(f)(1), 707(b)(1), 267(b). In the control group context the degree of control is expanded to 20% "commonality" from the usual 50%.
49. IRC Sec. 702.
50. IRC Sec. 707(c).
51. Reg. §1.736-1(b)(5).
52. Reg. §1.736-1(b)(5)(iii).
53. This is governed by Code section 755.
54. Reg. §1.755-1(a).
55. Reg. §1.755-1(b).

56. IRC Sec. 734(b).
57. Reg. §1.755-1(c).
58. IRC Sec. 754.
59. See for example Delaware at 6 D.C.A. §18-305.
60. The payment is income in respect of a decedent or IRD. IRD items do not get a step-up in basis and are taxable to the recipient. See Reg. §1.753-1(b) and IRC Sec. 691.
61. 1983-2 CB 158. The ruling follows closely the favorable decision in *Estate of Knipp v. Comm.*, 25 TC 153 (1955).
62. 1959-1 CB 237.

Chapter 7

EMPLOYEE BENEFIT PLANNING

QUALIFIED PLANS

For most purposes, the qualified plan of a limited liability company will function much the same as the qualified plan of a corporation. Noncorporate qualified plans are referred to as Keogh, or HR-10 plans. The designation HR-10 came from the original designation number of the bill that ultimately became Tax Equity and Fiscal Responsibility Act of 1982 (TEFRA), which changed the treatment of these plans. "Keogh" was the name of the Congressman who sponsored the bill.

In most respects, Keogh plans are subject to the same rules as qualified plans of a corporation. For example, in the area of Code section 415 limits, which govern the amounts of contributions and benefits that may be provided, the same limits apply to corporate and noncorporate plans. On the other hand, rules that formerly applied only to self-employed individuals became part of the corporate requirements, now generally described as the top-heavy rules. These rules impose additional requirements when a disproportionate amount of benefits accrue to key employees.[1] The top-heavy rules are applied in addition to the nondiscrimination rules of Section 401(a). The purpose of all these rules is to limit the amount of benefits or contributions going disproportionately to key employees.

The following general rules apply to Keogh plans, as well as qualified plans of corporations:

- The minimum distribution rules.[2]
- Limits on Social Security integration (i.e., permitted disparity).[3]
- A limit on the amount of compensation that can be taken into account in providing a contribution or benefit.[4]
- A three-year 100% vesting requirement for top heavy plans.[5]

In spite of the attempts at parity, a few distinctions still exist between corporate and noncorporate plans. Since most LLCs or FLPs will be taxed as partnerships, these distinctions should exist between most LLC or FLP plans and most corporate plans.

First, in a noncorporate business entity, a self-employed person's compensation is his net income from self-employment.[6] This amount is total compensation reduced by all applicable deductions, including the deduction for contributions to qualified plans.[7] The limit on annual additions to a defined contribution plan is an amount equal to the lesser of 25% of compensation or $35,000, for 2001 plan years, as indexed for inflation.[8] (For plan years beginning before January 1, 2001, the dollar amount for this purpose was $30,000.) Thus, a corporate employee with an income of $100,000 could receive a contribution of $25,000 in a defined contribution plan. In the case of an LLC or FLP member, this amount would be $20,000, because the deduction for the contribution to the plan has to be subtracted from gross compensation to arrive at net compensation. Thus, the base compensation is $100,000 minus $20,000, or $80,000. Twenty-five percent of $80,000 is equal to a contribution of $20,000, which may be deductible by the employer.[9] Stating this mathematically, the limit for members of an LLC or FLP would effectively be 20%, instead of 25%.

Another limitation in noncorporate plans lies in the ability to purchase accident, health or life insurance within the plan for self-employed individuals such as LLC or FLP members.[10]

The most important difference lies in the area of prohibited transactions. ERISA mandates that the prohibited transaction exemptions found in the statute do not apply between a qualified plan and an owner-employee.[11] As such, the statutory exemptions that exist for a corporate plan will not exist in a plan for an LLC or FLP engaging in any of the following transactions between the plan and a self-employed member:

- The lending of any part or corpus of the plan.[12]
- The payment for services rendered to the plan.[13]
- The sale or purchase of any property from the plan.[14]

Of the above prohibited transactions, probably the most important difference between the LLC or FLP plan and the normal corporate plan is the prohibition against making loans to LLC or FLP members.

Another limitation is that separation from service cannot be a qualifying event for a lump sum distribution for self-employed individuals.[15] The reason for this is that many self-employed people never actually retire. They may always keep their hand in the business. Since it is so difficult to assess when such a person has a separation from service, the potential favorable tax treatment of a lump sum distribution is denied. Also, in terms of assessing reasonable compensation, the deduction for a qualified plan is not factored out in determining compensation.[16] In other words, compensation for determining reasonable compensation for a self-employed person includes the amount contributed on his behalf to any qualified plan.

The planner must take into account the top-heavy rules in many plans involving LLCs or FLPs. A plan is top-heavy if the present value of the cumulative accrued balances for a defined benefit plan, or aggregate account balances for a defined contribution plan for *key employees*, exceeds 60% of the cumulative accrued benefits or aggregate account balance for all employees.[17]

A key employee is an employee, who for this plan year or any of the preceding four plan years, was or is:

- An officer of the employer having an annual compensation from the employer greater than 50% of the limits prescribed in Section 415(b)(1)(A).[18] Code section 415(b)(1)(A) is the dollar limitation in effect for defined benefit plans for the calendar year in which the plan year ends; or

- An employee having annual compensation from the employer in excess of the defined contribution limit contained in Section 415(c)(1)(A) and who owns both more than ½ percent interest and one of the 10 largest interests in the employer;[19] or

- A more than 5% owner in the employer;[20] or

- A more than 1% owner who also has annual compensation exceeding $150,000.[21]

If a plan is deemed to be top-heavy, then it must comply with three additional requirements in addition to the usual requirements mandated by Section 401.

These additional requirements are:

- A top-heavy plan must vest accrued benefits for employees either on the basis of 100% vesting after three years or utilize six-year graded vesting. In six-year graded vesting, the employee must be 20% vested after two years. Twenty percent additional vesting must occur each year thereafter so that the employee is 100% vested after six years.[22]

- The plan must make a minimum contribution or provide for a minimum benefit for *non-key* employees. In the case of a defined benefit plan, each non-key employee must be provided an accrued benefit of not less than the employee's average compensation multiplied by the *lesser* of 2% for each year of service or 20%.[23] For a defined contribution plan, the minimum contribution, including forfeitures, for non-key employees must be the employee's compensation multiplied by the *lesser* of 3% or the highest percentage rate used for a key employee.[24]

NONQUALIFIED DEFERRED COMPENSATION BENEFITS

In recent years, the interest in nonqualified plans has dramatically increased. This has occurred because of a number of factors. Individuals are living longer, combined with a corresponding need to provide sufficient assets to maintain their life style for this longer period of time. In addition, the Revenue Reconciliation Act of 1993 decreased the amount of compensation that could be taken into account in designing the qualified plan. The includable compensation limit was decreased from $200,000 ($235,800 as adjusted for cost of living increases) to $150,000.[25] Further compounding this decrease was the change in the method of calculating cost of living increases. Old law had simply multiplied the includable compensation limit by the consumer price index inflator on an annual basis. The new cost of living adjustment provides for a delay of any increase until there is an increase totaling $10,000 and then the amount is rounded down to the nearest $10,000 amount.[26] This will result in the cost of living increase actually serving as a decrease in the future if it is examined on a constant dollar basis.

The great appeal of nonqualified plans lies in the great variety of plan design and construction available. Nonqualified deferred compensation plans can be divided into two broad categories – true deferral plans and salary continuation plans. Both types receive similar tax treatment. In a "true deferral" plan, the employer and employee agree that the employee will give up a portion of his current compensation in exchange for the employer's promise to pay a benefit at some future date. A "salary continuation" plan, on the other hand, provides a benefit in addition to all other forms of compensation. That is, the employer promises to pay a benefit in the future, but there is no reduction in the employee's compensation. For example, a "SERP" (Supplemental Employee Retirement Plan) is a plan for a selected group of executives, which generally provides extra retirement benefits. An "excess benefit plan" is a special kind of plan that provides benefits in excess of those allowed under the limits of Section 415.

In the case of LLCs or FLPs, it is important to differentiate between these various designs. Unlike a true deferral plan, it is possible to provide a salary continuation-type benefit under the guaranteed payment provisions of the Internal Revenue Code. A guaranteed payment is a payment made by an entity taxed as a partnership, such as an LLC or FLP, to one of its owners where the payment is not based on the entity's income.[27] Thus, it is possible to provide post-retirement benefits to a member on a fixed amount or other standard basis. If the entity were a C corporation, these payments would be characterized as salary continuation payments. In the LLC or FLP context, if these payments are determined without regard to the LLC or FLP's income, they will be guaranteed payments. The term guaranteed payments is really a misnomer, since the payments do not have to be guaranteed. They simply have to be fixed in an amount that does not cross-reference the income or profits of the LLC or FLP.

The concept of guaranteed payments occurred as a result of some difficult allocation problems existing prior to the enactment of that provision of the 1954 Internal Revenue Code. Prior to 1954, if an income-type payment was made to a partner and the partnership did not have sufficient income to cover the payment, the payment was deemed to be a capital distribution from all other partners' capital accounts. In 1954, Congress sought to come up with a scheme that was no longer an "...unnecessary and complicated law."[28] If the payments met the tests of Section 707, then they were treated the same as payments to an outsider.

As such, the payment is deductible to the extent that it would be deductible under some other Internal Revenue Code section. Thus, it is possible to structure guaranteed payments to replicate salary continuation-type deferred compensation payments.

In order to be a guaranteed payment, the following five tests must be met:

- The LLC or FLP must be taxed as a partnership.

- The payment must be made from the LLC or FLP to a member.[29] If the member has ceased to be a member then he will be deemed to be an outsider. If the payments are made based on LLC or FLP activity when the member was a member then the payments are deemed to be made to a member.[30]

- The guaranteed payment must be for the rendering of services or the furnishing of capital to the LLC or FLP.[31] In the case of a salary continuation-type payment, obviously the rendering must be for services.

- The payment must be made without any reference to LLC or FLP income.[32]

- The partner must be acting in his capacity as a partner. Over past years, the distinction between partner capacity payments and non-partner capacity payments engendered serious discussions. Amendments in 1984 served only to cloud the issue even further. In the case of salary continuation-type payments, they would clearly seem to be payments in a partnership capacity or payments for services rendered. However, the issue would seem to have virtually little practical importance and any distinction between partner capacity and non-capacity would make very little difference. Indeed, one commentator has suggested that the issue is practically moot and as such should no longer even be a requirement.[33]

The concept of the guaranteed payment may serve to make salary continuation type payments into the future. It is important to note that such payments will be deemed ordinary income to the member. Likewise, deductibility is not guaranteed. In order to ensure a deduction, the payment must be deductible under other Internal Revenue Code sections.[34] For deferred compensation purposes, these would be Code sections 162 and 404. The payments must be reasonably based on the working life of the member.

MEDICAL AND HEALTH INSURANCE

Under Code section 162, an employer who provides for a plan of medical and health insurance can deduct the amounts of any premiums paid and the employee does not have to report the premiums as income.[35] However, this deduction is not available to self-employed individuals. Self-employed individuals are defined as those who have net earnings from self-employment.[36] The IRS has specifically ruled that partners in a partnership are self-employed for this purpose.[37] The same rule would seem to apply to an LLC or FLP taxed as a partnership. In the case of a self-employed person, the deduction is limited to 60% in 2001 of the amount paid for medical or health *insurance* on the individual, his spouse and dependents. (The deduction is scheduled to increase to 70% in 2002 and then to 100% in 2003 and later years.)[38] No deduction is allowed to the extent that it exceeds the individual's earned income derived from the trade or business providing the health or medical care coverage. In the case of an LLC or FLP taxed as a partnership, net earnings from self-employment includes a member's distributive share[39] as well as guaranteed payments.[40]

The structure of how taxation occurs is interesting. The LLC or FLP can deduct the full amount of the premiums under Code section 162(a). The members must fully report the income under Section 61(a) as a guaranteed payment. The deduction under Section 162(l) then accrues to each member personally provided all of the Section 162(l) requirements are met.[41]

GROUP TERM LIFE INSURANCE

An employer may provide employees with up to $50,000 of group term life insurance protection each year on a tax-free basis.[42] Any amount above $50,000 is taxed pursuant to a table contained in the regulations.[43] The insurance is deductible under Section 162(a).

Following are four basic requirements that must be met in order for a plan to qualify as group term coverage:

- The coverage must provide a general death benefit.[44] This means that travel insurance or other policies that pay a death benefit only under certain circumstances will not qualify.

- The coverage must be provided to a group of employees.[45] If the group consists of fewer than 10 employees special non-discrimination rules apply. These rules essentially mandate that coverage must be for all full-time employees and the amount of coverage is either a uniform percentage of compensation or consists of a series of brackets where no bracket exceeds 2½ times the next lower bracket and the lowest bracket provides at least 10% of the coverage of the highest bracket.[46]

- The coverage is under a policy carried directly or indirectly by the employer.[47]

- The amount of coverage is based on a formula that precludes individual selection.[48]

An employee for purposes of group term life coverage is a person performing services in an employer-employee relationship. The key test is that the employer have "the right to control and direct the individual who performs the services."[49] This test will obviously generally exclude LLC or FLP members. However, it would appear that members in a member-managed LLC or FLP who are also employees could qualify.

The LLC or FLP is not at a total disadvantage here. This regulation would generally exclude partners in a partnership as well as S corporation shareholders.[50] There may even be difficulties in a C corporation. An employee who is an officer that provides minimal services or an employee who is also a director will generally not be considered an employee for this purpose.[51] Likewise, certain professionals such as "physicians, lawyers, dentists, veterinarians, contractors"[52] will not be considered employees because of their ability to control how they provide their services. Furthermore, there are very stringent rules for plans that provide disproportionate benefits to key employees. Income tax free coverage is available to key employees only if the plan does not discriminate in favor of key employees with regard to type as well as amount of coverage. The amount of coverage must be limited to either a flat amount for all persons covered or be based on a uniform percentage of compensation.[53] For these purposes, a key employee is the same as described above and defined in Code section 416.

It is possible for an LLC or FLP to provide group term coverage for all true employees.[54] However, as is true with virtually all other business organizations, providing coverage to owners is much more difficult or much less advantageous. For owners such as members, split dollar and bonus plans will be much more attractive.

SPLIT DOLLAR PLANS

Split dollar plans can be very attractive for LLC or FLP members. Generally, there is little income advantage to members of an LLC or FLP who are insured under a split dollar plan. The premium will be non-deductible under Section 264 and for all intents and purposes will be paid with after-tax dollars. The plan, from the member's standpoint, should always be a contributory plan. If it is an employer-pay-all plan, then fictional or phantom income will be created. The economic benefit, or PS 58 cost, will be income in excess of that generated by the LLC or FLP. If the plan is contributory, meaning the employee contributes the economic benefit or PS 58 cost, then this phantom income problem is eliminated. The employee is able to receive the amount to contribute as a distribution from the LLC or FLP. As long as basis exceeds this amount, this distribution will be income tax free.

If there is no income tax advantage (or disadvantage), then why should an LLC or FLP consider split dollar? The answer lies in the gift tax ramifications. The gift tax consequences are measured the same way as the income tax consequences through the economic benefit or PS 58 cost calculation.[55] When an irrevocable life insurance trust is used, there may be a number of situations where there is difficulty in utilizing the annual exclusion to shelter the premium cost from gift tax. The policy may be large or highly rated so that the premium is a relatively high amount. The trust may have few natural beneficiaries, or the grantor may have used the bulk of the annual exclusion through making other gifts. In all three situations, it is desirable to measure the insurance gift not by the full amount of the premium, but rather by the imputed term cost represented by the economic benefit or PS 58 cost. In other words, one is able to generate a larger death benefit gift in a trust through the use of the annual exclusion if one uses a term-based rate rather than a full premium rate.

It is important to note that an LLC or FLP has none of the equity split dollar problems that confront C corporations. In late January of 1996 the IRS issued a technical advice memorandum (TAM) regarding equity split dollar.[56] While this TAM is incomplete at best, it at least raises the specter of Section 83 treatment in equity split dollar plans. An equity split dollar plan is one where the business is returned the cash value, up to the business' contributions, upon death or upon surrender of the policy. At some point, when the cash value exceeds these contributions, any excess accrues to the employee's portion of the policy. Historically, this equity cash value in the hands of the employee has not created an additional tax event. Since this amount has been treated as part of the term benefit accruing to the employee, and since this amount was taxed by means of the economic benefit or PS 58 cost, the perception was that no additional tax consequences would occur. In TAM 9604001, the IRS raises the possibility of Section 83 creating an additional taxable event to the employee on this equity cash value.

None of these problems should pertain to split dollar in the LLC or FLP context. The key reason for this is that traditional, non-equity split dollar is such an effective planning tool in LLC or FLPs. In the traditional split dollar approach, the LLC or FLP will receive all of the cash value upon death or surrender. The reason for this lies in Section 705(a)(1)(B), which provides that the basis in a member's interest in an LLC or FLP taxed as a partnership is increased by any income exempt from tax. Presumably, this would include the cash value increase above basis in the life insurance contract. The annual increase in cash value represents income to the LLC or FLP in an "accounting" sense. It is an investment return. However, Section 72 would result in this return not being taxable. Thus, the members will receive an increase in their respective bases as a result of this cash value increase. To an LLC or FLP member, an increase in basis is one of the most important events that can occur. As has been previously discussed, a member can withdraw amounts up to one's basis tax-free.[57] Thus, if the cash value of the split dollar plan increases one's basis, this serves as a shelter in enabling the same member to make higher withdrawals from the LLC or FLP. In some ways this is really "super" equity split dollar. In a regular corporate split dollar program, the equity may be vested in an irrevocable life insurance trust. However, there may be difficulties in accessing this equity. In the LLC or FLP context, it can be effectively utilized by making distributions of other LLC or FLP property. The actual equity in the life insurance policy is not touched; it merely enables the tax-free distribution of other amounts from the LLC or FLP.

BUSINESS OWNED LIFE INSURANCE

If the cash value of a split dollar plan represents an opportunity to increase basis, then obviously having the LLC or FLP own an entire life insurance policy can also represent a tremendous planning opportunity. Just as the cash value increase increases basis (without tax), the death benefit can accomplish the same thing.[58] Thus business owned life insurance (BOLI) could present all kinds of interesting planning opportunities. Most of these opportunities result from leverage that occurs as a result of the tax-free nature of life insurance, yet having the concomitant increase in basis as a result of the cash surrender value and/or the death benefit. The following proposals just scratch the surface of some interesting planning opportunities.

The use of salary continuation-types of plans is coupled with life insurance. As described above, a salary continuation-type payment will be deductible to an LLC or FLP in two situations. If the recipient is an employee who is not a member, then the payment will simply be a deductible expense to the LLC or FLP. If it is a member who receives the payments then the payment can be structured as a guaranteed payment and deductible as such. In either case there is a deduction. The actual cash used to fund the program may occur by means of a life insurance policy. The growth in cash value will increase basis. When amounts are withdrawn from the policy, normal tax rules should apply. Assuming the contract is not a modified endowment contract (MEC),[59] amounts may be withdrawn tax free up to basis and tax-free loans can be made thereafter. These amounts will not affect the LLC or FLP in any way. The net effect is that the LLC or FLP receives an increase in basis because of the insurance and also receives a deduction when the payments are made. This represents the best of all possible worlds.

Along similar lines, key employee coverage not only protects the business from loss of key employees, but the death benefit will increase basis.

Further, the buy sell opportunities are endless. As described in Chapter 6, there is considerable leeway in treating the distribution as either a basis distribution or as a deductible expense-includable income item. The insurance proceeds may serve to increase basis before any basis reduction occurs in a tax-free distribution scenario. Stated another way, the life insurance preserves the basis in the hands of all of the survivors even if a basis reduction type of distribution occurs. If the payment is tax deductible, then the leverage situation occurs of creating a deduction by means of tax-free income. Again, this represents the best of all possible worlds.

Care should be exercised in structuring these arrangements. Any life insurance proceeds distribution should be treated as a distribution of future earnings or a draw. The reason for this is that basis adjustments through the insurance will occur at the end of the year. If the distribution occurs before the end of the year, there may be a distribution without a basis increase. If the distribution exceeds basis, then the excess is taxable as capital gain.[60] If the distribution is deemed an advance, then the transaction will remain open until the end of the tax year. The basis increase and decrease will occur at the same time, on the last day of the tax year. As such, no inadvertent capital gains problems should exist.

FRINGE BENEFITS

Because of the inherent passthrough rules of an LLC or FLP taxed as a partnership, the opportunity exists to create a deductible fringe benefit at the LLC or FLP level that is not income to the LLC or FLP member. The rules are constructed to include all fringe benefits as taxable under Section 61 subject to an exclusion contained in Section 132.[61]

Code section 132 contains a list of six categories of fringe benefits that are exempt from income taxation. The six categories are:

- No-additional-cost services.[62]
- Qualified employee discounts.[63]
- Working condition fringes.[64]
- De minimis fringes.[65]

- Qualified transportation fringes.[66]

- Qualified moving expense reimbursement.[67]

Even though it occurs third on the list, the most important exception is the working condition fringe benefit. This exception recognizes that there are many factors that go into an employee successfully completing his job. The section defines a working condition fringe as "...any property or services provided to an employee of the employer to the extent that, if the employee paid for such property or services, such payment would be allowable as a deduction under Section 162 or 167."[68] This section is important in that it simply provides that the expense has to meet the regular rules of business deductibility; it must be ordinary and necessary. Thus, items such as the company car, deduction for office rent, business supplies and support staff expenses are generally deductible. However, the provision ignores the fact that in reality, at the employee level, the expense may effectively not be deductible because of other Code provisions. For example, if the employee does not itemize deductions, it would be of little use. Likewise, at the employee level the deduction may be minimized by the 2% of adjusted gross income floor or the reduction in itemized deductions for certain high income taxpayers. In other words, all such expenses are fully deductible at the LLC or FLP level if the LLC or FLP provides the benefits. Thus, it is possible to structure benefits to be fully deductible through the LLC or FLP that would only be partially deductible if taken as personal deductions. This can represent a sizable tax planning opportunity and can more than cover the additional expenses of setting up and running the LLC or FLP.

FOOTNOTE REFERENCES

1. Most of the top-heavy rules are in Code section 416.
2. IRC Sec. 401(a)(9).
3. IRC Sec. 401(a)(5).
4. IRC Secs. 401(a)(17), 404(l).
5. IRC Sec. 416(b).
6. IRC Sec. 401(c) contains a series of definitions. Under these, members in an LLC or FLP will be deemed to be self-employed persons.
7. IRC Sec. 401(c)(2).
8. IRC Sec. 415(c)(1), IR 2000-82.
9. See IRC Sec. 404(a)(8).
10. IRC Sec. 404(e).
11. ERISA Sec. 408(d); ERISA is PL 93-406 (9/2/74).

12. ERISA Sec. 408(d)(1).
13. ERISA Sec. 408(d)(2).
14. ERISA Sec. 408(d)(3).
15. IRC Sec. 402(e)(4)(A).
16. IRC Sec. 404(a)(8)(C).
17. IRC Sec. 416(g).
18. IRC Sec. 416(i)(A)(i).
19. IRC Sec. 416(i)(A)(ii).
20. IRC Sec. 416(i)(A)(iii).
21. IRC Sec. 416(i)(A)(iv).
22. IRC Sec. 416(b).
23. Reg. §1.416-1, M-4.
24. Reg. §1.416-1, M-7, M-8, M-9.
25. IRC Secs. 401(a)(17)(A), 404(l).
26. IRC Sec. 401(a)(17)(B).
27. IRC Sec. 707.
28. H.R. Conf. Rep. No. 1337, 83rd Congress, 2nd Sess.
29. Reg. §1.707-1(c).
30. See Rev. Rul. 56-326, 1956-2 CB 100.
31. IRC Sec. 707(c).
32. *Id.*
33. See Postlewaite & Cameron, "Twisting Slowly in the Wind: Guaranteed Payments after the Tax Reform Act of 1984," 40 *Tax Lawyer* 649 (1987).
34. See *Cagle v. Comm.*, 539 F.2d 409 (5th Cir. 1976), *aff'g.* 63 TC 86 (1974)
35. IRC Sec. 106.
36. IRC Sec. 401(c)(1).
37. Rev. Rul. 91-26, 1991-1 CB 184.
38. IRC Sec. 162(l).
39. IRC Sec. 702(a)(8).
40. Rev. Rul. 91-26, 1991-1 CB 184; IRC Sec. 707(c).
41. See Rev. Rul. 91-26, 1991-1 CB 184.
42. IRC Sec. 79(a).
43. Reg. §1.79-3, Table I.
44. Reg. §1.79-1(f)(3).
45. Reg. §1.79-0.
46. Reg. §1.79-1(c).
47. Reg. §1.79-1(a).
48. Reg. §1.79-1(a)(4).
49. Reg. §31.3401(c)-1(b).
50. IRC Sec. 1372.
51. Reg. §31.3401(c)-1(f).
52. Reg. §31.3401(c)-1(c).
53. Reg. §1.79-1(d).
54. See IRC Sec. 31; Reg. §31.3401(c)-1(e).
55. Rev. Rul. 78-420, 1978-2 CB 67; TAM 9604001.
56. TAM 9604001.
57. IRC Sec. 731(a).
58. The death benefit is tax-free income under IRC Sec. 101(a) and, thus, increases basis.
59. IRC Sec. 7702A.
60. IRC Sec. 731(a).
61. See IRC Sec. 61; IRC Sec. 132.
62. IRC Sec. 132(a)(1).

63. IRC Sec. 132(a)(2).
64. IRC Sec. 132(a)(3).
65. IRC Sec. 132(a)(4).
66. IRC Sec. 132(a)(5).
67. IRC Sec. 132(a)(6).
68. IRC Sec. 132(d).

Chapter 8

SECURITIES, BANKRUPTCY AND OTHER FEDERAL LAW ISSUES

SECURITIES LAW

The federal securities laws apply to transactions involving securities. The definition of securities is very broad. In the seminal United States Supreme Court case, an investment contract was defined as "a contract, transaction, or scheme whereby a person invests his money in a common enterprise and is led to expect profits solely from the efforts of the promoter or a third party."[1]

Limited liability company interests would seem to meet most of the requirements of this test. Clearly, most members are making an investment and expecting a profit from that investment. The critical issue becomes the last part of the definition. Are the members relying "solely on the efforts" of someone else? If they are, it is a security. On the other hand, if the profit arises from their own efforts it is not a security. While there are no cases on this matter involving LLCs, there are a number of cases involving partnerships and it would seem that these cases are instructive by analogy.

A number of cases have held that a general partnership cannot meet the "solely on the efforts of others" test given the nature of a general partner.[2] The key issue is one of control and since a general partner has the power to control decisions of the general partnership, such a general partner cannot be said to rely on the efforts of others. It appears that under this analysis actual control is not needed, rather simply having the potential to be involved in the decision-making process will remove the general partner from the "efforts of others" category.

The Fifth Circuit Court of Appeals has held that this reasoning is not absolute. The court found that "the mere fact that an investment takes the form of a general partnership or joint venture does not inevitably insulate it from the reach of securities law."[3] The court held that while it would be a significant burden to overcome the presumption of control and hence be characterized as a security, it could happen. The court looked at three hypothetical possibilities where this could occur. The first possibility would be a partnership agreement that provided the general partners had little power, where the general partner was more akin to a limited partner. The second possibility would be an inexperienced partner who would be unable to exercise any real control due to the lack of experience. The third possibility discussed would be a partner who is dependent upon some unique entrepreneurial ability of a third party.

The Fourth Circuit Court of Appeals has had the ability to look at both the control issue and the *Williamson* language. In *Rivanna Trawlers Unlimited v. Borchardt*, the court started with the basic assumption that a general partnership will not be deemed a security because of the ability of the general partner to control the decision-making process.[4] In reiterating that only under limited circumstances could a general partnership be deemed a security, the court effectively followed the view of *Williamson*. However, it appears that the fourth circuit sought to limit *Williamson* to only the first of the three hypothetical situations. The court, in effect, held that the key in determining if a general partnership was a security would lie in the examination of the partnership agreement. If on the face of the agreement the powers of a general partner were specific and unambiguous, then the general partnership would not be a security since the powers would indicate the requisite element of control. The court further held that a partnership would be deemed to be a security only where it would not be possible for the general partners to exercise *any* control.

As a result, it would appear that only in extremely anomalous cases will a general partnership be deemed to be a security.

In the case of a limited partnership, the same control reasoning seems to cut the other way, namely, that limited partnerships *are* securities. There are a few cases that have held limited partnerships are not securities. These cases have generally been characterized by the limited partners having some voice in the control of the partnership, as well as being few in number. For example, a federal district court held that a limited partnership was not a security where the limited partner "had a say in the operation" of the partnership.[5] Some courts have focused on the number of limited partners as being a critical issue. If the limited partnership has only a few limited partners, it most likely will not be classified as a security.[6] Conversely, the second circuit has held that the presence of a large number of limited partners will be a factor in finding that the partnership is a security.[7]

Analogies to a general partnership or limited partnership would seem to be appropriate in the LLC context. As such, the control issue becomes as critical for LLCs as it is for partnership classifications. Therefore, the issue becomes one of determining whether there is sufficient control in the members so that the LLC will not be deemed to be a security. In this regard, there is much more flexibility with an LLC than with a limited partnership. The limited partnership rules basically provide that if a limited partner has too much of a say in the partnership, the partner loses limited liability and is deemed to be a general partner.[8] There is no similar prohibition for LLCs. Indeed, all members have limited liability regardless of their participation.

It would appear that a member-only LLC would not be a security. The reason for this is that, absent provisions to the contrary, state statutes provide that management vests with the members. Once the members have management capabilities, they must also be deemed to have control. Once the members have control, there is no delegation to others and the *Howey* test cannot be met.

In the case of an LLC that has managers, the issue would not be as clear. If the members in such an arrangement have no powers whatsoever, then the LLC could possibly be construed as a security. It would seem that such a situation would be very rare. There seems to be a gray area in between. If the members have no managers and have a voice in the operation of an LLC, it will clearly not be a security. The other extreme, where a few managers have complete control with a large number of silent members, probably will result in the LLC meeting the investment contract test and being classified as a security. Unlike the limited partnership, the LLC can strike a middle ground. Control rights may be allocated to members even in an LLC that has managers. According to the available case law, the courts have generally examined the operating agreement. To the extent that the operating agreement provides some control element to all members, this should be sufficient to remove the LLC from the sphere of being deemed a security.

The ability to structure some degree of control in an LLC, even where the managers have the bulk of operating responsibility, is a real plus for the LLC form of business. It gives the LLC a decided advantage over a limited partnership where similar flexibility does not exist. If the LLC is not a security, then most of the securities law issues are obviated. If the

LLC is not a security, then the formation of the LLC and the sale of interests therein will be much easier and less expensive. One will not have to worry about falling within one of the exemptions from registration. Even if the LLC were to fall into such an exemption, it is still very expensive to accomplish the due diligence to arrive at the point that an exemption is available. Issuers that have not complied with such due diligence will not have to worry that purchasers may be able to rescind the sale for a failure to so register a security. Likewise, the fraud and material misrepresentation actions under federal securities law will not be available. Any action that commences will be brought in state court under common law principles as opposed to being brought in federal court as a federal securities law issue.

The nonsecurities status of an LLC can be an important consideration. If the entity is a corporation and sells stock, stock is clearly a security. Since an LLC does not have stock and it is possible to give every member some element of control, the classification as a security can be avoided.

BANKRUPTCY LAW

Any person may be a debtor under the bankruptcy laws.[9] A "person" for this purpose is defined as including individuals, partners and corporations. While an LLC is clearly a person under this definition, it is not clear whether it is classified as a corporation or a partnership for bankruptcy purposes. The Bankruptcy Code defines a corporation as an "association having a power or privilege that a private corporation...possesses" and a "partnership association organized under a law that makes the capital subscribed responsible for the debts of such associations."[10] It would seem that under either definition, an LLC would be classified as a corporation for bankruptcy purposes. It would appear that the aspect of limited liability would be a "privilege that a corporation possesses." Likewise, partnership associations were precursors of LLCs that existed in a number of midwestern states. Also, capital in an LLC is responsible for the LLC's debts. Again, this arises, in part, because of the limited liability nature of an LLC. Because of limited liability, the members are not responsible for the debts of the LLC because the LLC itself is responsible. This result makes sense since if an LLC was deemed to be a partnership, the bankruptcy laws could result in individual members being forced to contribute to its debts.[11] Such a result would substantially negate the attribute of limited liability.

Providing that an LLC is a corporation for bankruptcy purposes preserves the essential character of an LLC – limited liability.

If an LLC is characterized as a corporation for bankruptcy proceedings, then the LLC can be a debtor under the law. The corporate characterization however, may cause further difficulties. The bankruptcy law is silent on the issue of whether a corporation can file for voluntary bankruptcy. On the other hand, the general partner can file a petition for voluntary bankruptcy in a limited partnership. In the case of a general partnership, if all general partners approve, then the petition is deemed to be voluntary. On the other hand, a petition by less than all partners is deemed to be involuntary.[12] It would seem that a bankruptcy court could apply similar rules to an LLC by analogy. However, the exact nature of what a court would actually do remains unclear.

Under the Bankruptcy Code, officers and directors of a corporation are deemed to be insiders.[13] It would seem that managers in a member-manager LLC would also be insiders. Likewise, general partners in a partnership are insiders.[14] It would appear that all members in a member-only LLC would be deemed to be insiders. However, in a member-manager LLC it would further appear that members only would not be treated as insiders.

FOREIGN LLCs AND INTERSTATE COMMERCE

A foreign LLC is one organized in one state and doing business in another state. This generally does not refer to an LLC organized in a foreign country.

The interstate commerce clause of the United States Constitution provides the specific underpinnings allowing an LLC organized in one state to do business in another. Under this clause, states are prevented from prohibiting LLCs or providing undue restrictions on LLCs or any other business engaging in interstate business. A state statute that attempts to hinder interstate commerce will be declared unconstitutional and void.[15] On the other hand, a state may exercise reasonable control over foreign LLCs. This can be justified under the police power of the state as well as the fact that states can regulate intrastate commerce. As a result, most LLC statutes have provisions for foreign LLCs. The trend has been to define foreign LLCs very broadly. Older statutes simply allowed foreign LLCs to register.[16] Newer statutes seem to be expanding this to include any organization affording limited liability to its members whether or not it is officially denominated an LLC.[17]

The process of allowing an LLC formed in one state to do business in another is generally called qualification. Qualification generally consists of filing an application containing basic LLC information and the designation of a registered agent within the state. In general, the application asks for information on the name of the LLC, the name and address of any mangers and the type of business engaged in by the LLC. In addition, some states require a certification that the LLC is valid in the original state of registration and that it remains in good standing in that state.[18]

Interestingly enough, most states allow the LLC to adopt any name that it wants in the foreign state. The name cannot be deceptively similar to any other business name in the foreign state. Most states allow for the reservation of a name. The sole requirement is that the business must use the LLC indicia or something similar even if it is not officially an LLC in the state of original jurisdiction.[19] Maine requires that the full limited liability company be used with no abbreviation.[20] The LLC generally must designate a registered agent based in the state where the LLC is registering as a foreign LLC.

Most states limit a foreign LLC to activities that are legal for domestic LLCs. Some states contain a laundry list of activities deemed to be isolated transactions that do not require the full registration of a foreign LLC. One such statute allows sales through independent contractors, making loans, maintaining a bank account and soliciting orders through the mail to be isolated transactions which, if the business of the LLC is limited to these activities, does not necessitate full registration as a foreign LLC.[21]

A foreign LLC may be subject to a fine if it does not register with the state. Likewise, the attorney general of the state may file an injunction to prohibit the LLC from doing business there. If an LLC does business in a foreign state and does not register, generally suit may be brought against it by filing notice of the action with the foreign state's secretary of state.[22] On the other hand, an unregistered foreign LLC is generally denied access to the courts of the foreign state to initiate suit.[23] Contracts entered into by the unregistered LLC are unaffected by its failure to register.[24] While such an LLC cannot initiate a suit, it can defend itself in a suit brought by others.[25] It would seem that contracts entered into *after* an attorney general has received an injunction against the foreign LLC would have questionable validity, although this is not clear at this time.[26]

One of the most important issues governing foreign LLCs is the choice of law question. Which state law applies? Is it the law of the domestic state or the law of the foreign state? In the case of *transactions* involving the foreign state, generally the place of the transaction will govern which state law is applicable. On the other hand, a number of statutes specifically provide that the law of the domestic state of formation applies to internal management and workings of the LLC.[27] It would seem that absent such a specific provision, the same result should occur. Under basic federal principles, it seems that the foreign state would have to give full faith and credit to the domestic state in matters governing the internal workings of the LLC. It would also seem that the provisions for limited liability would themselves be an internal issue. Delaware specifically provides that the domestic state governs on all issues involving the applicability of limited liability.[28] This, of course, poses at least the potential for forum shopping on the liability issue. While it does not appear that there is a great discrepancy between the states on the limited liability protection issue, if one were to develop in the future, this type of provision may result in certain states being favored for formation even though actual operations lie elsewhere. In essence, this type of provision makes the various state laws portable. Formation can occur in one state that would have very protective laws on the liability issue, while actual operations are conducted in a less stringent state. The more comprehensive provision on liability would, in effect, be transferred to the foreign state.

It remains to be seen exactly how such a provision will play out for professional LLCs. Professional LLCs are generally permitted. However, one must be sure the professional governing body has recognized the validity of the professional LLC. For example, usually state supreme court approval is needed for an LLC to be formed for attorneys. Most states have complied with these provisions, but it is important to note any extra governing provisions provided by the regulatory body for the particular profession.

A further issue exists in the case of foreign LLCs doing business in a jurisdiction that either has no LLC statute or has a statute that is silent regarding the nature and effect of a foreign LLC. Four arguments seem to require the validity of the foreign LLC.

The first argument rests under the common law principle of comity. Comity is defined as "courtesy, complaisance and respect."[29] Comity is an imprecise term and apparently falls somewhere between ironclad obligation to recognize the other state's law and a mere courtesy to the other state. While it appears that comity never is a sufficient reason by itself to recognize the validity of another state's law, it can be used to bolster other arguments in favor of validity.[30]

The second argument relates to the full faith and credit clause of the United States Constitution. This clause requires every state to give full faith and credit to the laws of every other state. In general, states do not have to give credence to all laws of another state. On the other hand, states are obligated to give full faith and credit to those laws that are *not* arbitrary or blatantly unfair.[31] Assuming that such prosaic material as LLC legislation will not be construed as blatantly unfair, it would appear that states would recognize the LLC legislation of other states.

The third argument relates to the *Restatement of Laws (Second Edition) of the Conflict of Laws*. This is the most recent edition of a learned treatise on the subject of how one state's laws are valid in another state. While there is currently no LLC provision in this book, Section 307 states that in the corporate area a foreign state should recognize the domestic state's laws on limited liability. By analogy, a similar result should occur with an LLC.

The fourth argument relates back to the interstate commerce clause. In recent years, the courts have reinvigorated the commerce clause and invalidated a number of state statutes designed to be applied against foreign businesses. For example, in one case an Ohio statute that applied only to foreign entities that acquired Ohio corporations was struck down.[32] The gist of these cases seems to be that the interstate commerce clause requires states to treat both their internal business ventures and external business ventures the same. One cannot create an unfair home advantage by discriminating against foreign businesses. This strong anti-discrimination theme would seem to apply in the LLC context as well.

FOOTNOTE REFERENCES

1. *SEC v. W.J. Howey Co.*, 328 U.S. 293, 298-299 (1946).
2. See *Goodwin v. Elkins & Co.*, 730 F.2d 99 (3rd Cir. 1984); *Odom v. Slavik*, 703 F.2d 212 (6th Cir. 1983); *Frazier v. Manson*, 651 F.2d 1078 (5th Cir. 1981).
3. *Williamson v. Tucker*, 645 F.2d 404, 422 (5th Cir. 1981).
4. 840 F.2d 236 (1988).
5. *Bamco 18 v. Reeves*, 675 F.Supp. 826 (S.D.N.Y. 1987).
6. See *Bank of American Nat'l Trust v. Hotel Rittenhouse*, 595 F. Supp. 800 (E.D. Pa. 1984).
7. *Mayer v. Oil Field Systems Corp.*, 721 F.2d 59 (2nd Cir. 1983).
8. Uniform Limited Partnership Act, Sec.6; Revised Uniform Limited Partnership Act, Sec. 303 (1991 Supp.).
9. 11 U.S.C. §109.
10. 11 U.S.C. §101(9).
11. 11 U.S.C. §548(b).
12. 11 U.S.C. §303(b)(3).
13. 11 U.S.C. §101(30)(A).
14. 11 U.S.C. §101(30)(B).
15. *Dahnke-Walker Milling Co. v. Bondurant*, 257 U.S. 282 (1921).
16. See Delaware: 6 D.C.A. §18-901.
17. See Maine: 31 M.R.S.A. §602(6).
18. Delaware: 6 D.C.A. §18-902(1)(b); Maine: 31 M.R.S.A. §712(3)(H).
19. Delaware: 6 D.C.A. §18-904(a).
20. Maine: 31 M.R.S.A. §605(4).
21. Maine: 31 M.R.S.A. §712(1)(A) through (N).
22. Delaware: 6 D.C.A. §18-911.
23. Maine: 31 M.R.S.A. §718(1).
24. Delaware: 6 D.C.A. §18-907(b)(1).
25. Delaware: 6 D.C.A. §18-907(b)(3).
26. See Maine: 31 M.R.S.A. §719(1).
27. Maine: 31 M.R.S.A. §711(1).
28. Delaware: 6 D.C.A. §18-901.1.
29. Black's Law Dictionary p. 267 (1990).
30. See *Hilton v. Guyot*, 159 U.S. 113 (1895).
31. *Allstate Ins. Co. v. Hague*, 449 U.S. 302 (1981).
32. *Campeau Corp. v. Federated Dep't Stores*, 679 F. Supp. 735 (S.D. Oh. 1988).

Chapter 9

MERGERS AND CONVERSIONS

OVERVIEW

The limited liability company is obviously a very attractive business vehicle. Other business forms include C corporations, S corporations and partnerships. This chapter looks at the conversion and merger strategies and consequences involved in changing from one of these business forms to an LLC.

TERMINOLOGY AND STATE STATUTES

"Conversion" generally means the changing from a partnership to an LLC. For taxation purposes, the goal is to do this with as few negative tax ramifications as possible. Potential tax consequences include the taxation of any gain, and changes to the owners' basis in the LLC (usually referred to as outside basis) and the basis of the assets that constitute the LLC (usually referred to as inside basis). The term "merger" usually means the combination of two separate entities into one, for example a partnership and an LLC being merged into one LLC.

In general, most, but not all, LLC statutes use the term merger. Some statutes refer to this process as merger and consolidation.[1] In most states other entities are permitted to merge into an LLC. For example, Delaware specifically allows for a merger between a "corporation,...business trust or association,...real estate investment trust,...common law trust,...unincorporated business,...partnership (including a registered limited liability partnership) or...foreign limited liability company, and...domestic limited liability company."[2] The Maine statute, on the other hand, only refers to the merger of an LLC into another LLC.[3] Virtually no statutes use the word conversion.

The importance of these language distinctions may eventually lie in the tax treatment of the merger or conversion. For example, the transaction usually can be structured in one of three ways. Consider an example where the old entity is referred to as Oldco and the new entity as LLC. First, Oldco can be merged into the LLC with the interests in the LLC distributed in liquidation to Oldco's owners. Second, Oldco can be liquidated to its members with the formation of a new LLC with the distributed assets. Finally, Oldco can sell its assets to the LLC. The LLC interests are then distributed to Oldco's owners in liquidation of Oldco. In a state that does not allow a merger, presumably the second and third options will still be available. In a state allowing a merger, all three options should be available. The problem occurs in considering whether the tax results should be different depending upon which of the three forms the merger utilizes. Unfortunately, there is little IRS guidance on this point. If ultimately all three transactions have the same tax result, then this problem is interesting only from a theoretical possibility. On the other hand, if different tax results arise from different structures, then the state statutes, as well as the planning route chosen, will be critical. Obviously, tax traps for the unwary will exist in such a situation. This subject will be discussed in greater detail below.

In a number of states the LLC must file a certificate of merger. Generally, this certificate asks for the same basic information that is provided in the articles of organization as well as submission of a filing fee.[4] In most states there must be a recitation in the certificate that both entities have voted for and approved the merger.

MERGER OF CORPORATIONS AND LLCs

In general, it makes little tax sense to merge either a C or an S corporation into an LLC. In the case of a C corporation, a double taxation results. First, the corporation will recognize gain on the assets of the corporation.[5] Then the assets will be deemed distributed to the owners of the corporation and the owners will have gain as well.[6] Finally, the transaction will be characterized as a contribution to the new LLC.[7] This result will occur no matter how it is structured. In all events, the sale of assets (creating gain to the corporation) followed by a liquidation to the shareholders (creating gain to the shareholders) will occur. There is really no way to avoid this problem.

In the case of an S corporation there will be a single level of tax occurring at the shareholder level. A private letter ruling recently addressed an S corporation merging with an LLC.[8] The letter ruling states that the basic single level of taxation rule applies to the S shareholders. The difference between their basis in the S corporation and the fair market value of the assets received by the LLC was deemed to be the measure of gain subject to taxation. Presumably, if the holding period of Code section 1223 is met, then the tax would be at capital gains rates. For S corporations there may be a capital gains tax at the corporate level as well. Code section 1374 provides for an S corporation level capital gains tax when the corporation has converted from a C corporation within a 10-year time period and the corporation had built-in gains at the time of the conversion. This point should be considered with care for any S corporation considering conversion into an LLC.

One important exception does apply. Code section 337 allows for the merger of a subsidiary into another entity on a tax-free basis. In another private letter ruling, the IRS had the opportunity to examine a corporate subsidiary merging into an LLC.[9] In essence, the IRS found that the merger would be tax free since the Section 337 provision had been met. This ruling poses an interesting merger approach with the desired tax consequences, albeit in a somewhat limited form, since it will only apply in the case of a subsidiary merging with the LLC.

CONVERSIONS OF PARTNERSHIPS

The most common planning situation that will occur is when a partnership converts to an LLC.

In Revenue Ruling 84-52, the IRS had the opportunity to examine the conversion of a general partnership to a limited partnership.[10] The ruling concluded the following:

- The IRS treated the transaction as a contribution by the partners of their general partnership interests for interests in the limited partnership. The IRS further concluded that Code section 721 would apply to this transaction so that no gain would be recognized by the general partners.

- The business of the partnership was not terminated under Code section 708. As such, there was no need to file a final return, close the tax year, or modify any accounting treatment.

- The transaction had to be examined under Code section 752 with regard to the assumption of liabilities. If there is no change in the liabilities, then there is no change in any of the partners'

> adjusted bases. If there is a change in a partner's share of liabilities causing a deemed contribution by the partner, then the adjusted basis of that partner's interest shall be increased by the amount of such deemed contribution. Likewise, the decrease of any liabilities would be equivalent to a cash distribution from the partnership to the LLC, reducing basis. If this amount exceeded basis, then the partner would recognize gain on the excess.

The IRS has recently found that the precepts of Revenue Ruling 84-52 would apply when a partnership converts to an LLC.[11] The specific facts of the ruling involve the conversion of a domestic partnership to a domestic LLC taxed as a partnership. In essence, the ruling serves to adopt the principles of Revenue Ruling 84-52 and apply it to the conversion to the LLC. In Revenue Ruling 95-37, there is considerable discussion of the fact that the tax year of the partnership does not close. In essence, for taxation purposes, it is as if absolutely nothing has changed with the old partnership. This makes sense, since the new LLC is taxed as a partnership, the old partnership was taxed as a partnership, so the result is nothing more than the continuation of the old partnership.

In Revenue Ruling 95-55, the IRS also recently ruled on the conversion of a partnership to a limited liability partnership (LLP).[12] A number of states allow for a limited partnership to be an LLP by simply filing a certificate to that effect. In many ways the conversion automatically results in the LLP being taxed as a partnership. Another way of saying this is that the tax treatment of an LLP is similar to an LLC formed under a bulletproof statute. That is, regardless of what is done the entity must be taxed as a partnership. This is opposed to an LLC that may be taxed either as a corporation or as a partnership. Thus, for conservative individuals, the LLP conversion may be attractive since partnership taxation will necessarily occur. Revenue Ruling 95-55 reiterates the principles of no taxation and no change in any tax attributes that were contained in Revenue Rulings 84-52 and 95-37.

PROFESSIONAL LLCs

The early LLC statutes did not draw any distinction between LLCs in general and professional LLCs in particular. This has changed and later statutes specifically contain provisions allowing professionals to form

LLCs. This can be done by separate provisions for professionals,[13] or by incorporating the state's professional corporation statute by reference.[14]

A number of states formerly had prohibitions against professionals being able to form LLCs. Many of these have been repealed.[15] Only Rhode Island and California appear to have statutes that currently prohibit professionals from using the LLC form. California is considering a repeal of its prohibition.[16]

The use of LLCs by professionals is appealing for a number of reasons. First and foremost is the limited liability aspect. In general, professionals in a corporation are liable for their own negligence, but not for the negligence of their fellow professionals. This treatment has been afforded only if the professional practice was a corporation, which resulted in the negative double taxation consequences that a corporation incurs coupled with the onerous personal service corporation rules.[17] The LLC enables a professional practice to be afforded the liability protection desired along with the favorable taxation rules of a partnership. It is this flexibility that is the second important factor for professionals utilizing an LLC. Among the chief features here is the ability to characterize payments to retiring members as either deductible or nondeductible in nature.[18] As a result, many professional practices are selecting the LLC form of doing business.

It appears that many existing professional partnerships will probably be examining a conversion to the LLC form of business. The IRS has issued a private letter ruling on the conversion of a professional partnership to a professional LLC.[19] The ruling is an excellent reference source. The first part of the ruling examines the classical classification issues relating to an LLC being taxed as a partnership. The ruling then reiterates the tax consequences of the conversion following the precepts of Revenue Rulings 84-52 and 95-37. Both rulings are summarized in excellent form. The letter ruling makes it very clear that the members' basis in the LLC will carry over from their basis in the partnership. The ruling reemphasizes that such a conversion is a non-event tax wise. For example, the ruling notes that the capital gains holding period does not start anew. Likewise, the tax accounting methodology of the partnership (it was a cash basis taxpayer) will continue unabated. The Code section 708 non-termination rules are also restated with the conclusion that the conversion is not a termination.

The ruling is interesting in another regard. All of the other rulings have examined the various basis carryover provisions. One issue that has not been discussed in any previous ruling is the determination of the basis of assets in the LLC. Does the inside basis of assets in the partnership carry over to the LLC? The ruling says that indeed it does.

The ruling specifically states "[t]he basis of the PLLC assets will equal the basis of those assets in P immediately before the conversion." What makes this interesting is that it would appear that Code section 723 would mandate a different result. Code section 723 could be interpreted to provide that in the conversion the members' outside basis in the partnership becomes the inside basis of the assets in the LLC. The ruling obviously rejects that approach. The net effect is very similar to what occurs in the corporate merger situation under so-called "F" reorganizations.[20] Under the F reorganization analogy, the conversion is an event that creates no taxable events, and all attributes such as basis carry over in all respects. Given its all around importance, Letter Ruling 9538022 is reproduced in Appendix B.

FOOTNOTE REFERENCES

1. For example, both Maine and Delaware use this term.
2. Delaware: 6 D.C.A. §18-209.
3. Maine: 31 M.R.S.A. §741.1.
4. See Delaware: 6 D.C.A. §18-209(c).
5. IRC Sec. 336(a).
6. IRC Sec. 331(a).
7. IRC Sec. 721.
8. Let. Rul. 9543017.
9. Let. Rul. 9409014.
10. 1984-1 CB 157.
11. Rev. Rul. 95-37, 1995-1 CB 130. This ruling is reproduced in its entirety in Appendix B.
12. 1995-2 CB 313.
13. New Hampshire: N.H.R.S.A. Chap. 304-D.
14. Maine: 31 M.R.S.A. §645.3.
15. See for example, Maryland Corps. & Assns. Code Ann. §4A-201, which was modified by S.B. 547 effective 5/27/93.
16. Rhode Island: G.L.R.I. §7-16-3.
17. IRC Sec. 269A.
18. See Chapter 6 for a full discussion of this feature.
19. Let. Rul. 9538022.
20. Code section 368(a)(1)(F) provides that a "mere change of identity" is a completely tax-free transaction where no gain is recognized and where all basis carries over. It is the ultimate tax "non-event."

Chapter 10

ESTATE PLANNING

As is the case in many other areas, an LLC also combines the best attributes of corporations and partnerships in the area of estate planning. Just as partnerships are becoming very attractive estate planning vehicles, LLCs can also be very attractive estate planning vehicles. There are a number of tax and non-tax reasons that make an LLC attractive. The tax advantages are numerous and the flexibility of the LLC will allow any individual to maximize these advantages.

VALUATION

A key aspect of any estate plan is to minimize values for estate and transfer tax purposes. The classic estate plan result is a freeze. Generally, a freeze may be characterized by three different aspects. The first aspect is to transfer the property during one's lifetime. In other words, the key is to make a lifetime transfer or gift. Gifts have two advantages over transfers at death. While the goal has been to create a unified transfer tax system, this result has never been fully achieved.[1] For this reason, the gift tax has two advantages over the estate tax system. First, the estate tax is tax inclusive while the gift tax is tax exclusive. Another way of stating this is that the tax paid for the estate tax is part of the calculation of the estate tax itself. This "tax upon a tax" characteristic is not present in the gift tax area. This result can be demonstrated by comparing a $1,000,000 estate tax calculation with a $1,000,000 gift tax calculation. Assuming a 55% marginal bracket with no available credits, the estate tax will be 55% x $1,000,000 or $550,000. The $550,000 tax was part of the tax base (the $1,000,000). In the gift tax scenario, the $1,000,000 is split into a gift of $645,161 and a tax (at 55%) of $354,839. The tax is not part of the gift.

The second advantage of the gift tax is the availability of the annual exclusion. This provision allows tax-free gifts up to $10,000 (as indexed) per year per donee.[2] In the case of a husband and wife, each couple may make a split gift of up to $20,000 per year per donee. While this amount does not seem like much, judicious use over time can result in a substantial amount of wealth being transferred tax free.

The third advantage of making a gift is that any appreciation on the value of the property after the gift is made escapes tax. If a $1,000,000 gift is made and the property appreciates to $2,000,000 at the death of the donor, there is no recapture of tax on the $1,000,000 gain that occurred after the gift was made. There are only a limited number of situations where recapture applies and those are limited to situations where death occurs within three years of the transfer.[3]

Property will be valued at its fair market value for both gift tax and estate tax purposes. Fair market value is generally what a buyer and seller in an arm's length transaction would agree as to price.[4] The issue of valuation was litigated a number of times in the 1980s and 1990s. The courts generally found that fair market value could be decreased for a number of discount factors. These factors include discounts for lack of control (minority discounts), lack of marketability, lack of liquidation rights, lack of voting rights and lack of liquidity. At the same time, practitioners were devising various freeze techniques. These techniques generally involved fractionalizing business interests into various parts. The donor would retain an income interest that represented the bulk of the business's value. This was generally construed as a preferred or senior equity interest. A common or junior interest would be given away at little current value. However, all of the appreciation would occur in this junior interest, which would subsequently acquire all of the appreciation. The donor would retain control and the economic rights while at the same time freezing the value for estate tax purposes.

After an aborted attempt to address this problem in 1988,[5] a second attempt at resolving valuation issues commenced in 1990 resulting in new Chapter 14 of the Internal Revenue Code.

CHAPTER 14

Chapter 14 is the shortest chapter in the Internal Revenue Code. It consists of only four individual sections, Code sections 2701 through 2704.

Code section 2701 is designed to address the freeze situations as well as establish the basic tenets of Chapter 14. Under this section, if a transferor transfers an interest in a family business to a family member and retains an applicable retained interest in the business, the value of the applicable retained interest is deemed to be zero.[6] A transfer with the donor retaining an applicable retained interest will be deemed to be a transfer of the full business interest at full fair market value. Among the types of applicable retained interests are "a distribution right"[7] and "a liquidation, put, call, or conversion right."[8]

On the other hand, if the distribution right is a qualified payment, then its value may be discounted from the value of the gift.[9] A qualified payment is a distribution right that is fixed in amount or percentage. The percentage can itself be either a fixed or variable rate based "on a specified market interest rate."[10] In addition, the right must be cumulative, meaning that if it is not paid in one year it must be paid in the next. Likewise, a liquidation, put, call or conversion right may be taken into account to reduce value if the right is fixed,[11] or is a right to convert.[12] A fixed right is a right that can be exercised only for a specific time and specific amount. The right to convert is a non-lapsing right to convert interests that are the same as the transferred interest.

Code section 2702 applies these basic rules to non-business situations such as trusts. Code section 2703 imposes special rules on buy-sell agreements involving family members. Basically, such transactions must be at fair market value.[13] Code section 2704 contains miscellaneous rules, including special rules for liquidation rights. Liquidation rights are discussed below.

LIQUIDATION RIGHTS

The string of taxpayer victories during the 1980s was probably capped by the famous case of *Estate of Harrison v. Commissioner*.[14] In this case, the decedent owned an interest in a limited partnership. The interest was worth $60,000,000, based on its liquidation value. Liquidation value means the value of the underlying assets that would accrue to the partner if the partnership were dissolved and the property distributed to the partners. However, the decedent partner lacked a right to compel liquidation. Because of this inability to cause a liquidation, the estate claimed that the value of the interest was worth $33,000,000, not $60,000,000. The Tax Court agreed with the estate. In response to this case, Congress enacted Code sections 2704(a) and 2704(b) to eliminate any future *Harrison* situations.

Code section 2704(a) imposes a gift tax or estate tax if a person holds a liquidation right that lapses and is transferred to another family member. The fair market value of the right is deemed to be the value of the gift or, if this occurs at death, the estate tax value. Code section 2704(b) represents the converse of Section 2704(a). It is in essence the legislative repeal of *Harrison*. This provision states that a liquidation right is to be disregarded for valuation purposes unless there is a valid commercial reason for the right.[15] The restriction applies only if the liquidation right will lapse in the hands of the transferor, or if it can be removed after a transfer to a member of the transferor's family.[16] If the right never lapses or cannot be removed, then it can be taken into account for valuation purposes. In addition, if the right is "imposed by any Federal or State law" it is *not* to be disregarded.[17] Such a provision may be taken into account in reducing value. This is of critical importance in the LLC context. If the right in the LLC's operating agreement is not more restrictive than the appropriate state statute, such restriction may be utilized to reduce the valuation of the LLC interest.

The final aspect of Code section 2704 relates to the legislative repeal of another valuation case. In *Estate of Watts v. Commissioner*, the Tax Court was faced with examining two different methods of valuation.[18] One was the liquidation value. The other was the going concern value. Going concern value essentially is a capitalization of earnings of the business. In *Watts*, the going concern value was less than the liquidation value. The IRS argued that the higher liquidation value should be utilized in this case. The Tax Court, however, sided with the estate and imposed only the going concern value. The Tax Court examined the business agreement, which provided that the business could not be liquidated at the death of any of the owners. As such, the Tax Court felt that use of the liquidation method of valuation would be inappropriate. The legislative history of Code section 2704(b) makes it clear that the section is meant to apply in a situation like the one in *Watts*. The idea is that by denying the use of liquidation restrictions, the Tax Court, or any other valuing body, is free to apply the liquidation method. This is particularly true when liquidation value is significantly higher than going concern value.

The regulations specifically provide that there is to be no double taxation consequences through the interaction of these various liquidation provisions. For example, a liquidation right disregarded for gift tax purposes (meaning that the gift includes the value of the right) cannot also create a taxable event if it lapses under Code section 2704.[19]

MINORITY DISCOUNTS

The above material is silent regarding the availability of minority discounts. Indeed, the legislative history of Code section 2704 specifically states that it does *not* apply to minority discounts.[20] The IRS had lost cases on this issue, specifically cases involving obtaining minority discounts where the transferees were family members of the transferor. The IRS argued a sort of common law attribution rule. This argument centered on the fact that since the recipients were family members of the transferor, control still existed if one looked at the family as a unit. However, the Tax Court and two federal circuit courts disagreed with the IRS and allowed a minority discount for the transfer of a minority interest to a family member.[21]

Given the language in the Conference Reports and the lack of judicial success, the IRS "threw in the towel" on this issue with the issuance of Revenue Ruling 93-12.[22] This ruling is one of the most important rulings that the IRS has issued in many years. The facts of the ruling are very simple. A taxpayer owned 100% of a business. He made a gift of 20% of the business to each of his five children. The IRS found that a minority discount was available on the value of the gift where each recipient received a minority interest even though the recipients were family members of the transferor.

This is a very important planning technique because it can result in a discount of anywhere from 25% to 50%. The figure that is usually utilized is 35%. While this amount cannot be applied in every situation, it does show the potential magnitude of the importance of this tool.

INCOME TAX CONSIDERATIONS

Originally, family limited partnerships were used as devices to split income among family members. The IRS challenged the concept of putting assets into a partnership and making gifts to family members as being an effective device to split up income among family members. The IRS lost these arguments in the Supreme Court case of *Commissioner v. Culbertson.*[23] The precepts of *Culbertson* became part of the Internal Revenue Code when Congress enacted Code section 704(e) in 1954.

This section provides that a family limited partnership will be respected if the following requirements are met:

- The partnership is one where capital is a material income producing factor.
- The partnership interest was created by purchase or gift.
- The distributive share of each partner is included in his gross income.

Splitting income among family members has become less important in recent years. Part of the reason has been the emphasis of the family partnership as an estate planning device, with little concern for income tax results. Another reason has been the imposition of the so-called "kiddie tax" where income of individuals under 14 years of age is taxed at their parents' rate.[24]

In addition, the regulations make it clear that if the donor in a family limited partnership retains control over making distributions to the partners, then the donor will be taxed on all the income.[25]

The goal of income splitting has become less important in recent years. Because of the "kiddie tax" rules, it may not be available. Given the relatively flat marginal brackets it may not be important. This may be advantageous. If income is distributed to a child, but taxed to the parent, it will not be a taxable gift. Thus, it may be characterized as a gift tax-free transfer. That result may outweigh any income shifting desires.

Where the income control question does become important is in the context of Code section 2036. This estate tax section provides that if someone transfers property and retains income, or the right to designate who is to receive income, then the assets come back into the transferor's estate. The question then becomes does this apply to a family limited partnership situation? The IRS has said that it does not. The IRS indicated in two recent private letter rulings that the fiduciary duties owed by a general partner would preclude estate tax includability.[26] The same rule should apply if there is a family limited liability company since fiduciary powers are established in the LLC context similar to those of the limited partnership.

THE FAMILY LIMITED LIABILITY COMPANY

Putting all these concepts together, it is easy to see the attractiveness of using a family limited liability company as an estate planning device.

The family LLC should be constructed so it will be classified as a partnership for federal income tax purposes. This will mean that all of the family limited partnership rules will apply. The family LLC has an advantage over the family limited partnership.

The following points are critical in establishing the family LLC:

- The creator of the family LLC should be its only manager. The manager is analogous to a general partner and should own at least one percent of all LLC items of "income, gain, loss, deduction or credit."[27] Since it is an LLC, the manager, unlike the general partner, will not have unlimited personal liability. Whatever percentage of ownership the manager owns will be included in his estate.[28]

- Only the creator should transfer assets to the LLC members by gift. If there is more than one transferor and the assets are investments, then there is the possibility that the LLC will be deemed to be an investment company.[29] In such a situation, the gain on the investments is taxed at the time of transfer.

- Revenue Procedure 95-10, 1995-1 CB 501, should be followed in order to classify the LLC as a partnership. Revenue Procedure 95-10 is reproduced in its entirety in Appendix A.

- The interests of the members (i.e., family) should be created by gift.[30] The IRS has ruled that gifts to limited partners will qualify for the annual exclusion.[31] By analogy, it should also be available to LLC members.

- Where minor children are members, a guardian or trust should be appointed to own the interest on their behalf. While the regulations[32] and one case[33] allow for the minor to own the interest outright if "[he] is competent to manage property," prudence would seem to dictate that a trust or guardian be appointed. A trust provides a sensible vehicle in this situation.

- The members, as donees of the LLC interests, should have no management rights in the LLC.[34]

- Strict compliance should be followed in all LLC formalities such as proper filings, operating agreements, filing of tax returns, etc.[35]

- The strictures of Chapter 14, as well as the partnership allocation rules, should be examined in any proposed LLC structure.

ASSET PROTECTION

One advantage to using an LLC as opposed to a partnership is that the creator of the entity can still have limited liability. In other words, individual members are not subject to the liabilities of the LLC. Another question involving asset protection is if an individual LLC member is sued, can the creditor pursue the LLC member's interest in order to satisfy the obligation? This is, in essence, a question of individual liability being transferred to the LLC.

In general, LLC statutes provide that if there is an assignment of an LLC interest, the assignee has no rights in the management of the LLC and is entitled to only share in its profits and losses.[36] Indeed, the member still remains a member, even though his interest is assigned. This applies until the members agree that the assignee shall become a member.[37]

A number of statutes specifically provide that the rights of a judgment creditor are simply that of an assignee and nothing more.[38] Thus, such a creditor has no ownership or voting rights, only a right to share in profits and losses. If the LLC makes distributions discretionary, this further means that such a creditor will have the taxable consequence of profits or losses. The taxable consequences consist of having to report his share of distributive income. Thus, the creditor may wind up having to report taxable income without ever being assured of getting actual distributions. Since the creditor is an assignee and not a member, he has no right to compel distributions. Thus, the creditor may have the tax responsibility without the assets to pay the tax. This result, which is well known to many creditors, makes the LLC a very potent asset protection device. Under this rule, proceeding against an LLC interest may result in acquiring only a tax bill and nothing more. This serves to insulate most LLC interests from attachment by creditors and results in the LLC's ability to serve as an asset protection vehicle.

MEDICARE AND MEDICAID PLANNING

A number of commentators have suggested that a family limited partnership may be an ideal Medicare or Medicaid asset protection vehicle.[39] The intent would be to structure a family limited partnership or family LLC in such a way that the underlying assets are not accessible and not counted for purposes of the Medicaid assets test. Since the assets would be locked up in the LLC it could be argued that they are unavailable.

The use of an LLC in this way is entirely untested. Under the OBRA rules, it appears that an LLC would be tested under the trust rules.[40] This would serve to create an examination of the income rules, as well as the resource rules. Under the income rules, the income of the recipient is also examined. If the LLC pays income out to the recipient, it will be reported to the IRS as part of the Schedule K-1 of Form 1065. However, under these rules, spouses' incomes are treated as separate assets so that it may be possible to shift income to the healthy spouse.

Another problem may be in the estate recovery rules. At least the mandatory one percent interest would be estate includable and subject to recapture. This may be avoided by using something like a revocable trust. However, it would appear that these solutions may not be very practical. Great care must be exercised in any planning activities in this area.

LLC VERSUS A TRUST

An LLC would appear to be more advantageous than a trust in many situations. A family limited partnership was used in place of a marital trust in one very interesting private letter ruling.[41] In that ruling, the husband transferred a 98% limited partnership interest to his wife while retaining a one percent general partnership interest. As the only general partner, he was in control of the investment decisions. The ruling concluded that there would be a present interest for purposes of the lifetime gift marital deduction since the wife would always have a 99% interest (she had owned one percent prior to the transfer). While the interest may be made up of different assets, the percentage of the interest in the partnership could not be changed after the transfer. The ruling also concluded that there would be no retained interest that would trigger a reinclusion for estate tax purposes. The interest could be sold by the wife or otherwise disposed of by her. As such, the husband retained nothing, even though he had the investment control power, since he was the only general partner. A similar result would be achieved through a family LLC.

Interestingly enough, it would appear that there would be a similar result for a transfer at death. At least the possibility exists that an LLC could be an estate tax marital deduction planning vehicle. We will have to wait and see if there are any future developments in this regard.

Another important use of an LLC for family gift purposes will be the ability to use the LLC in place of a Uniform Gifts to Minors Act (UGMA) disposition. A disposition utilizing an LLC member-only interest will not evolve into total and unbridled ownership, at age 18 or 21, as would happen under the UGMA. With an LLC, it would be possible to remove any restriction upon a member's interest at any time. Such removal, however, may have additional gift tax consequences. Even with the additional gift tax consequences, the LLC would seem to be a much better choice than a UGMA disposition.

THE LIFE INSURANCE LLC

One of the ongoing concerns of both partnerships and LLCs has been the question of whether an entity taxed as a partnership can own life insurance as its only asset. The issue has revolved around the requirement contained in the former classification regulations that the entity must have a "business objective." In a recent private letter ruling, a valid partnership was found where "[t]he partnership…engage[s] in the purchase and acquisition of life insurance policies on the lives of its partners. [The] [p]artnership [has] ownership rights in the policies and…manage[s] a portfolio of insurance policies."[42] On the other hand, more recently, in revenue procedures, the IRS has stated that it would not rule on "whether in connection with the transfer of a life insurance policy to an unincorporated organization, (i) the organization will be treated as a partnership under Sections 761 and 7701."[43] Further compounding this issue is the idea that courts have historically examined the business objective test as only necessitating a review of the organizational documents, and not an examination of the actual operations of the entity. In other words, so long as the business organizational documents delineated a business purpose then the business objective test was met.

A recent article in *Tax Lawyer* stated, "[t]hat the participants never actually engage in business or exercise the permitted business powers is irrelevant, as long as the documents indicate a possible business objective and bestow the requisite business powers."[44] Likewise, a recent Tax Court case reiterated the concept that the business objective test is met by examining the documents. In *Allen v. Commissioner*, the court stated that "[a] trust has a business objective if it is created to enable the parties to carry on a business enterprise and divide the gains which accrue from the common enterprise. [*citations omitted*] We look to the trust document to determine the purpose for which a trust entity was formed. The purpose cannot be different or narrower than provided by the document."[45]

In spite of the above discussion, some commentators have been uncomfortable with an entity taxed as a partnership having its sole purpose to own life insurance.

With the advance of the classification regulations, it would appear that these concerns are even less founded. The business objective requirement ceases to exist under these regulations. Rather, the entity has to be a joint undertaking. "A joint venture or other contractual arrangement may create a separate entity for federal tax purposes if the participants carry on a trade, business, financial operation, or venture, and divide the profits therefrom."[46] Under this construct, it would seem that life insurance would qualify as a financial operation or venture, though, of course at this juncture there is no formal statement on this issue. However, in light of the above history and court decisions, coupled with the proposed regulations, it would appear likely that a limited liability company formed to own life insurance would be viable.

After examining the business objective issue, the discussion then turns to why one would rather have life insurance owned in an LLC as opposed to a more standard irrevocable life insurance trust.

There appear to be two chief advantages of the insurance LLC as opposed to the insurance trust. First, and perhaps foremost, is the issue of control. If an insured is a trustee of an irrevocable life insurance trust and the trust owns a policy on the insured's life, then the full amount of the proceeds will be included in the insured's estate. This is regardless of the fact that the policy is owned by the life insurance trust. Historically, there has been a slight difference in interpretation among the United States Courts of Appeals regarding this application. The Fifth Circuit Court of

Appeals has held that the possession of any incident of ownership over the policy as trustee, no matter how small, is sufficient to warrant full estate tax includability.[47] The Second Circuit Court of Appeals has held that there is estate tax includability if the insured trustee decedent has an incident of ownership if the insured is the transferor or the insured has trust powers sufficient to benefit himself, herself or the insured's estate. On the other hand, if the transferor is not the insured, the transfer is not part of a plan, and the insured cannot benefit himself, herself or the insured's estate, then there is no estate tax includability.[48] The Sixth Circuit Court of Appeals has held that possession of incidents of ownership will result in estate tax includability only if the insured trustee can benefit himself, herself or the insured's estate.[49] For the Sixth Circuit Court of Appeals, the source of the incidents of ownership is irrelevant.

The official IRS position is an amalgamation of the above opinions. In Revenue Ruling 84-179, the IRS held that an insured would have an incident of ownership as a trustee where the trust owned a policy on the life of the insured and either the trustee could benefit personally from the trust or the insured transferred the policy outright to the trust or as part of a prearranged plan.[50]

In the case of an LLC owning a policy, the rules are similar to the corporate rules. If the proceeds are payable to the LLC then the "incidents of ownership" rules do not apply.

Instead of Code section 2042 applying, it is Section 2033 that controls. Code section 2033, in its entirety, states that: "[t]he value of the gross estate shall include the value of all property to the extent of the interest therein of the decedent at the time of his death." In other words, if the insured member owns a two percent interest in the LLC, then two percent of the proceeds will be included in his estate. Whatever percentage the insured owns, that percentage gets translated into the amount of estate tax includability. It is important to reiterate that this includability occurs not through the incident of ownership rules of Code section 2042, but rather through the fact that the value of the LLC is increased by the insurance proceeds. The IRS and the courts have been very consistent in this treatment. For example, this result is reached in the older Tax Court case of *Estate of Knipp v. Commissioner*.[51] Likewise, Revenue Ruling 83-147 reaches the same conclusion.[52] Finally, in a very recent private letter ruling, the same analysis was used to reach the same conclusion.[53]

Thus, the insured LLC has a distinct advantage over the insured trust. If the insured is a one percent owner, and if the insured is the only member-manager, the LLC will be recognized as a partnership for taxation purposes. Further, the insured as the member-manager will be the only person with control over the assets of the LLC, that is, the life insurance policy. The cost for this control will be one percent of the proceeds included in the value of the LLC, which will be included in the insured's estate under Code section 2033. If a similar arrangement were attempted with a trust, in all likelihood 100% of the proceeds would be includable, since Section 2042 and not Section 2033 would apply.

The other key advantage is it is much easier to obtain an annual exclusion in the LLC context. In the trust context one is always faced with the problem of qualifying the transfer as a present interest. The Internal Revenue Code requires that to avail oneself of the annual exclusion for gift tax purposes, the transfer must be a "present interest."[54] The regulations specifically provide that the payment of premiums on a life insurance policy owned by a trust is a future interest.[55] The problem can be alleviated by creating withdrawal or demand powers pursuant to the holding in the *Crummey* decision.[56] However, the IRS has placed a number of hurdles to overcome in using these demand powers. One such hurdle is that in order to qualify, one should have an interest in the trust other than the demand power.[57] Another requirement is that notice must be sent each year to each beneficiary in order to validate the withdrawal power.[58] Finally, since the demand power is a general power of appointment, when it ceases to be applicable, there is a gift to fellow beneficiaries through the lapse of a general power provisions.[59] This results in either limiting the power to the greater of $5,000 or 5% of the trust corpus (the so called 5 or 5 power) or by using "hanging" or special testamentary powers. Each of these approaches creates further problems.[60]

On the other hand, the payment of a premium in a life insurance LLC will be deemed to be a present interest obviating the need for all of the administrative gymnastics that the trust requires. In *Estate of Wooley v. U.S.*, the district court held that so long as any contributions were reflected in the capital accounts and a member could control distributions from his capital account, the end result would be that any transfer would be a present interest, automatically qualifying for the annual exclusion.[61] The IRS has gone even further. In a private letter ruling, the general partner had the right to control distributions pursuant to the partnership agreement.[62]

Regardless, the IRS held that any transfer would qualify as a present interest. The IRS reasoned that since the general partner owed fiduciary duties to the limited partners, the right of withdrawal could not be unreasonably withheld. As such, the transfer would still qualify as a present interest. Using this as an analogy to LLCs, if the transfer is to an LLC, since most states have similar fiduciary duties in the LLC context, the transfer should achieve present interest status, limiting the need for demand powers. These transfers should include premium payments.

THE FAMILY LLC VERSUS THE FAMILY LIMITED PARTNERSHIP

In most instances, family LLCs and family limited partnerships will operate exactly the same. The family LLC does have two advantages. The first advantage is obvious. A general partner in a partnership has unlimited liability. Thus, if the partnership is sued in contract or tort, the personal assets of the general partner can be reached to satisfy any resulting judgment. In the LLC context, the analogy is that a member-manager has essentially the same rights and responsibilities as a general partner. However, in an LLC all members of the LLC, including member-managers, have limited liability. The net result is that personal assets of the member-manager cannot be reached by the LLC's creditors.

The other advantage is not so obvious. In the limited partnership context, the limited partners cannot have any say in management decisions. Even if their input is limited, any management or control capabilities will result in the limited partner losing limited liability. There is much greater flexibility in the LLC context. Members can have complete management and control capabilities, no management or control capabilities, or anything in between. In all instances limited liability will be preserved. Therefore, there is much greater flexibility in using the LLC since a few, many or no management rights can be given to the "limited" members of an LLC without affecting their limited liability.

FOOTNOTE REFERENCES

1. Former Assistant Secretary of the Treasury Stanley S. Surrey is credited with first expressing the concept of a unified transfer tax system. Surrey served many years as a professor at Harvard Law School and authored a classic series of textbooks and treatises.

2. IRC Sec. 2503(b).
3. IRC Sec. 2035. Since 1986, this provision applies only to a relatively few and very specialized transactions.
4. Regs. §§20.2031-1(b) and 25.2512-1.
5. IRC Sec. 2036(c), as in effect prior to December 17, 1987.
6. IRC Sec. 2701(b)(1).
7. IRC Sec. 2701(b)(1)(A).
8. IRC Sec. 2701(b)(1)(B).
9. IRC Sec. 2701(c)(3).
10. IRC Sec. 2701(c)(3)(B).
11. IRC Sec. 2701(c)(2)(B).
12. IRC Sec. 2701(c)(2)(C).
13. IRC Sec. 2703(a)(1).
14. 52 TC Memo 1306 (1987).
15. IRC Sec. 2704(b)(3)(A).
16. IRC Sec. 2704(b)(2).
17. IRC Sec. 2704(b)(3)(B).
18. 823 F.2d 483 (11th Cir. 1987) *aff'g* 51 TC Memo 60 (1985).
19. Reg. §25.2704-1(c)(2)(ii).
20. H.R. Conf. Rep. No. 964, 101st Cong, 2nd Sess., PL 101-508 §11602(a), 1991-2 CB 481.
21. See *Estate of Andrews v. Comm.*, 79 TC 938 (1982); *Estate of Lee v. Comm.*, 69 TC 860 (1978); *Estate of Bright v. U.S.*, 658 F.2d 999 (5th Cir. 1981); *Estate of Propstra v. U.S.*, 680 F.2d 1248 (9th Cir. 1982).
22. 1993-1 CB 202, *rev'g* Rev. Rul. 81-253, 1981-2 CB 187.
23. 337 US 733 (1949).
24. IRC Sec. 1(g).
25. Reg. §1.704-1(e)(2)(ii).
26. Let. Ruls. 9546006 and 9546007.
27. Rev. Proc. 92-88 1992-2 CB 496. See also Rev. Proc. 89-12 1989-1 CB 798.
28. IRC Sec. 2033.
29. IRC Sec. 721(b); Reg. §1.351-1(c).
30. IRC Sec. 704(e)(2).
31. Let. Ruls. 9131006 and 9415007.
32. Reg. §1.704-1(e)(2)(viii).
33. *Woodbury v. Comm.*, 49 TC 180 (1967).
34. Reg. §1.704-1(e)(2)(ix).
35. Reg. §1.704-1(e)(2)(vi).
36. Delaware: 6 D.C.A. §18-702.
37. Delaware: 6 D.C.A. §18-702(b).
38. Delaware: 6 D.C.A. §18-703; Maine: 31 M.R.S.A. §686.
39. See for example, Mazart, G. "The Family Limited Partnership: Opportunities for Disability and Government Benefits Planning," *Elder Law Reporter*, June 1994 at pp. 1-4.
40. 42 U.S.C. Sec. 1396p(d)(6) applies the word "trust" to any "legal device."
41. Let. Rul. 9310039.
42. Let. Rul. 9309021.
43. Rev. Proc.2000-3, 2000-1 IRB 103.
44. Brier, K.P. and Darby, III, J.P. "Famly Limited Partnerships: Decanting Family Investment Assets Into New Bottles," *Tax Lawyer*, Vol. 49, No. 1, Fall 1995, p. 127 at page 144.
45. TC Memo 1991-452.

46. Reg. §301.7701-1(a)(2).
47. *Rose v. U.S.*, 511 F.2d 259 (5th Cir. 1975); *Terriberry v. U.S.*, 517 F.2d 286 (5th Cir. 1975).
48. *Skifter v. U.S.*, 468 F.2d 699 (2nd Cir. 1972).
49. *Fruehauf v. Comm.*, 427 F.2d 80 (6th Cir. 1970).
50. 1984-2 CB 195, *revk'g* Rev. Rul. 76-261, 1976-2 CB 276.
51. 25 TC 153 (1955).
52. 1983-2 CB 158.
53. Let. Rul. 9623024.
54. IRC Sec. 2503(b).
55. Reg. §25.2503-3(c), Ex. 2.
56. *Crummey v. Comm.* 397 F.2d 82 (9th Cir. 1968).
57. See *Estate of Cristofani v. Comm.*, 97 TC 74 (1991). The IRS has indicated that it will litigate "abuses" in excess of the *Cristofani* fact pattern. (AOD 1996-010).
58. Rev. Rul. 81-7, 1981-1 CB 474; Let. Rul. 9532001.
59. IRC Sec. 2514(e).
60. See for example Let. Rul. 8901004.
61. 736 F.Supp. 1506 (DC IN 1990).
62. Let. Rul. 9131006.

Chapter 11

VALUATION

As discussed in the last chapter, one of the critical elements common to both LLCs and family limited partnerships is the ability to obtain a discount as part of the transfer process. What this means is that the gift or transfer tax value is less than the actual fair market value of the property. This chapter will examine the various techniques used to obtain such discounts.

OVERVIEW

There are many different statements on valuation sprinkled throughout the Internal Revenue Code. However, for transfer taxes the basic rules are relatively uniform. The fair market value of property as of the date of death or the alternate valuation date governs value for estate tax purposes.[1] Likewise, fair market value at the time of transfer is the measure of value for gift tax purposes.[2]

The term fair market value is defined for purposes of both the estate tax and gift tax regulations as the price at which property would change hands between a willing buyer and a willing seller where neither is under any compulsion to sell or buy and both have reasonable knowledge of all relevant facts.[3]

In valuing a business interest such as the ownership in an LLC, the basic starting point is Revenue Ruling 59-60.[4] This ruling acknowledges that there is no single method for reaching value. All the facts and circumstances of a particular case must be examined. The ruling provides "that all available financial data, as well as all relevant factors affecting the fair market value" should be taken into account.[5] The ruling then goes on to list eight specific intrinsic factors that should be considered. These factors are discussed below.

The Nature and History of the Business

The logical starting point to evaluate a business is in a detailed analysis of the history of both the business and the industry in which it operates. Courts have followed this approach that the history of the business and industry commence all valuation discussions.[6] Among the key points to be discerned by the history is the degree of risk in the business, which includes such factors as the stability, growth and diversity of the business operations.[7] This approach can be important in businesses and securities that are cyclical in nature. The Tax Court has specifically recognized cycles in business valuation.[8] Likewise, the history of the business will affect other factors used to value a business. For example, the history of the business can affect earnings capacity in both a positive and negative sense.

Economic Conditions

The economic outlook for the business can be a very important factor. In one of the most famous valuation cases of recent note, *Estate of Newhouse v. Commissioner*, economic conditions of the business were critical in the valuation process.[9] In this case, advertising and newspaper companies were among the assets to be valued. The Tax Court reviewed such data as the decline in the number of newspapers as well as the effect of television on newspaper profits. In another well known case, *Northern Trust Company v. Commissioner*, the general economic conditions facing the construction industry were evaluated in assessing value.[10]

Financial Condition

It is obvious that the business's financial condition is critical in establishing its value. Usually this approach involves the examination of financial records for a number of years. The trends established in examining these records can be a most important factor in valuing the business. Revenue Ruling 59-60 establishes the concept that operating assets are to be given a higher weight than non-operating assets.[11]

In reviewing financial conditions, one of the most widely discussed areas is the relevance of book value. Obviously, book value represents the underpinning of a financial analysis, yet it is not the sole reference. Revenue Ruling 59-60 points out that the income statement is also a very important document for establishing value.

In general, the courts have given little weight to book value when the business consists of an operating company where such factors as goodwill become very important. For example, the book value of a fast food franchise may have little direct connection to actual value in light of the high degree of goodwill involved in such a business. Likewise, for professionals who depend on services rather than capital assets, the book value of the business will have little direct correlation to actual or fair market value. The Tax Court afforded book value little weight in the case of *Sirloin Stockade, Inc. v. Commissioner*, even going as far as to call book value "inappropriate."[12]

On the other hand, book value can be a useful indicator of value in a holding company or a situation where the assets of the business consist of items such as marketable securities. In addition, where earnings are not a relevant factor book value may come to the forefront as a valuation device.[13] In a corporation where 95% of its assets were equities and real estate, the Tax Court utilized book value as practically the exclusive valuation methodology.[14]

When an LLC is being used as a family LLC and the assets are largely investment assets, book value of the underlying assets will be the normal starting point for valuation purposes. If the LLC is an operating business, then most likely the other factors will come into play. Chief among these factors is earnings, which is discussed below.

Earnings

Revenue Ruling 59-60 makes it clear that the most important factor in ascertaining the value of an operating business is the earnings capacity of the business. In keeping with its view that trends are very important, Revenue Ruling 59-60 states that five or more previous years should be used to assess earnings.[15] In general, earnings are capitalized to reach fair market value. To capitalize earnings, one must divide the earnings by a capitalization rate. The determination of a capitalization rate is one of the most important aspects of determining value. There is no sole method for determining a capitalization rate, but the risk of the business is generally the most important factor in determining a capitalization rate. Other factors include the inherent nature of the business as well as the volatility of earnings. As stated in Revenue Ruling 59-60, the capitalization rate is often reached by comparing the capitalization rates for similar publicly traded companies. This approach was specifically validated by the Tax Court in *Estate of Feldmar v. Commissioner*.[16] The capitalization rate of comparable companies is generally only a starting point. The rate must be adjusted for the particular business to be evaluated. For example, in *Estate of Rodriguez v. Commissioner* the rate was adjusted to reflect the loss of a key employee.[17]

Cash Flow

Over the last few years cash flow and "Discounted Cash Flow"[18] (DCF) analyses have come to the forefront. Part of the reason has been the ability of mathematicians to devise mathematical formulas which work with great precision in assessing value. This method essentially values the business based on the discounted values of future free cash flows. Free cash flow is defined as being equal to the after- tax operating earnings of the company, plus non-cash charges, less investments in operating working capital, property, equipment and other "hard" assets. For consistency, the discount rate is equal to the "Weighted Average Cost of Capital) or WACC. WACC adjusts the opportunity of investment cost by examining the rate of return for each capital item., and weighting the result on the basis of where the maximum opportunities for profit lie.

As was described various economic models have been devised pursuant to the DCF methodology. One such formula is the Miller-Modigliani formula, first devised in the 1960s. The formula is :

$$\text{VALUE OF ENTITY} = \frac{\text{NOPLAT}}{\text{WACC}} + K * (\text{NOPLAT} * N * \frac{[\text{ROIC-WACC}]}{\text{WACC}* (1+\text{WACC})}$$

WHERE:

NOPLAT = Net Operating Profits Less Taxes

WACC = Weighted average cost of capital

ROIC = Rate of return on investment capital

K = Percentage of NOPLAT to be invested in new projects

N = Number of years company will invest in new projects.

Goodwill

Under the reasoning of Revenue Ruling 59-60, goodwill is an intangible asset that is closely aligned to earning capacity.[19] Under this argument, goodwill would be earnings that exceed an industry norm or average. The idea is that equal businesses will earn equal amounts. However, the presence of goodwill will cause the earnings to be higher. Revenue Ruling 68-609 provides a formula for calculating goodwill.[20] The formula is constructed on the following basis:

1. Determine the value of the tangible assets in a business. Assume for hypothetical purposes that this amount is $1,000,000.

2. Determine the average earnings of a business over a period of at least five previous years. Assume in our hypothetical that this amount is $100,000.

3. Determine the rate of return in a similar business or businesses. For our example, assume this is 9 percent.

4. Calculate the return based on the similar business percentage described in number 3. Another way of stating this is to multiply the percentage in number 3 by the tangible assets determined under number 1. In our case this would be $1,000,000 times 9 percent or $90,000.

5. Determine the excess earnings. This is the actual average earnings minus the earnings calculated based on the industry average. Another way of stating this is to subtract the amount calculated in number 4 from the amount determined in number 2. In our example, this would be $100,000 minus $90,000 or $10,000. This is the amount of excess earnings attributable to goodwill.

6. Capitalize the amount of excess earnings. If we assume a 15% capitalization rate, we have $10,000 divided by 15% or $66,667.

7. The capitalized excess earnings are added to the tangible assets. This is the result of adding number 6 to number 1. In our example this would be $1,000,000 plus $66,667 or $1,066,667.

The application of goodwill to increase business value is generally used only where the goodwill is transferable. Thus, if the goodwill is attributable to the reputation of a key employee, the value of the goodwill may be lost at the death of that employee.[21]

COMPARABLES

Another important consideration in Revenue Ruling 59-60 is the use of comparable businesses to establish value.[22] In utilizing comparables, it is necessary to determine what is or is not really a comparable business. Two cases illustrate this point. In *Estate of Miller v. Commissioner*, the Tax Court was faced with having to determine the value of a hotel chain.[23] The court found that national hotel chains were not comparable for purposes of business valuation. In *Estate of Hall v. Commissioner*, the court was trying to determine the fair market value of Hallmark cards.[24] The court relied on an expert that considered, among others, Coca-Cola and Avon Products as comparable companies. The court based this rationale on the fact that Coca-Cola and Avon, like Hallmark, were the leading companies in their respective industries. Another expert considered Hallmark in light of 15 other companies. Interestingly enough, the court rejected an appraiser who considered as comparable the only other major marketer of greeting cards in the United States.

RECONCILING THE VARIOUS FACTORS

Given the number of factors taken into account to establish business value, two questions often occur. These involve the question of averaging the different values obtained through the different methodologies and the weight to be afforded the various factors.

Revenue Ruling 59-60 points out that there is no point in attempting to construct a mathematical formula for reconciling the various factors. Specifically mentioned is that it is inappropriate to average any of the factors. The weight to be assigned to the various factors is determined on a case by case basis. While all factors should be considered, certain factors will be paramount depending upon the type of case involved. This determination is part of what an expert does in establishing value. The bottom line is that this is a judgment call based on experience and common sense.

DISCOUNTS FOR A MINORITY INTEREST

As mentioned in the chapter on estate planning, one of the advantages in using a family LLC or family limited partnership is the availability of obtaining discounts from the fair market value. Very early on, the courts recognized the validity of discounting the value of an interest in an enterprise where that interest is a minority interest.

A famous quotation from a 1935 case says "[m]inority stock interests in a 'closed' corporation are usually worth much less than the proportionate share of assets to which they attach."[25] The reason for this concept lies in two separate factors that are usually interrelated. One discount is for lack of control, that is, the inability to unilaterally "call the shots." This discount is usually referred to as a minority discount. The second factor relates to the fact that such an interest may not be liquid. There may be little motivation to purchase an interest that does not control the enterprise's activities. The discount here is for lack of marketability, which is discussed below.

In the case of a minority discount, various approaches are used depending on which method is being used to value the underlying enterprise.

For example, probably the most common valuation method utilized is the earnings approach. As discussed above, in this approach the earnings of the company are divided by a capitalization percentage to achieve a value for the enterprise. Since the minority owner can neither compel a distribution of earnings nor establish the amount of earnings to be distributed, the earnings attributable to the minority owner's interest are reduced. The effect of this reduction of earnings for the minority owner is to reduce the overall value of the minority owner's interest. A factor that is sometimes used to reduce these earnings is the extent that a majority owner or owners overcompensate themselves since they are in control. In essence, this overcompensation amount is subtracted from the earnings attributable to the minority owner.

Another common approach is the financial condition approach. As was described above, this approach is useful when valuing an enterprise that is made up of investment assets with which a total net asset value can be computed by simply adding up the respective values of the underlying assets. Usually the interest of a minority owner is discounted by some percentage when computing the minority discount in a situation using the financial condition as a base. The starting point is to assess the entire value of the enterprise. This amount is then multiplied by the percentage of ownership that the minority owner possesses. Finally, from this amount a further percentage is applied to represent the amount of the minority discount. A critical determination is how much of a percentage should be taken. As with all other valuation issues, there is no hard and fast rule. Some appraisers look at the number of different control factors from which a minority owner may be excluded. The more factors that the owner is excluded from, the greater the minority discount.

Following are some control factors to consider:

- Appointment of directors.
- Appointment of managers.
- Determining compensation for officers, managers and directors.
- Liquidation of all or part of the business.
- Obtaining loans, or otherwise recapitalizing and refinancing the business.
- Allowing distributions or dividends from the company.
- Changing articles of organization, by-laws or other business documents.
- Vetoing any action.

These items become very important in drafting the LLC's articles of organization. If the LLC is to be used for estate planning purposes and a large minority discount is desired, then the minority members of the LLC should have as little power and control as possible. Specific attention should be paid to the items listed above.

Another important technique used to evaluate the amount of a minority discount is to utilize comparables. One may use past transactions involving the actual entity's securities or use comparables from other industries. In recent years, appraisers have paid particular attention to a database involving mergers. This database traces public companies that sell or otherwise transfer at least 10% of their worth and the purchase price is at least $1,000,000. This publication is known as the *Mergerstat Review*.[26] The *Mergerstat* data is published as a "control premium," that is, it is based on the amount by which the acquisition price exceeds the market price. The control premium can be converted to a minority discount through a mathematical formula.[27] This is the same as saying that the sales price is the same as the fair market value and that the value without the control premium is the same as the discounted value. On this basis, the data for 1994 is that the average minority discount for this sample was 29.5%. The median discount was 25.9%. It is interesting to note that in the *Mergerstat* data there is a strong correlation between control premium and the overall strength of the financial markets. The higher the market, as measured by price/earnings ratios, the greater the control premium. This means that minority discounts will also tend to be greater during strong economic times. However, even with a greater minority discount, the intrinsic value of the minority interest may be greater than it would be otherwise. Even though the discount may be higher, the base against which it is applied may be higher still, so that in real dollar terms the value of the interest may be overpriced, even with the higher discount.

A third approach is sometimes referred to as the bottom-up approach. This approach basically tries to value the minority interest on its own terms without trying to discount from some other value. Two factors are generally taken into account when valuing a minority interest by its own terms. One factor examines the possibility of cash distributions. The other factor looks at the potential for capital appreciation. If the interest has income or appreciation potential, its worth will be greater.

It is important to note two further studies on the subject of minority discounts. One study appearing in *Trusts and Estates* concluded that the average discount for minority interest in real estate partnerships was 44%.[28] Interestingly enough, the same study found that in about one-quarter of the partnerships the discount exceeded 60%! Another, older study appeared in *Estate Planning* magazine.[29] This study concluded that the average discount was 36%. About 20% of the sales had discounts less than 20%; 53% had discounts between 22% and 48%; and 23% had discounts between 48% and 78%.

DISCOUNT FOR LACK OF MARKETABILITY

The idea of marketability really deals with the issue of liquidity. This refers to how fast or easily the interest can be sold. There are two components to this concept. One is how *fast* the interest can be sold. An ability to sell quickly involves an active and enthusiastic market for the security or interest. The other concept involves the *ease* of sale. The focus is on selling the interest easily without involving such complicating issues as owner financing and other types of guarantees to facilitate the sale.

It is clear that both marketability and minority discounts are related. Obviously, a minority interest with little control has less market appeal than one that has a controlling issue. Because of this, the percentage decreases for marketability and minority are multiplicative and not additive. For example, suppose a security has a value of $100 and there is a 40% discount for a minority interest and a 40% discount for lack of marketability. The total discount is *not* 80% (40% + 40%), but is 64%. It is calculated on the following basis:

Fair Market Value	$100.00
Discount for Minority	40%
Discount	$ 40.00
Value After Discount	$ 60.00
Discount for Marketability	40%
Discount	$24.00
Net Value	$36.00
Percentage Discount	64%

However, it is important to note that the Tax Court has used the additive approach in one case. In *Martin v. Commissioner*, the IRS valued an interest with a 35% discount for minority and a 35% discount for marketability.[30] The court agreed with these values and established an overall reduction of 70%.

The marketability approach also focuses on an equivalency with public securities. The measuring public security value is often referred to as the publicly traded equivalent value or simply the equivalent value. Because of the vastness of the United States public securities market, there is ample room for various empirical studies on this issue. The studies take two different forms. The first study compares the value of publicly traded securities with the value of securities that are restricted as to sale. Restricted securities are sometimes referred to as letter stock. In general, restricted stock comes about in situations where the issuing company does not want to register it. This stock cannot be sold to the public since it is not registered. However, it can be sold in a private transaction under certain conditions. As such, restricted stock is sometimes issued in merger and acquisition situations where a company simply does not have the time to go through a full registration. Likewise, some companies may have the original founders holding onto restricted stock that was issued at the formation of the business. As a result, the difference in prices between restricted and public stock serves as a good measure to assess the value of marketability and liquidity.

Usually the process of obtaining the percentage of a discount for lack of marketability is done on the basis of comparables. A similar industry security is examined on the basis of the differential between the marketable and the restricted values. There are a number of sources available for obtaining these differentials.

An older study that is still used sometimes is the SEC Institutional Investor Study.[31] This study, as would be expected, found that marketability discounts were less for New York Stock Exchange Companies, more for AMEX companies, more still for the predecessor of NASDAQ and the most for all others. The overall discount for all groups was 25.8%. For the non-reporting companies this discount increased to about 33%.

Two studies have appeared in *Taxes* magazine. A study by Robert Moroney appeared in March, 1973.[32] It examined 146 different transactions and found an average discount of 35.6% and a median discount of 33%. A second study by J. Michael Maher appeared in 1976.[33] This study, also comparing restricted and unrestricted stock sales, found an average discount of 35.4% and a median discount of 34.7%.

More recent studies show that these percentages have remained fairly constant. A study by Willamette Management Associates found a median discount of 31.2% for transactions that took place primarily in the early 1980s.[34]

Another recent study appeared in *Financial Analysts Journal*.[35] This study analyzed 69 private placement situations and determined the discount to be on average 33.75%. This amount is obviously very consistent with the previous studies.

Another empirical approach that has been reported in a few instances involves companies that have gone public. The methodology is one where security prices are compared after a company has gone public with prices before the company went public. Willamette Management Associates has done 12 studies over recent years.[36] The Willamette study was unique in that adjustments were made for different stock indices and for changes in securities P/E ratios. The end result was median discounts in a range between 32% and 80%. These figures were somewhat higher than the restricted stock analysis described above.

One final approach has been utilized. In a *Journal of Taxation* article, Thomas Solberg examined how the courts have treated the discount for restricted securities.[37] This study examined 15 different cases. The range for discounts was from 10% to 90%. The median discount was 38.9%, with an average discount of 37.4%. The Solberg study was further updated by Phillip W. Moore in an article for *Trusts and Estates*.[38] In this study involving cases from 1969 to 1982, Moore separated the cases into three groups. The first group consisted of cases from 1969 to 1976, the second group was from 1976 through 1979 and the final group was from 1980 until 1982. What Moore found was that the average discount increased over each of the three time spans. The average for the first span was 18.75%. This increased to 24% for the second group and 28.60% for the third group.

Since this study there have been three well-known cases in the Tax Court examining the issue of a discount for lack of marketability.

In *Estate of Gallo v. Commissioner*, the Tax Court was faced with valuing a decedent's interest in the holding company that owned the Gallo wineries.[39] The IRS first valued the interest at over $1,000 per share. The estate appraiser valued each share at $290. The appraiser then reduced it by a 36% discount for lack of marketability. The Tax Court agreed with the estate appraiser and ultimately valued the stock at $235 per share, which included the 36% discount for lack of marketability.

The second important case is *Estate of Watts v. Commissioner*.[40] This case involved the valuation of timberland and other assets where the liquidation value of the underlying property was higher than the going concern value. The going concern value is essentially based on a capitalization of earnings. The Tax Court accepted this earnings approach as opposed to the liquidation value. In addition, a discount for lack of marketability of 35% was taken as well. This case is important since it allows a discount on what is essentially a capitalization based approach.

The third case is *Estate of Hall v. Commissioner*.[41] The valuation in this case involved a large minority block in Hallmark Cards, Inc. The ultimate valuation that was accepted by the Tax Court was based upon a buyout formula provision. The Tax Court allowed a discount for lack of marketability of 35%, which had been the amount recommended by the appraiser.

CONCLUSION

As mentioned in the chapter on estate planning, the availability of discount factors makes the LLC appealing as an estate planning device. This chapter has focused on the mechanics of obtaining these discounts. In the LLC context, it is important to note that the operating agreement must be carefully drafted with provisions that will serve to maximize these discounts.

FOOTNOTE REFERENCES

1. Reg. §20.2031-1(b).
2. Reg. §25.2512-1.
3. Regs. §§20.2031-1(b) and 25.2512-1.
4. 1959-1 CB 237.
5. Rev. Rul. 59-60, Sec. 4.01, 1959-1 CB 237.
6. See *Hall v. Commissioner*, 92 TC 312 (1989).
7. Rev. Rul. 59-60, Sec. 4.02(a), 1959-1 CB 237.
8. *Est. of Giselman v. Comm.*, TC Memo 1988-391.
9. 94 TC 193 (1990), *nonacq.*, 1991-1 CB 1.
10. 87 TC 349 (1986).
11. Rev. Rul. 59-60, Sec. 4.02(c), 1959-1 CB 237.
12. TC Memo 1980-303.
13. See for example, *Est. of Heckscher v. Comm.*, 63 TC 485 (1975).
14. *Est. of Lee v. Comm.*, 69 TC 860 (1978).
15. Rev. Rul. 59-60, Sec. 4.02(d), 1959-1 CB 237.
16. TC Memo 1989-429.
17. TC Memo 1989-13.
18. For greater analysis, please see Copeland T., Koller T., and Murrin J., *VALUATION: Measuring and Managing the Value of Companies*, John Wiley & Sons, New York, 1996.
19. Rev. Rul. 59-60, Sec. 4.02(f), 1959-1 CB 237.
20. 1968-2 CB 327.
21. *Zorniger v. Comm.*, 62 TC 435 (1974).

22. Rev. Rul. 59-60, Sec. 4.02(h), 1959-1 CB 237.
23. TC Memo 1977-39.
24. 92 TC 312 (1989).
25. *Cravens v. Welch*, 10 F.Supp. 94, 95 (1935).
26. Published by Houlihan, Lokey, Howard and Zukin, Los Angeles, CA.
27. The formula is:

$$1 - \frac{1}{(1 + \text{Control Premium})}$$

28. Thompson and Spunt, "The Widespread Overvaluation of Fractional Ownership Positions, " *Tr. & Est.*, June 1993 at page 63.
29. Coolidge, "Fixing Value of Minority Interests in Business: Actual Sales Suggest Discount as High as 70%," *Est. Plan.*, Spring, 1975 at page 141.
30. TC Memo 1985-424.
31. "Institutional Investor Study Report of the Securities and Exchange Commission," 92nd Congress Sess. 1, Document No. 92-64, U.S. Government Printing Office, 1971.
32. Moroney, "Most Courts Overvalue Closely Held Stocks," *Taxes*, March, 1973 at page 144.
33. Maher, "Discounts for Lack of Marketability for Closely-Held Business Interests," *Taxes*, September 1976 at page 562.
34. Pratt, Reilly and Schweihs, *Valuing a Business: The Analysis and Appraisal of Closely Held Companies*, Irwin Professional Publishing, 1996 at page 341.
35. Silber, "Discounts on Restricted Stock," *Fin. Analysts J.*, July-August, 1991 at page 60.
36. Pratt, Reilly and Schweihs at page 343.
37. Solberg, "Valuing Restricted Securities," *J. Tax'n*, September, 1979 at page 150.
38. Moore, "Valuation Revisited," *Tr. & Est.*, February, 1987 at page 48.
39. TC Memo 1985-363.
40. TC Memo 1985-595, *aff'd* 823 F.2d 483 (11th Cir. 1987).
41. 92 TC 312 (1989).

Chapter 12

DISCOUNTS

OVERVIEW

As was mentioned previously, valuation includes discounts for possession of a minority interest and lack of marketability. These concepts represent economic concepts, and, as we all know, economic concepts do not necessarily translate into taxation concepts. In the case of utilization of discounts from a tax perspective the IRS has fought a rearguard type of action. This recalcitrant view on the part of the IRS is contained in several announcements and rulings that state it will closely scrutinize valuation discounts of closely held business interests, especially those taken for family limited partnerships, which are not operating companies but instead hold a pool of investments (typically a public security portfolio or a portfolio of real estate investments).[1] Among the concepts of these attacks are the following arguments:

- Transfer into the partnership results in loss of value on the interests retained because of the various discounts and thus there is a gift on formation of a family limited partnership;

- Any restrictions on use of partnership property should be ignored because the partnership agreement does not meet the requirements of IRC Section 2703(b); and

- The limited partner has a complete and unconditional withdrawal right under the applicable state partnership law, and thus any restrictions on the exercise of such withdrawal right should be ignored pursuant to IRC Section 2704(b).

Unfortunately for the IRS, (and fortunately for estate planners), these arguments have all been rejected by the courts. In many of the court decisions, the courts have both gone out of their way to chastise the IRS and to go out of their way to find in favor of the taxpayers.

The initial starting point in this dispute, and where the courts have supported taxpayer views is the case of *Estate of Bright v. Commis-*

sioner.[2] For many years, prior to this case the IRS fought the concept of taking discounts in family owned limited partnerships or corporations. The IRS theory was a kind of "quasi-attribution" rule, namely that in a family situation, all members of the family would agree on a course of action, and hence there could be no minority interests in such a setting. The Court of Appeals vigorously disagreed with the IRS on this point, both on tax and judicial reasons. Perhaps most importantly, the court stressed a theme that resounds to this day. This theme is that the concept of discounts has been in place for many years, and as such, under the doctrine of adhering to judicial precedence, the courts will not overturn the concept.

The court in *Bright* specifically stated: "Our final reason for rejecting family attribution is based upon the important policy that the law should be stable and predictable. This policy is especially important in the tax laws, because there is widespread reliance by taxpayers upon established principles in planning their affairs."[3]

Bright is important since it represented the last in a series of cases that the IRS had summarily lost on this issue. Indeed, the trial court in *Bright* essentially held that to relitigate this issue over and over, (and to continually lose) was tantamount to IRS harassment triggering the IRS to incur taxpayer costs in the litigation. As a result, the IRS decided to "throw in the towel" on this issue in Revenue Ruling 93-12.[4]

The ruling makes the following, important holding: "If a donor transfers shares in a corporation to each of the donor's children, the factor of corporate control in the family is not considered in valuing each transferred interest for purposes of section 2512 of the Code. For estate and gift tax valuation purposes, the Service will follow *Bright*, *Propstra*, *Andrews*, and *Lee* in not assuming that all voting power held by family members may be aggregated for purposes of determining whether the transferred shares should be valued as part of a controlling interest. Consequently, a minority discount will not be disallowed solely because a transferred interest, when aggregated with interests held by family members, would be a part of a controlling interest. This would be the case whether the donor held 100 percent or some lesser percentage of the stock immediately before the gift."

THE STRUCTURE OF THE TRANSACTION

Revenue ruling 93-12 was the creative force that spurred on the use of family limited partnerships for estate planning purposes.

The concept of the FLP is fairly straight forward. Under various revenue procedures,[5] the IRS has held that in order to be a valid partnership for taxation purposes, a general partner must own at least 1% of the partnership. Since a general partner is in control of the partnership, a 1% sole general partner would be in complete control, even though the percentage of ownership is only 1%.

In a normal transaction, an individual would create the FLP or the Family Limited Liability Company (FLLC). As has been previously described, the key advantage of the FLLC will be the fact that the member-manager (analogous to a general partner) has insulation from personal liability in the FLLC format, but not in the FLP format. The individual would then transfer assets to the FLP or FLLC, in return for all of the units in the FLP or FLLC. The individual keeps the general partnership unit for control, and then makes gifts of the limited partnership (or "member" units) to family members. These units are then "discounted" for gift tax valuation purposes. The discounts are based on the twin keystones of the fact that they are not marketable (and hence are also "illiquid") and also that they are restricted interests. By restricted interests, it is meant that the limited partners have no control or no "voice" in the operation of the FLP or FLLC. This is analogous to having a "minority" interest in a corporate context.

While discounts are thought of in the FLP or FLLC context, it is important to note that they can be utilized in other situations. For example, in a family buy-sell agreement, IRC 2703 mandates that value be at "fair market value". However, fair market value incorporates the concepts of discounting. As such, these concepts are also applicable for buy-sell agreements. Finally, the concept of discounting can be used in establishing the value of assets for purposes of filing the estate tax return.[6]

THE MINORITY DISCOUNT

The courts have supported the concept of a minority discount since the earliest days of taxation. For example, in the 1940 case of *Hooper v.*

Commissioner,[7] the Tax Court first applied a minority discount in the estate tax valuation arena. In the case of *Ward v. Commissioner,*[8] the Tax Court applied a 33⅓% minority discount in an early FLP case. The court went on to describe the long history of minority discounts with the following paragraph:

> The courts have long recognized that the shares of stock of a corporation which represent a minority interest are usually worth less than a proportionate share of the value of the assets of the corporation. Estate of Bright v. United States, 658 F.2d 999 (5th Cir. 1981) (en banc); Harwood v. Commissioner, supra; Estate of Andrews v. Commissioner, supra; Estate of Zaiger v. Commissioner, 64 T.C. 927 (1975); Estate of deGuebriant v. Commissioner, 14 T.C. 611 (1950), rev'd. on other grounds sub nom. Claflin v. Commissioner, 186 F.2d 307 (2d Cir. 1951); Hooper v. Commissioner, supra; Sundquist v. United States, an unreported case (E.D. Wash. 1974, 34 AFTR 2d 74-6337, 74-2 USTC par. 13,035); Obermer v. United States, 238 F. Supp. 29 (D. Hawaii 1964); Drybrough v. United States, 208 F. Supp. 279 (W.D. Ky. 1962). The minority discount is recognized because the holder of a minority interest lacks control over corporate policy, cannot direct the payment of dividends, and cannot compel a liquidation of corporate assets. See Harwood v. Commissioner, 82 T.C. at 267; Estate of Andrews v. Commissioner, 79 T.C. at 953; Drybrough v. United States, 208 F. Supp. at 287-288[8]. A lack of marketability discount, on the other hand, reflects the fact that there is no ready market for shares in a closely held corporation. Estate of Andrews v. Commissioner, 79 T.C. at 953.

The justification for a minority discount is explained very well in the important case of *Estate of Furman v. Commissioner.*[9] The court states: "A minority interest discount reflects the minority shareholder's inability to compel either the payment of dividends or liquidation in order to realize a pro rata share of the corporation's net earnings or net asset value."

Thus, the minority discount has a long history and it constitutes one of the building blocks of discounts.

LACK OF MARKETABILITY

While it is often coupled with the discount for a minority, the concept of a discount for lack of marketability is actually a separate concept. In essence, it simply means that the number of willing purchasers of the property are limited. As such, a discount should be available.

A good description of the discount occurs in the aforementioned *Furman* case, where the court states:

> A lack of marketability discount reflects the fact that there is no ready market for shares in a closely held corporation. Ascertaining the appropriate discount for limited marketability is a factual determination. Critical to this determination is an appreciation of the fundamental elements of value that are used by an investor in making his or her investment decision. Some of the relevant factors include: (1) The cost of a similar company's stock; (2) an analysis of the corporation's financial statements; (3) the corporation's dividend-paying capacity and dividend payment history; (4) the nature of the corporation, its history, its industry position, and its economic outlook; (5) the corporation's management; (6) the degree of control transferred with the block of stock to be valued; (7) restrictions on transferability; (8) the period of time for which an investor must hold the stock to realize a sufficient return; (9) the corporation's redemption policy; and (10) the cost and likelihood of a public offering of the stock to be valued.

NEW DISCOUNT THEORIES: POTENTIAL LOSS OF A KEY EMPLOYEE

As has been previously described, the courts have been unwilling to accept the restricted view of the IRS on discounts. Recently courts have been willing to go even further and to create new theories to *increase* the amount of discounts. Previously cited has been the *Furman* case. In *Furman*, the Tax Court increased the amount of discount because of the fact that the business was essentially being run by a key employee. The court recognized that the potential loss of that key employee could result in a substantial loss of value for the business. The court explained its rationale as follows:

> Where a corporation is substantially dependent upon the services of one person, and where that person would no longer be able to perform services for the corporation by reason of death or incapacity, an investor would expect some form of discount below fair market value when purchasing stock in the corporation to compensate for the

loss of that key employee. See Estate of Huntsman v. Commissioner, 66 T.C. 861 (1976); Estate of Mitchell v. Commissioner, supra; Estate of Feldmar v. Commissioner, T.C. Memo 1988-429; Estate of Yeager v. Commissioner, T.C. Memo. 1986-448. Although FIC could have purchased key-person life insurance on Robert's life, a minority shareholder could not compel FIC to purchase such insurance, and FIC had no such insurance in effect.

We have found as facts that Robert was a key person in the management of FIC, that FIC had no second layer of management, and that Robert's contacts, experience, and managerial expertise were critically important to the success of FIC. While the operation of a franchised Burger King restaurant might appear to be formulaic, FIC was a growing organization, and Robert's responsibilities extended well beyond the operation of existing restaurants. Moreover, since BKC had considerable control over FIC's costs, expansion opportunities, competition, and ultimately profits, Robert's personal relationships with the founders of BKC were very helpful to the success of FIC. We therefore agree with petitioners and find that a key-person discount of 10 percent was appropriate in determining the value of FIC stock as of February 1980 and August 1981.

Accordingly, we allow a total discount of 46 percent in valuing the FIC common stock transferred by decedents in 1980 and 1981, reflecting a combined minority and marketability discount of 40 percent and a key-person discount of 10 percent.

NEW DISCOUNT THEORIES: POTENTIAL CAPITAL GAINS TAXATION

Another new theory with regards to discounts relates to potential capital gains taxation. The theory here is that when assets are transferred via an FLP or FLLC, the basis of the assets remains the same as it was in the hands of the transferor or creator of the FLP or FLLC.[10] Thus, if an FLP or FLLC were to distribute assets and then the assets were sold by the limited partner or partners, the partner would have to pay a capital gains tax. In the "high-profile" case of *Estate of Davis v. Commissioner*,[11] Mr. Davis was a co-founder of the Winn-Dixie supermarkets and the assets in question in the case were shares of Winn-Dixie stock that had been transferred to a corporate equivalent of an FLP. The court allowed a discount based on the following line of thought:

> We are convinced on the record in this case, and we find, that, even though no liquidation of ADDI&C or sale of its assets was planned or contemplated on the valuation date, a hypothetical willing seller and a hypothetical willing buyer would not have agreed on that date on a price for each of the blocks of stock in question that took no account of ADDI&C's built-in capital gains tax. We are also persuaded on that record, and we find, that such a willing seller and such a willing buyer of each of the two blocks of ADDI&C stock at issue would have agreed on a price on the valuation date at which each such block would have changed hands that was less than the price that they would have agreed upon if there had been no ADDI&C's built-in capital gains tax as of that date.

NEW DISCOUNT THEORIES: POOR PORTFOLIO DIVERSITY

In a very recent case, *Adams v. United States*,[12] the Fifth Circuit Court of Appeals validated the concept that a discount would be allowed for poor portfolio diversity. The specific language that the court used is as follows:

> We discern a very real possibility that, as a matter of law, the holder of an assignee interest in the partnership could be stuck with an unmarketable interest in a partnership that owns a poorly diversified mix of assets and over which the assignee has no legal control. If this proved to be the case, the fair market value of the 25 percent assignee interest would be substantially less than a straight, ratable 25 percent share of the partnership's NAV, thereby reflecting these undesirable characteristics.

CURRENT DEVELOPMENTS: SEPARATE INTERESTS

A recent case posed an interesting question for purposes of looking at the potential to combine interests to eliminate a minority discount. In the case of *Estate of Mellinger v. Commissioner*, [13] the issue was whether stock owned by a decedent should be aggregated with stock in which the decedent was the beneficiary. The court refused to aggregate the QTIP stock with the personal stock, so as to eliminate a minority interest discount. The court held:

> Section 2044 was amended by the Technical Corrections Act of 1982, Pub. L. 97-448, sec. 104(a)(1)(B), 96 Stat. 2365, 2380. The legislative history accompanying that amendment provides no additional guidance on whether the interests involved in this case should be aggregated. Rather, "The bill clarifies that QTIP property included in a deceased donee spouse's estate is treated as passing from that spouse, for purposes of the estate tax, including the charitable and marital deductions." S. Rept. 97-592, at 20 (1982), 1983-1 C.B. 475, 483. In addition, the legislative history to the amendment does not suggest that Congress intended that section 2044 property be treated as being owned by the second spouse to die for purposes of aggregation and does not provide for aggregation with other fractional interests in the same property included in the decedent's estate under section 2033. Neither section 2044 nor the legislative history indicates that decedent should be treated as the owner of QTIP property for this purpose.

CURRENT DEVELOPMENTS: NON-APPLICATION OF SECTION 2704(b)

As was described above, one argument that the IRS has formulated to eliminate discounts is to interpose Code section 2704(b) as a device to eliminate the discount. The argument is based on the theory that the limited partner has a complete and unconditional withdrawal right under the applicable state partnership law, and thus any restrictions on the exercise of such withdrawal right should be ignored pursuant to Section 2704(b). In general, Section 2704(b) generally provides that, where a transferor and his family control a corporation or partnership, a restriction on the right to liquidate the corporation or partnership shall be disregarded in determining the value of an interest that has been transferred from the transferor to a family member if, after the transfer, the restriction on liquidation either lapses or can be removed by the family. However, Section 2704(b)(3)(B) excepts from the definition of an applicable restriction "any restriction on liquidation imposed, or required to be imposed, by any Federal or State law." In the recent case of *Kerr v. Commissioner*,[14] the issue was whether provisions, which provided for the FLP to dissolve and liquidate on the earlier of (1) December 31, 2043, (2) by agreement of all the partners, or (3) on the occurrence of certain narrowly defined acts of dissolution, could be utilized to reduce estate tax value. The critical issue was whether or not these provisions were more restrictive than state law. The applicable state law was Texas. The court found that under Texas law,[15] a Texas limited partnership could be dissolved on the earlier of: (1) the occurrence of events specified in the partnership agreement to cause dissolution; (2) the written consent of all partners to dissolution; (3) the withdrawal of a general partner; or (4) entry of a decree of judicial dissolution. As a result, the court concluded that the restrictions were not more restrictive than that allowed by Texas law. As such, the provisions in the agreement would be allowed to reduce value.

The court made the conclusion, as follows:

> On the basis of a comparison of . . . the partnership agreements and [Texas law], we conclude that section 10.01 of the partnership agreements does not contain restrictions on liquidation that constitute applicable restrictions within the meaning of section 2704(b). We reach this conclusion because Texas law provides for the dissolution and liquidation of a limited partnership pursuant to the occurrence of events specified in the partnership agreement or upon the written consent of all the partners, and the restrictions contained in section 10.01 of the partnership agreements are no more restrictive than the limitations that generally would apply to the partnerships under Texas law. Consequently, these provisions are excepted from the definition of an applicable restriction pursuant to section 2704(b)(3)(B) and section 25.2704-2(b), Gift Tax Regs.

Since Texas law in this interest is similar to the law in other states, it appears that the IRS will have difficulty in making this argument in any jurisdiction. Thus, if liquidation restrictions are spelled out in the agreement they should be given weight in reducing value and in allowing for a discount based on these rights.

FOOTNOTE REFERENCES

1. See Letter Rulings 9736004, 9730004, 9725002, 9723009, 9719006, and 9735003.
2. 658 F.2d 999 (5th Cir. 1981).
3. Id. At p. 1006.
4. 1993-1 CB 202. This ruling is reproduced in the appendix.
5. See for example, Rev. Proc. 89-12, 1989-1 CB 798.

6. Form 706.
7. 41 BTA 114 (1940).
8. 87 TC 78 (1986).
9. TC Memo 1998-157. This case represents a good "textbook" for the understanding the tax basis for discounts.
10. IRC Sec. 1015.
11. 110 TC 530 (1998).
12. -F.3d-; No. 99-10497 (5th Cir. 7/5/00).
13. 112 TC 26 (1999).
14. 113 TC 449 (1999).
15. Texas Revised Limited Partnership Act, Section 8.01.

Appendix A

REVENUE PROCEDURE 95-10
1995-1 CB 501

Section 7701 — Definitions
Statement of Procedural Rules
Full Text

SECTION 1. PURPOSE

.01 This revenue procedure specifies the conditions under which the Internal Revenue Service (Service) will consider a ruling request that relates to classification of a domestic or foreign limited liability company (LLC) as a partnership for federal tax purposes. This revenue procedure modifies Rev. Proc. 89-12, 1989-1 CB 798, which specifies the conditions under which the Service will consider a ruling request that relates to the classification of an organization as a partnership for federal tax purposes. Rev. Proc. 89-12 applies to organizations formed as partnerships and also applies to other organizations seeking partnership classification. It also provides that any reference to a "limited partnership" includes an organization formed as a limited partnership under applicable state law and any other organization formed under a law that limits the liability of any member for the organization's debts and other obligations to a determinable fixed amount. Rev. Proc. 89-12 no longer applies to LLCs. See section 6 of this revenue procedure.

.02 This revenue procedure applies to all organizations that are formed as LLCs under the laws of the United States or of any State or the District of Columbia (domestic law) providing for or allowing limited liability to any of their members and that are not incorporated organizations, trusts, or partnerships formed under statutes corresponding to the Uniform Partnership Act or the Revised Uniform Limited Partnership Act. This revenue procedure also applies to all organizations formed under a law other than domestic law (foreign law or foreign statute), where the foreign law or foreign statute provides for or allows limited liability to any of their members (whether or not the foreign organization is "incorporated" under a foreign statute). See Rev. Rul. 88-8, 1988-1 CB 403. This revenue procedure does not apply to a publicly traded LLC treated as a corporation under section 7704 of the Internal Revenue Code.

.03 Unless the context clearly indicates otherwise, references to the LLC's operating agreement include the articles of organization and all other controlling documents, however designated, entered into by the members of the LLC. If the applicable statute allows for management by one or more designated persons, managers are those persons designated or elected by the members to act on behalf of the LLC.

.04 The Service may decline to issue a ruling under this revenue procedure when warranted by the facts and circumstances of a particular case and when appropriate in the interest of sound tax administration.

SECTION 2. BACKGROUND

.01 Section 7701(a)(2) defines the term partnership to include a syndicate, group, pool, joint venture, or other unincorporated organization, through or by means of which any business, financial operation, or venture is carried on, and which is not, within the meaning of the Code, a trust or estate or a corporation. Sections 301.7701-2 and 301.7701-3 of the Procedure and Administration Regulations set forth rules for determining whether an organization is classified as a partnership or as an association taxable as a corporation for federal tax purposes.

.02 Rev. Rul. 73-254, 1973-1 CB 613, provides that the classification of a foreign unincorporated business organization for federal tax purposes will be determined under section 7701 and the regulations thereunder. However, it is the local law of the foreign jurisdiction that must be applied in determining the legal relationships of the members of the organization among themselves and with the public at large, as well as the interests of the members of the organization in its assets. Rev. Rul. 88-8 provides that an entity organized under foreign law is considered to be "unincorporated" for purposes of section 301.7701-2(a)(3) and, therefore, is classified for federal tax purposes solely on the basis of the characteristics set forth in section 301.7701-2.

.03 Rev. Proc. 94-1, 1994-1 CB 378, as updated annually, sets forth procedures for taxpayer requests and Service issuance of advance rulings; however, Rev. Proc. 94-3, 1994-1 CB 447, and Rev. Proc. 94-7, 1994-1 CB 542, as updated annually, list areas in which the Service will not issue, or will not ordinarily issue, advance rulings.

SECTION 3. INFORMATION TO BE SUBMITTED WITH RULING REQUEST

.01 Section 8 of Rev. Proc. 94-1 outlines general requirements concerning the information to be submitted as part of a ruling request, including a classification ruling request. For example, an LLC classification ruling request must contain a complete statement of all facts relating to the classification issue. Among those facts to be included in the statement are the items of information specified in this revenue procedure; therefore, the ruling request must provide all items of information specified below, or at least account for all the items. For example, if no registration statement is required to be filed with the U.S. Securities and Exchange Commission (SEC), the ruling request should so state.

.02 Submission of the documents and supplementary materials required by section 3.04 of this revenue procedure does not satisfy the information requirements contained in section 3.03 of this revenue procedure or in section 8 of Rev. Proc. 94-1. All material facts in documents, including those items required by section 3.03 of this revenue procedure, must be included in the ruling request and may not merely be incorporated by reference therein. All submitted documents and supplementary materials must contain applicable exhibits, attachments, and amendments.

.03 REQUIRED GENERAL INFORMATION. The following information must be included in the request for a ruling:

(1) The name and taxpayer identification number (if any) of the LLC;

(2) The business of the LLC;

(3) The date and place of filing of the LLC's articles of organization, or the anticipated date and place of filing;

(4) The identification of the domestic or foreign jurisdiction whose law controls the formation and operation of the LLC;

(5) A representation that the LLC has been, and will be at all times, in conformance with the controlling laws of the domestic or foreign jurisdiction;

(6) The nature, amount, and timing of capital contributions made and to be made by the members to the LLC;

(7) The extent of participation of the members and the managers in profits and losses of the LLC, including any possible shift in the profit and loss sharing ratios over time;

(8) A description of the relationships, direct and indirect, between the members and the managers (whether or not also members) that would suggest that the managers, individually or in the aggregate, may not at all times act independently of the members (because of individual or aggregate influence or control by the members in their capacity as such over the managers). These relationships include: (a) ownership by non-manager members of 5 percent or more of the stock or other beneficial interests in a manager; (b) control by non-manager members of 5 percent or more of the voting power in a manager; (c) ownership of 5 percent or more of the stock or other beneficial interests in any manager and in any non-manager members by the same person or persons acting as a group; and (d) control of 5 percent or more of the voting power in any manager and in any non-manager members by the same person or persons acting as a group. A person is considered to own any beneficial interest owned by a related person and is considered to control any voting power controlled by a related person. A person is treated as related to another person if they bear a relationship to each other specified in section 267(b) or section 707(b)(1). The relationships defined in the first sentence of this section 3.03(8) may also include a debtor-creditor relationship and an employer-employee relationship;

(9) If it is asserted that the LLC lacks the corporate characteristic of limited liability: (a) a description of the legal arrangements

supporting the assertion that the LLC lacks limited liability, (b) a representation of the net worth (based on assets at current fair market value) of the member or members assuming personal liability for all obligations of the LLC (assuming member), excluding interests in the LLC held by that member or members, (c) a description of the assuming member's or members' assets and liabilities arising from transactions with the LLC or with a person related to any member or members under section 267(b) or section 707(b)(1), and (d) a description of all other organizations in which the member or members have an interest;

(10) A detailed description of how each of the applicable provisions of section 5 of this revenue procedure are satisfied;

(11) If the Service has issued a revenue ruling on the applicable domestic or foreign law, a discussion of how the revenue ruling applies to the taxpayer's ruling request.

.04 REQUIRED COPIES OF DOCUMENTS AND SUPPLEMENTARY MATERIALS. The following copies of documents and materials must be submitted with the ruling request:

(1) The LLC's articles of organization filed or to be filed with the domestic or foreign jurisdiction in which the LLC is formed;

(2) The LLC's operating agreement (exclusive of the articles of organization);

(3) The registration statement (or comparable document under foreign law) filed or to be filed with the SEC or comparable foreign regulatory body. (A draft that is final in all material respects is acceptable);

(4) If a registration statement (or comparable document under foreign law) is not required to be filed with the SEC or comparable foreign regulatory body, the documents filed or to be filed with any domestic federal or state (or comparable foreign) agency engaged in the regulation of securities and any private offering memorandum (or comparable documents un-

der foreign law). (Drafts that are final in all material respects are acceptable);

(5) A copy of the applicable domestic or foreign law, and amendments, under which the LLC was or will be formed;

(6) An outline or copies of all promotional material used to sell interests in the LLC, highlighting statements about probable domestic and foreign tax consequences and the effect of the requested ruling upon the tax consequences;

(7) An English translation of all documents in a foreign language.

SECTION 4. GENERAL PROVISIONS AND OWNERSHIP TESTS

.01 GENERAL. The Service will consider a ruling request that relates to classification of an LLC as a partnership for federal tax purposes only if the LLC has at least two members and, to the extent applicable, the conditions in sections 4 and 5 of this revenue procedure are satisfied. The determination of whether the LLC has at least two members is based on all the facts and circumstances. Section 5.01 relates solely to the corporate characteristic of continuity of life described in section 301.7701-2(b); section 5.02 relates solely to the corporate characteristic of free transferability of interests described in section 301.7701-2(e); section 5.03 relates solely to the corporate characteristic of centralized management described in section 301.7701-2(c); and section 5.04 relates solely to the corporate characteristic of limited liability described in section 301.7701-2(d). Section 4.02 through 4.05 of this revenue procedure provides minimum ownership requirements that must be satisfied if the taxpayer requests a ruling that the LLC lacks continuity of life under section 5.01(1) (pertaining to dissolution events relating solely to member- managers), free transferability of interests under section 5.02(1) (pertaining to consent to transfer solely by member-managers), or limited liability under section 5.04. Failure to satisfy any of the above sections only precludes a ruling that the LLC lacks the particular corporate characteristic addressed by the relevant section and does not necessarily preclude the issuance of a partnership classification ruling by the Service. If the LLC is issued a ruling under this revenue procedure that it is classified as a partnership and the LLC subsequently has only one member, the letter ruling ceases to be effective because the LLC's status as a partnership for federal tax purposes terminates as of the relevant date specified in section 708 and section 736.

.02 GENERAL RULE AS TO PROFIT AND LOSS INTERESTS. Unless section 4.03 of this revenue procedure applies, if the taxpayer requests a ruling that the LLC lacks continuity of life under section 5.01(1) or free transferability of interests under section 5.02(1), the member-managers in the aggregate must own, pursuant to the express terms of the operating agreement, at least a 1 percent interest in each material item of the LLC's income, gain, loss, deduction, or credit during the entire existence of the LLC. Further, unless section 4.03 applies, if the taxpayer requests a ruling that the LLC lacks limited liability under section 5.04, the assuming member or members must in the aggregate own, pursuant to the express terms of the operating agreement, at least a 1 percent interest in each material item of the LLC's income, gain, loss, deduction, or credit during the entire existence of the LLC. However, it will generally not be considered a violation of this section 4.02 if a required allocation under either section 704(b) or section 704(c), or corresponding Income Tax Regulations, temporarily causes less than 1 percent of the LLC's income, gain, loss, deduction, or credit to be allocable to the party otherwise required under this section 4.02 to receive the allocation; in these cases, the ruling request must describe any required allocations and explain why the allocation is required under section 704(b) or section 704(c), as appropriate. Any other temporary allocation causing less than 1 percent of any material item of the LLC's income, gain, loss, deduction, or credit to be allocable to the necessary parties will be considered a violation of this section 4.02, unless the LLC clearly establishes in the ruling request that the member-managers or the assuming members (as the case may be) have a material interest in net profits and losses over the LLC's anticipated life. For this purpose, a profits interest generally will not be considered material unless it substantially exceeds 1 percent and will be in effect for a substantial period of time during which the LLC reasonably expects to generate profits. For example, a 20 percent interest in profits that begins 4 years after the LLC's formation and continues for the life of the LLC generally would be considered material if the LLC is expected to generate profits for a substantial period of time beyond the initial 4-year period.

.03 EXCEPTION TO GENERAL RULE AS TO MINIMUM PROFITS AND LOSS INTERESTS. If the LLC has total contributions exceeding $50 million, the member-managers (or assuming members) need not meet the 1 percent standard in section 4.02 of this revenue procedure. However, except for a temporary allocation or nonconformance specified in section 4.02, the member-managers (or assuming members) in the aggregate must maintain an interest at all times during the existence of the LLC in each material item of at least 1 percent divided by the ratio of total contributions to $50 million, and the LLC's operating agreement must expressly incorporate at least the computed percentage. For example, if total contributions are $125 million, the interest in each material item must be at least .4 percent, that is, 1 percent divided by 125/50. In no event, however, other than as a result of a temporary allocation or nonconformance specified in section 4.02, may the member-managers' (or assuming members') aggregate interest at any time during the existence of the LLC in any material item be less than .2 percent.

.04 GENERAL RULE AS TO CAPITAL ACCOUNT BALANCES. Unless section 4.05 of this revenue procedure applies, if the taxpayer requests a ruling that the LLC lacks continuity of life under section 5.01(1), or free transferability of interests under section 5.02(1), the member-managers, in the aggregate, must maintain throughout the entire existence of the LLC a minimum capital account balance equal to the lesser of 1 percent of total positive capital account balances or $500,000. Further, unless section 4.05 applies, if the taxpayer requests a ruling that the LLC lacks limited liability under section 5.04, the assuming member or members must maintain a minimum capital account balance in accordance with the rules of the preceding sentence. Whenever a non-managing member (or non-assuming member) makes a capital contribution, the member-managers (or assuming members) must be obligated, pursuant to the express terms of the operating agreement, to contribute immediately to the LLC capital equal to 1.01 percent of the non-managing members' (or non-assuming members') capital contributions or a lesser amount (including zero) that causes the sum of the member-managers' (or assuming members') capital account balances to equal the lesser of 1 percent of total positive capital account balances for the LLC or $500,000. If no member has a positive capital account balance, then the member-managers (or assuming members) in the LLC need not have a positive capital account balance to satisfy this section 4.04. Capital accounts and the value of contributions are determined under the rules of section 1.704-1(b)(2)(iv) of the Income Tax Regulations.

.05 EXCEPTION TO GENERAL RULE OF MINIMUM CAPITAL ACCOUNT BALANCES. If at least one member-manager (or assuming member) otherwise required under section 4.04 of this revenue procedure to have and maintain a minimum capital account balance has contributed or will contribute substantial services in the capacity as a member, apart from services for which guaranteed payments under section 707(c) are made, the capital account standard in section 4.04 does not apply to any of the member-managers (or assuming members). However, the operating agreement of the LLC must expressly provide that, upon the dissolution and termination of the LLC, the member-managers (or assuming members) will contribute capital to the LLC in an amount equal to the lesser of: (1) the aggregate deficit balance, if any, in their capital accounts, or (2) the excess of 1.01 percent of the total capital contributions of the non-managing members (or non-assuming members) over the aggregate capital previously contributed to the LLC by the member-managers (or assuming members). Those services that do not relate to day-to-day operations in the LLC's primary business activity, such as services related to the organization and syndication of the LLC, accounting, financial planning, general business planning, and services in the nature of investment management, will be closely scrutinized by the Service to determine if they are in fact substantial services. In making this determination, the nature of the LLC and its activities will be taken into account.

SECTION 5. RULING GUIDELINES FOR SPECIFIC CORPORATE CHARACTERISTICS

.01 CONTINUITY OF LIFE.

(1) DISSOLUTION EVENTS RELATING SOLELY TO MEMBER-MANAGERS. If the members of the LLC designate or elect one or more members as managers and the controlling statute, or the operating agreement pursuant to the controlling statute, provides that the death, insanity, bankruptcy, retirement, resignation, or expulsion of any member-manager causes a dissolution of the LLC without further action of the members, unless the LLC is continued by the consent of not less than a majority in interest of the remaining members, the Service will generally rule that the LLC lacks continuity of life. For purposes of the preceding sentence all the member-managers must be subject to the specified dissolution events. For example, if the LLC is managed by A, B, and C, it must be provided that a dissolution event with respect to A, B, or C will

dissolve the LLC, and not a dissolution event with respect to only one of the named managers (i.e., a dissolution event only with respect to A but not B or C).

(2) DISSOLUTION EVENTS RELATING TO MEMBERS. If the members of the LLC do not designate or elect one or more members as managers (or if the LLC requests a ruling under this section 5.01(2) despite the presence of member-managers) and the controlling statute, or the operating agreement pursuant to the controlling statute, provides that the death, insanity, bankruptcy, retirement, resignation, or expulsion of any member dissolves the LLC without further action of the members, unless the LLC is continued by the consent of not less than a majority in interest of the remaining members, the Service generally will rule that the LLC lacks continuity of life. For purposes of the preceding sentence, all the members must be subject to the specified dissolution events.

(3) MAJORITY IN INTEREST. See Rev. Proc. 94-46, 1994-28 IRB 129, pertaining to majority in interest, for purposes of applying section 5.01(1) and (2) of this revenue procedure.

(4) LIMITATION ON DISSOLUTION EVENTS. If the controlling statute, or the operating agreement pursuant to the controlling statute, provides that less than all of the dissolution events listed above with respect to the member-managers (when applying section 5.01(1)) or the members (when applying section 5.01(2)) dissolves the LLC, the Service will not rule that the LLC lacks continuity of life unless the taxpayer clearly establishes in the ruling request that the event or events selected provide a meaningful possibility of dissolution.

.02 FREE TRANSFERABILITY OF INTERESTS.

(1) CONSENT TO TRANSFER SOLELY BY MEMBER-MANAGERS. If the members of the LLC designate or elect one or more members as managers, and the controlling statute, or the operating agreement pursuant to the controlling statute, provides that each member, or those members owning more than 20 percent of all interests in the LLC's capital, income, gain, loss, deduction, and credit, does not have the power to confer upon a non-member all the attributes of the member's interests in the LLC without the consent of not less than a majority of the non-transferring member-managers, the Service will generally rule that

the LLC lacks free transferability of interests. See Rev. Proc. 92-33, 1992-1 CB 782.

(2) CONSENT TO TRANSFER BY MEMBERS. If the members of the LLC do not designate or elect one or more members as managers (or if the LLC requests a ruling under this section 5.02(2) despite the presence of member-managers), and the controlling statute, or the operating agreement pursuant to the controlling statute, provides that each member, or those members owning more than 20 percent of all interests in the LLC's capital, income, gain, loss, deduction, and credit, does not have the power to confer upon a non-member all the attributes of the member's interests in the LLC without the consent of not less than a majority of the non-transferring members, the Service will generally rule that the LLC lacks free transferability of interests. See Rev. Proc. 92-33.

(3) MAJORITY DEFINED. For purposes of applying sections 5.02(1) and 5.02(2) of this revenue procedure, consent of a majority includes either a majority in interest (see Rev. Proc. 94-46 pertaining to majority in interest), a majority of either the capital or profits interests in the LLC, or a majority determined on a per capita basis.

(4) MEANINGFUL CONSENT. The Service will not rule that the LLC lacks free transferability of interests unless the power to withhold consent to the transfer constitutes a meaningful restriction on the transfer of the interests. For example, a power to withhold consent to a transfer is not a meaningful restriction if the consent may not be unreasonably withheld.

.03 CENTRALIZATION OF MANAGEMENT.

(1) MEMBERS MANAGE LLC WITHOUT MANAGERS. If the controlling statute, or the operating agreement pursuant to the controlling statute, provides that the LLC is managed by the members exclusively in their membership capacity, the Service generally will rule that the LLC lacks centralized management.

(2) MEMBERS DESIGNATED OR ELECTED AS MANAGERS. If the members of the LLC designate or elect one or more members as managers of the LLC, the Service will not rule that the LLC lacks centralized management unless the member-managers in the aggregate

own at least 20 percent of the total interests in the LLC. However, even if the aggregate ownership requirement is satisfied, the Service will consider all the relevant facts and circumstances, including, particularly, member control of the member-managers (whether direct or indirect), in determining whether the LLC lacks centralized management. The Service will not rule that the LLC lacks centralized management if the member-managers are subject to periodic elections by the members, or, alternatively, the non-managing members have a substantially non-restricted power to remove the member-managers.

.04 LIMITED LIABILITY.

The Service generally will not rule that an LLC lacks limited liability unless at least one assuming member validly assumes personal liability for all (but not less than all) obligations of the LLC, pursuant to express authority granted in the controlling statute. In addition, the Service generally will not rule that an LLC lacks limited liability unless the assuming members have an aggregate net worth that, at the time of the ruling request, equals at least 10 percent of the total contributions to the LLC and is expected to continue to equal at least 10 percent of total contributions to the LLC throughout the life of the LLC. In the case of an LLC in which the assuming members do not satisfy the safe harbor described in the preceding sentence, close scrutiny will be applied to determine whether the LLC lacks limited liability. In that connection, it must be demonstrated that an assuming member has (or the assuming members collectively have) substantial assets (other than the member's interest in the LLC) that could be reached by a creditor of the LLC. In determining the net worth of the assuming member (or assuming members), the principles contained in section 4.03 of Rev. Proc. 92-88, 1992-2 CB 496, are to be applied.

SECTION 6. EFFECT ON OTHER REVENUE PROCEDURES

Rev. Proc. 89-12 is modified so that it does not apply to ruling requests submitted by LLCs described in this revenue procedure.

SECTION 7. EFFECTIVE DATE

This revenue procedure applies to all ruling requests received in the National Office on or after January 17, 1995.

Drafting Information:

The principal author of this revenue procedure is D. Lindsay Russell of the Office of Assistant Chief Counsel (Passthroughs & Special Industries). For further information regarding this revenue procedure contact Mr. Russell at (202) 622-3050 (not a toll-free call).

Appendix B

REVENUE RULINGS AND LETTER RULINGS

REVENUE RULING 95-37

1995-1 CB 130

Section 706 –Partner-Partnership Tax Years
Full Text

Issues

(1) Do the federal income tax consequences described in Rev. Rul. 84-52, 1984-1 C.B. 157, apply to the conversion of an interest in a domestic partnership into an interest in a domestic limited liability company (LLC) that is classified as a partnership for federal tax purposes?

(2) Does the taxable year of the converting domestic partnership close with respect to all the partners or with respect to any partner?

(3) Does the resulting domestic LLC need to obtain a new taxpayer identification number?

Law and Analysis

In Rev. Rul. 84-52, a general partnership formed under the Uniform Partnership Act of State M proposed to convert to a limited partnership under the Uniform Limited Partnership Act of State M. Rev. Rul. 84-52 generally holds that (1) under section 721 of the Internal Revenue Code, the conversion will not cause the partners to recognize gain or loss under sections 741 or 1001, (2) unless its business will not continue after the conversion, the partnership will not terminate under section 708 because the conversion is not treated as a sale or exchange for purposes of section 708, (3) if the partners's shares of partnership liabilities do not change, there will be no change in the adjusted basis of any partner's interest in the partnership, (4) if the partners's shares of partnership liabilities change and cause a deemed contribution of money to the partnership by a partner under section 752(a), then the adjusted basis of such a partner's interest will be increased under section 722 by the amount of the deemed contribution, (5) if the partners's shares of partnership liabilities change and cause a deemed distribution of money by the partnership to a partner under section 752(b), then the basis of such a partner's interest will be reduced under section 733 (but not below zero) by the amount of the deemed distribution, and gain will be recognized by the partner under section 731 to the extent the deemed distribution exceeds the adjusted basis of the partner's interest in the partnership, and (6) under section 1223(1), there will be no change in the holding period of any partner's total interest in the partnership.

The conversion of an interest in a domestic partnership into an interest in a domestic LLC that is classified as a partnership for federal tax purposes is treated as a partnership-to-partnership conversion that is subject to the principles of Rev. Rul. 84-52.

Section 706(c)(1) provides that, except in the case of a termination of a partnership and except as provided in section 706(c)(2), the taxable year of a partnership does not close as the result of the death of a partner, the entry of a new partner, the liquidation of a partner's interest in the partnership, or the sale or exchange of a partner's interest in the partnership.

Section 706(c)(2)(A)(i) provides that the taxable year of a partnership closes with respect to a partner who sells or exchanges the partner's entire interest in a partnership. Section 706(c)(2)(A)(ii) provides that the taxable year of a partnership closes with respect to a partner whose interest is liquidated, except that the taxable year of a partnership with respect to a partner who dies does not close prior to the end of the partnership's taxable year.

In the present case, the conversion of an interest in a domestic partnership into an interest in a domestic LLC that is classified as a partnership for federal tax purposes does not cause a termination under section 708. See Rev. Rul. 84-52. Moreover, because each partner in a converting domestic partnership continues to hold an interest in the resulting domestic LLC, the conversion is not a sale, exchange, or liquidation of the converting partner's entire partnership interest for purposes of section 706(c)(2)(A). See Rev. Rul. 86-101, 1986-2 C.B. 94 (the taxable year of a partnership does not close with respect to a general partner when the partnership agreement provides that the general partner's interest converts to a limited partnership interest on the general partner's death because the decedent's successor continues to hold an interest in the partnership). Consequently, the conversion does not cause the taxable year of the domestic partnership to close with respect to all the partners or with respect to any partner.

Because the conversion of an interest in a domestic partnership into an interest in a domestic LLC that is classified as a partnership for federal tax purposes does not cause a termination under section 708, the resulting domestic LLC does not need to obtain a new taxpayer identification number.

Holdings

(1) The federal income tax consequences described in Rev. Rul. 84-52 apply to the conversion of an interest in a domestic partnership into an interest in a domestic LLC that is classified as a partnership for federal tax purposes. The federal tax consequences are the same whether the resulting LLC is formed in the same state or in a different state than the converting domestic partnership.

(2) The taxable year of the converting domestic partnership does not close with respect to all the partners or with respect to any partner.

(3) The resulting domestic LLC does not need to obtain a new taxpayer identification number.

The holdings contained herein would apply in a similar manner if the conversion had been of an interest in a domestic LLC that is classified as a partnership for federal tax purposes into an interest in a domestic partnership. The holdings contained herein apply regardless of the manner in which the conversion is achieved under state law.

This revenue ruling does not address the federal tax consequences of a conversion of an organization that is classified as a corporation into an organization that is classified as a partnership for federal tax purposes. See, e.g., sections 336 and 337.

Effect on Other Revenue Rulings

Rev. Rul. 84-52 and Rev. Rul. 86-101 are amplified.

Drafting Information:

The principal author of this revenue ruling is D. Lindsay Russell of the Office of Assistant Chief Counsel (Passthroughs and Special Industries). For further information regarding this revenue ruling contact Mr. Russell on (202) 622-3050 (not a toll-free call).

REVENUE RULING 93-12

Section 2512 – Valuation of property; in general
Full text

Issue

If a donor transfers shares in a corporation to each of the donor's children, is the factor of corporate control in the family to be considered in valuing each transferred interest, for purposes of section 2512 of the Internal Revenue Code?

Facts

P owned all of the single outstanding class of stock of X corporation. P transferred all of P's shares by making simultaneous gifts of 20 percent of the shares to each of P's five children, A, B, C, D, and E.

Law and Analysis

Section 2512(a) of the Code provides that the value of the property at the date of the gift shall be considered the amount of the gift.

Section 25.2512-1 of the Gift Tax Regulations provides that, if a gift is made in property, its value at the date of the gift shall be considered the amount of the gift. The value of the property is the price at which the property would change hands between a willing buyer and a willing seller, neither being under any compulsion to buy or to sell, and both having reasonable knowledge of relevant facts.

Section 25.2512-2(a) of the regulations provides that the value of stocks and bonds is the fair market value per share or bond on the date of the gift. Section 25.2512-2(f) provides that the degree of control of the business represented by the block of stock to be valued is among the factors to be considered in valuing stock where there are no sales prices or bona fide bid or asked prices.

Rev. Rul. 81-253, 1981-1 C.B. 187, holds that, ordinarily, no minority shareholder discount is allowed with respect to transfers of shares of stock between family members if, based upon a composite of the family members' interests at the time of the transfer, control (either majority voting control or de facto control through family relationships) of the corporation exists in the family unit. The ruling also states that the Service will not follow the decision of the Fifth Circuit in Estate of Bright v. United States, 658 F.2d 999 (5th Cir. 1981).

In Bright, the decedent's undivided community property interest in shares of stock, together with the corresponding undivided community property interest of the decedent's surviving spouse, constituted a control block of 55 percent of the shares of a corporation. The court held that, because the community-held shares were subject to a right of partition, the decedent's own interest was equivalent to 27.5 percent of the outstanding shares and, therefore, should be valued as a minority interest, even though the shares were to be held by the decedent's surviving spouse as trustee of a testamentary trust. See also, Propstra v. United States, 680 F.2d 1248 (9th Cir. 1982). In addition, Estate of Andrews v. Commissioner, 79 T.C. 938 (1982), and Estate of Lee v. Commissioner, 69 T.C. 860 (1978), nonacq., 1980-2 C.B. 2, held that the corporation shares owned by other family members cannot be attributed to an individual family member for determining whether the individual family member's shares should be valued as the controlling interest of the corporation.

After further consideration of the position taken in Rev. Rul. 81-253, and in light of the cases noted above, the Service has concluded that, in the case of a corporation with a single class of stock, notwithstanding the family relationship of the donor, the donee, and other shareholders, the shares of other family members will not be aggregated with the transferred shares to determine whether the transferred shares should be valued as part of a controlling interest.

In the present case, the minority interests transferred to A, B, C, D, and E should be valued for gift tax purposes without regard to the family relationship of the parties.

Holding

If a donor transfers shares in a corporation to each of the donor's children, the factor of corporate control in the family is not considered in valuing each transferred interest for purposes of section 2512 of the Code. For estate and gift tax valuation purposes, the Service will follow Bright,

Propstra, Andrews, and Lee in not assuming that all voting power held by family members may be aggregated for purposes of determining whether the transferred shares should be valued as part of a controlling interest. Consequently, a minority discount will not be disallowed solely because a transferred interest, when aggregated with interests held by family members, would be a part of a controlling interest. This would be the case whether the donor held 100 percent or some lesser percentage of the stock immediately before the gift.

Effect on Other Documents

Rev. Rul. 81-253 is revoked. Acquiescence is substituted for the nonacquiescence in issue one of Lee, 1980-2 C.B. 2.

Drafting Information:

The principal author of this revenue ruling is Deborah Ryan of the Office of Assistant Chief Counsel (Passthroughs and Special Industries). For further information regarding this revenue ruling, contact Ms. Ryan on (202) 622-3090 (not a toll-free call).

REVENUE RULING 59-60

Status: Modified by 65-193, Amplified by 77-287, Amplified by 80-213, Amplified by 83-120
Section 2031 – Valuation of stocks and bonds
(Also Section 2512.)
(Also Part II, Sections 811(k), 1005, Regulations 105, Section 81.10.)
Full Text

Section 1. Purpose.

The purpose of this Revenue Ruling is to outline and review in general the approach, methods and factors to be considered in valuing shares of the capital stock of closely held corporations for estate tax and gift tax purposes. The methods discussed herein will apply likewise to the valuation of corporate stocks on which market quotations are either unavailable or are of such scarcity that they do not reflect the fair market value.

Sec. 2. Background and Definitions.

.01 All valuations must be made in accordance with the applicable provisions of the Internal Revenue Code of 1954 and the federal Estate Tax and Gift Tax Regulations. Sections 2031(a), 2032 and 2512(a) of the 1954 Code (sections 811 and 1005 of the 1939 Code) require that the property to be included in the gross estate, or made the subject of a gift, shall be taxed on the basis of the value of the property at the time of death of the decedent, the alternate date if so elected, or the date of gift.

.02 Section 20.2031-1(b) of the Estate Tax Regulations (section 81.10 of the Estate Tax Regulations 105) and section 25.2512-1 of the Gift Tax Regulations (section 86.19 of Gift Tax Regulations 108) define fair market value, in effect, as the price at which the property would change hands between a willing buyer and a willing seller when the former is not under any compulsion to buy and the latter is not under any compulsion to sell, both parties having reasonable knowledge of relevant facts. Court decisions frequently state in addition that the hypothetical buyer and seller are assumed to be able, as well as willing, to trade and to be well informed about the property and concerning the market for such property.

.03 Closely held corporations are those corporations the shares of which are owned by a relatively limited number of stockholders. Often the entire stock issue is held by one family. The result of this situation is that little, if any, trading in the shares takes place. There is, therefore, no established market for the stock and such sales as occur at irregular intervals seldom reflect all of the elements of a representative transaction as defined by the term "fair market value."

Sec. 3. Approach to Valuation.

.01 A determination of fair market value, being a question of fact, will depend upon the circumstances in each case. No formula can be devised that will be generally applicable to the multitude of different valuation issues arising in estate and gift tax cases. Often, an appraiser will find wide differences of opinion as to the fair market value of a particular stock. In resolving such differences, he should maintain a reasonable attitude in recognition of the fact that valuation is not an exact science. A sound valuation will be based upon all the relevant facts, but the elements of common sense, informed judgment and reasonableness must enter into the process of weighing those facts and determining their aggregate significance.

.02 The fair market value of specific shares of stock will vary as general economic conditions change from "normal" to "boom" or "depression," that is, according to the degree of optimism or pessimism with which the investing public regards the future at the required date of appraisal. Uncertainty as to the stability or continuity of the future income from a property decreases its value by increasing the risk of loss of earnings and value in the future. The value of shares of stock of a company with very uncertain future prospects is highly speculative. The appraiser must exercise his judgment as to the degree of risk attaching to the business of the corporation which issued the stock, but that judgment must be related to all of the other factors affecting value.

.03 Valuation of securities is, in essence, a prophesy as to the future and must be based on facts available at the required date of appraisal. As a generalization, the prices of stocks which are traded in volume in a free and active market by informed persons best reflect the consensus of the investing public as to what the future holds for the corporations and industries represented. When a stock is closely held, is traded infrequently, or is traded in an erratic market, some other measure of value must be used. In many instances, the next best measure may be found in the prices at which the stocks of companies engaged in the same or a similar line of business are selling in a free and open market.

Sec. 4. Factors to Consider.

.01 It is advisable to emphasize that in the valuation of the stock of closely held corporations or the stock of corporations where market quotations are either lacking or too scarce to be recognized, all available financial data, as well as all relevant factors affecting the fair market value, should be considered. The following factors, although not all-inclusive are fundamental and require careful analysis in each case:

(a) The nature of the business and the history of the enterprise from its inception.

(b) The economic outlook in general and the condition and outlook of the specific industry in particular.

(c) The book value of the stock and the financial condition of the business.

(d) The earning capacity of the company.

(e) The dividend-paying capacity.

(f) Whether or not the enterprise has goodwill or other intangible value.

(g) Sales of the stock and the size of the block of stock to be valued.

(h) The market price of stocks of corporations engaged in the same or a similar line of business having their stocks actively traded in a free and open market, either on an exchange or over-the-counter.

.02 The following is a brief discussion of each of the foregoing factors:

(a) The history of a corporate enterprise will show its past stability or instability, its growth or lack of growth, the diversity or lack of diversity of its operations, and other facts needed to form an opinion of the degree of risk involved in the business. For an enterprise which changed its form of organization but carried on the same or closely similar operations of its predecessor, the history of the former enterprise should be considered. The detail to be considered should increase with approach to the required date of appraisal, since recent events are of greatest help in predicting the future; but a study of gross and net income, and of dividends covering a long prior period, is highly desirable. The history to be studied should include, but need not be limited to, the nature of the business, its products or services, its operating and investment assets, capital structure, plant facilities, sales records and management, all of which should be considered as of the date of the appraisal, with due regard for recent significant changes. Events of the past that are unlikely to recur in the future should be discounted, since value has a close relation to future expectancy.

(b) A sound appraisal of a closely held stock must consider current and prospective economic conditions as of the date of appraisal, both in the national economy and in the industry or industries with which the corporation is allied. It is important to know that the company is more or less successful than its competitors in the same industry, or that it is maintaining a stable position with respect to competitors. Equal or even greater significance may attach to the ability of the industry with which the company is allied to compete with other industries. Prospective competition which has not been a factor in prior years should be given careful attention. For example, high profits due to the novelty of its product and the lack of competition often lead to increasing competition. The public's appraisal of the future prospects of competitive industries or of competitors within an industry may be indicated by price trends in the markets for commodities and for securities. The loss of the manager of a so-called "one-man" business may have a depressing effect upon the value of the stock of such business, particularly if there is a lack of trained personnel capable of succeeding to the management of the enterprise. In valuing the stock of this type of business, therefore, the effect of the loss of the manager on the future expectancy of the business, and the absence of management-succession potentialities are pertinent factors to be taken into consideration. On the other hand, there may be factors which offset, in whole or in part, the loss of the manager's services. For instance, the nature of the business and of its assets may be such that they will not be impaired by the loss of the manager. Furthermore, the loss may be adequately covered by life insurance, or competent management might be employed on the basis of the consideration paid for the former manager's services. These, or other offsetting factors, if found to exist, should be carefully weighed against the loss of the manager's services in valuing the stock of the enterprise.

(c) Balance sheets should be obtained, preferably in the form of comparative annual statements for two or more years immediately preceding the date of appraisal, together with a balance sheet at the end of the month preceding that date, if corporate accounting will permit. Any balance sheet descriptions that are not self-explanatory, and balance sheet items comprehending diverse assets or liabilities, should be clarified in essential detail by supporting supplemental schedules. These statements usually will disclose to the appraiser (1) liquid position (ratio of current assets to current liabilities); (2) gross and net book value of principal classes of fixed assets; (3) working capital; (4) long-term indebtedness; (5) capital structure, and (6) net worth. Consideration also should be given to any assets not essential to the operation of the business, such as investments in securities, real estate, etc. In general, such nonoperating assets will command a lower rate of return than do the operating assets, although in exceptional cases the reverse may be true. In computing the book value per share of stock, assets of the investment type should be revalued on the basis of their market price and the book value adjusted accordingly. Comparison of the company's balance sheets over several years may reveal, among other facts, such developments as the acquisition of additional production facilities or subsidiary companies, improvement in financial position, and details as to recapitalizations and other changes in the capital structure of the corporation. If the corporation has more than one class of stock outstanding, the charter or certificate of incorporation should be examined to ascertain the explicit rights and privileges of the various stock issues including: (1) voting powers, (2) preference as to dividends, and (3) preference as to assets in the event of liquidation.

(d) Detailed profit-and-loss statements should be obtained and considered for a representative period immediately prior to the required date of appraisal, preferably five or more years. Such statements should show (1) gross income by principal items; (2) principal deductions from gross income including major prior items of operating expenses, interest and other expense on each item of long-term debt, depreciation and depletion if such deductions are made, officers' salaries, in total if they appear to be reasonable or in detail if they seem to be excessive, contributions (whether or not deductible for tax purposes) that the nature of its business and its community position require the corporation to make, and taxes by principal items, including income and excess profits taxes; (3) net income available for dividends; (4) rates and amounts of dividends paid on each class of stock; (5) remaining amount carried to surplus; and (6) adjustments to, and reconciliation with, surplus as stated on the balance sheet. With profit and loss statements of this character available, the appraiser should be able to separate recurrent from nonrecurrent items of income and expense, to distinguish between operating income and investment income, and to ascertain whether or not any line of business in which the company is engaged is operated consistently at a loss and might be abandoned with benefit to the company. The percentage of earnings retained for business expansion should be noted when dividend-paying capacity is considered. Potential future income is a major factor in many valuations of closely-held stocks, and all information concerning past income which will be helpful in predicting the future should be secured. Prior earnings records usually are the most reliable guide as to the future expectancy, but resort to arbitrary five-or-ten-year averages without regard to current trends or future prospects will not produce a realistic valuation. If, for instance, a record of progressively increasing or decreasing net income is found, then greater weight may be accorded the most recent years' profits in estimating earning power. It will be helpful, in judging risk and the extent to which a business is a marginal operator, to consider deductions from income and net income in terms of percentage of sales. Major categories of cost and expense to be so analyzed include the consumption of raw materials and supplies in the case of manufacturers, processors and fabricators; the cost of purchased merchandise in the case of merchants; utility services; insurance; taxes; depletion or depreciation; and interest.

(e) Primary consideration should be given to the dividend-paying capacity of the company rather than to dividends actually paid in the past. Recognition must be given to the necessity of retaining a reasonable portion of profits in a company to meet competition. Dividend-paying capacity is a factor that must be considered in an appraisal, but dividends actually paid in the past may not have any relation to dividend-paying capacity. Specifically, the dividends paid by a closely held family company may be measured by the income needs of the stockholders or by their desire to avoid taxes on dividend receipts, instead of by the ability of the company to pay dividends. Where an actual or effective controlling interest in a corporation is to be valued, the dividend factor is not a material element, since the payment of such dividends is discretionary with the controlling stockholders. The individual or group in control can substitute salaries and bonuses for dividends, thus reducing net income and understanding the dividend-paying capacity of the company. It follows, therefore, that dividends are less reliable criteria of fair market value than other applicable factors.

(f) In the final analysis, goodwill is based upon earning capacity. The presence of goodwill and its value, therefore, rests upon the excess of net earnings over and above a fair return on the net tangible assets. While the element of goodwill may be based primarily on earnings, such factors as the prestige and renown of the business, the ownership of a trade or brand name, and a record of successful operation over a prolonged period in a particular locality, also may furnish support for the inclusion of intangible value. In some instances it may not be possible to make a separate appraisal of the tangible and intangible assets of the business. The enterprise has a value as an entity. Whatever intangible value there is, which is supportable by the facts, may be measured by the amount by which the appraised value of the tangible assets exceeds the net book value of such assets.

(g) Sales of stock of a closely held corporation should be carefully investigated to determine whether they represent transactions at arm's length. Forced or distress sales do not ordinarily reflect fair market value nor do isolated sales in small amounts necessarily control as the measure of value. This is especially true in the valuation of a controlling interest in a corporation. Since, in the case of closely held stocks, no prevailing market prices are available, there is no basis for making an adjustment for blockage. It follows, therefore, that such stocks should be valued upon a consideration of all the evidence affecting the fair market value. The size of the block of stock itself is a relevant factor to be considered. Although it is true that a minority interest in an unlisted corporation's stock is more difficult to sell than a similar block of listed stock, it is equally true that control of a corporation, either actual or in effect, representing as it does an added element of value, may justify a higher value for a specific block of stock.

(h) Section 2031(b) of the Code states, in effect, that in valuing unlisted securities the value of stock or securities of corporations engaged in the same or a similar line of business which are listed on an exchange should be taken into consideration along with all other factors. An important consideration is that the corporations to be used for comparisons have capital stocks which are actively traded by the public. In accordance with section 2031(b) of the Code, stocks listed on an exchange are to be considered first. However, if sufficient comparable companies whose stocks are listed on an exchange cannot be found, other comparable companies which have stocks actively traded in on the over-the-counter market also may be used. The essential factor is that whether the stocks are sold on an exchange or over-the-counter there is evidence of an active, free public market for the stock as of the valuation date. In selecting corporations for comparative purposes, care should be taken to use only comparable companies. Although the only restrictive requirement as to comparable corporations specified in the statute is that their lines of business be the same or similar, yet it is obvious that consideration must be given to other relevant factors in order that the most valid comparison possible will be obtained. For illustration, a corporation having one or more issues of preferred stock, bonds or debentures in addition to its common stock should not be considered to be directly comparable to one having only common stock outstanding. In like manner, a company with a declining business and decreasing markets is not comparable to one with a record of current progress and market expansion.

Sec. 5. Weight to be Accorded Various Factors.

The valuation of closely held corporate stock entails the consideration of all relevant factors as stated in section 4. Depending upon the circumstances in each case, certain factors may carry more weight than others because of the nature of the company's business. To illustrate:

(a) Earnings may be the most important criterion of value in some cases whereas asset value will receive primary consideration in others. In general, the appraiser will accord primary consideration to earnings when valuing stocks of companies which sell products or services to the public; conversely, in the investment or holding type of company, the appraiser may accord the greatest weight to the assets underlying the security to be valued.

(b) The value of the stock of a closely held investment or real estate holding company, whether or not family owned, is closely related to the value of the assets underlying the stock. For companies of this type the appraiser should determine the fair market values of the assets of the company. Operating expenses of such a company and the cost of liquidating it, if any, merit consideration when appraising the relative values of the stock and the underlying assets. The market values of the underlying assets give due weight to potential earnings and dividends of the particular items of property underlying the stock, capitalized at rates deemed proper by the investing public at the date of appraisal. A current appraisal by the investing public should be superior to the retrospective opinion of an individual. For these reasons, adjusted net worth should be accorded greater weight in valuing the stock of a closely held investment or real estate holding company, whether or not family owned, than any of the other customary yardsticks of appraisal, such as earnings and dividend paying capacity.

Sec. 6. Capitalization Rates.

In the application of certain fundamental valuation factors, such as earnings and dividends, it is necessary to capitalize the average or current results at some appropriate rate. A determination of the proper capitalization rate presents one of the most difficult problems in valuation. That there is no ready or simple solution will become apparent by a cursory check of the rates of return and dividend yields in terms of the selling prices of corporate shares listed on the major exchanges of the country. Wide variations will be found even for companies in the same industry. Moreover, the ratio will fluctuate from year to year depending upon economic conditions. Thus, no standard tables of capitalization rates applicable to closely held corporations can be formulated. Among the more important factors to be taken into consideration in deciding upon a capitalization rate in a particular case are: (1) the nature of the business; (2) the risk involved; and (3) the stability or irregularity of earnings.

Sec. 7. Average of Factors.

Because valuations cannot be made on the basis of a prescribed formula, there is no means whereby the various applicable factors in a particular case can be assigned mathematical weights in deriving the fair market value. For this reason, no useful purpose is served by taking an average of several factors (for example, book value, capitalized earnings and capitalized dividends) and basing the valuation on the result. Such a process excludes active consideration of other pertinent factors, and the end result cannot be supported by a realistic application of the significant facts in the case except by mere chance.

Sec. 8. Restrictive Agreements.

Frequently, in the valuation of closely held stock for estate and gift tax purposes, it will be found that the stock is subject to an agreement restricting its sale or transfer. Where shares of stock were acquired by a decedent subject to an option reserved by the issuing corporation to repurchase at a certain price, the option price is usually accepted as the fair market value for estate tax purposes. See Rev. Rul. 54-76, C.B. 1954-1, 194. However, in such case the option price is not determinative of fair market value for gift tax purposes. Where the option, or buy and sell agreement, is the result of voluntary action by the stockholders and is binding during the life as well as at the death of the stockholders, such agreement may or may not, depending upon the circumstances of each case, fix the value for estate tax purposes. However, such agreement is a factor to be considered, with other relevant factors, in determining fair market value. Where the stockholder is free to dispose of his shares during life and the option is to become effective only upon his death, the fair market value is not limited to the option price. It is always necessary to consider the relationship of the parties, the relative number of shares held by the decedent, and other material facts, to determine whether the agreement represents a bonafide business arrangement or is a device to pass the decedent's shares to the natural objects of his bounty for less than an adequate and full consideration in money or money's worth. In this connection see Rev. Rul. 157 C.B. 1953-2, 255, and Rev. Rul. 189, C.B. 1953-2, 294.

Sec. 9. Effect on Other Documents.

Revenue Ruling 54-77, C.B. 1954-1, 187, is hereby superseded.

LETTER RULING 9538022

Section 7701 – Definitions
Full Text

Date: June 23, 1995

Dear * * *

This letter responds to your ruling request of February 5, 1995. You asked about the federal income tax consequences of P, a general partnership, converting into PLLC, a professional limited liability company.

The information submitted indicates that P is a State M general partnership engaged in the practice of law. P uses the cash receipts and disbursements method of accounting. To obtain additional liability protection, the partners of P have decided to convert P into PLLC, a professional limited liability company.

The conversion will consist of the P partners contributing their partnership interests to PLLC in exchange for identical PLLC interests. P will then dissolve and transfer all of its assets and liabilities to PLLC canceling all the P partnership interests. In exchange for transferring their partnership interests to PLLC, the members will have the same allocation of profits, losses, gains, capital, distributions and other items of income and tax credits as they had in P. In addition, the members will receive capital accounts in PLLC identical to the capital accounts they had in P.

P represents that PLLC, like P, will engage principally in the practice of law and will use the cash receipts and disbursements method of accounting. In addition, the members will organize and operate PLLC in conformity with State M's Act. In addition, the members of PLLC will execute an Operating Agreement providing for the operation of PLLC.

Classification

Section 7701 of the Code sets forth definitions to be used in determining the classification of an organization for federal tax purposes. Organizations are classified as associations taxable as corporations, as partnerships, or as trusts. The classification of any particular organization is determined under the tests and standards set forth in sections 301.7701-2 through 301.7701-4 of the Procedure and Administration Regulations.

Section 301.7701-2(a)(1) of the regulations enumerates six characteristics ordinarily found in a pure corporation that, taken together, distinguishes it from other organizations. These include: (1) associates, (2) an objective to carry on business and divide the gains therefrom, (3) continuity of life, (4) centralization of management, (5) liability for corporate debts limited to corporate property, and (6) free transferability of interests.

Section 301.7701-2(a)(2) of the regulations provides that characteristics common to partnerships and corporations are not material in attempting to distinguish between an association and a partnership. Because associates and an objective to carry on business and divide the gains therefrom are generally common to corporations and partnerships, an organization that has such characteristics will be classified as a partnership if it lacks at least two of the remaining characteristics. Section 301.7701-2(a)(3).

Section 301.7701-2(c)(1) of the regulations provides that an organization has the corporate characteristic of centralized management if any person (or group of persons that does not include all the members) has continuing exclusive authority to make management decisions necessary to conduct the business for which the organization was formed.

Section 301.7701-2(c)(4) of the regulations provides that there is no centralization of management decisions, unless the managers have sole authority to make such decisions. Because of the mutual agency relationship between members of a general partnership, a general partnership cannot achieve effective concentration of management powers and, therefore, centralized management. Usually, the act of any partner within the scope of the partnership business binds all the partners; and even if the partners agree among themselves that the powers of management shall be exclusively in a selected few, this agreement will be ineffective as against an outsider who had no notice of it.

Section 21.198(4401) of the Act provides that unless the articles of organization state that the business of the limited liability company is to be managed by managers, the business of the limited liability company will be managed by the members subject to any provisions in an operating agreement restricting or enlarging the management rights and duties of any member or group of members. If management is vested in the members: (a) the members will be considered to be managers for purposes of applying this Act unless the context clearly requires otherwise; and (b) the members have and are subject to all duties and liabilities of managers and to all limitations on liability and indemnification rights or managers.

Under section 21.198(4406) of the Act, every manager is an agent of the limited liability company for the purpose of its business, and the act of every manager, including the execution in the limited liability company name of any instrument, for apparently carrying on in the usual way the business of the limited liability company of which he or she is a manager binds the limited liability company, unless the manager so acting does not have the authority to act for the limited liability company in the particular matter and the person with whom he or she is dealing has the knowledge of the fact that he or she has no authority.

Section 6 of the proposed Operating Agreement provides that the business and affairs of PLLC will be managed by the members. No individual or group of individual members that does not include all of the members, will have any continuing, exclusive power or authority to make management decisions necessary to the conduct of the business for which PLLC was formed.

Accordingly, PLLC will lack the corporate characteristic of centralized management.

Section 301.7701-2(e)(1) of the regulations provides that an organization has the corporate characteristic of free transferability of interests if each of its members or those members owning substantially all of the interests in the organization have the power, without the consent of other members, to substitute for themselves in the same organization a person who is not a member of the organization. For this power of substitution to exist in the corporate sense, the member must be able, without the consent of other members, to confer upon the member's substitute all the attributes of the member's interest in the organization. The characteristic of free transferability does not exist if each member can, without the consent of other members, assign only the right to share in profits but cannot assign the right to participate in the management of the organization.

Section 21.198(4505) of the Act provides that except as provided in an operating agreement, a membership interest is assignable in whole or in part. Section 21.198(4506) provides that except as provided in an operating agreement, an assignee of a membership interest may become a member only if the other members unanimously consent.

Section 23 of the Operating Agreement forbids any member to sell, assign, hypothecate or otherwise transfer a member's interest in PLLC. In addition, no member has the power, without the consent of all of the other members, to substitute any other person for that member in PLLC.

Therefore, PLLC will lack the corporate characteristic of free transferability of interests.

PLLC will have associates and an objective to carry on business and divide the gains therefrom. Because PLLC will lack the corporate characteristics of centralized management and free transferability of interests, PLLC will be classified as a partnership for federal tax purposes.

Gain or Loss on Conversion

Section 708 of the Code provides that a partnership is considered continuing if it is not terminated. A partnership is terminated only if (1) no part of any business, financial operation, or venture of the partnership continues to be carried on by any of its partners in a partnership, or (2) within a 12-month period, there is a sale or exchange of 50 percent or more of the total interest in partnership capital and profits.

Section 1.708-1(b)(1)(ii) of the Income Tax Regulations provides, in part, that a contribution of property to a partnership does not constitute a sale or exchange for purposes of section 708.

Under section 721(a) of the Code, no gain or loss is recognized by a partnership or any of its partners upon the contribution of property to the partnership in exchange for an interest therein.

Under section 731(a) of the Code, if a partnership makes a distribution to a partner, gain will not be recognized to such partner, except to the extent that any money distributed exceeds the adjusted basis of such partner's interest in the partnership immediately before the distribution, and loss shall not be recognized to such partner, except upon the distribution of certain property in liquidation of a partner's interest in a partnership.

Rev. Rul. 84-52, 1984-1 C.B. 157, considers the federal income tax consequences of converting a general partnership into a limited partnership. Each partner's total percentage interest in the partnership's profits, losses, and capital remained the same after the conversion. Further, the business of the general partnership continued to be carried on after the conversion.

Rev. Rul. 84-52 treats the conversion as an exchange under section 721 of the Code. The revenue ruling holds that the general partnership is not terminated because the business of the general partnership will continue after the conversion and because, under section 1.708-1(b)(1)(ii), a transaction governed by section 721 is not treated as a sale or exchange for purposes of section 708.

Rev. Rul. 95-37, 1995-17 I.R.B. 10, examines the conversion of a domestic partnership into a domestic limited liability company classified as a partnership for federal tax purposes. Rev. Rul. 95-37 holds, in part, that the federal income tax consequences described in Rev. Rul. 84-52 apply to the conversion of a domestic partnership into a domestic limited liability company classified as a partnership.

The conversion of P into PLLC is analogous to the situation in Rev. Rul. 84-52. Assuming that P is properly classified as a partnership, we conclude that the conversion of P into PLLC will not terminate P under section 708(b) of the Code. In addition, PLLC will be considered a continuation of P. The partners' interests in capital, profits, and losses will remain the same after the conversion. Further, PLLC, its members, P, and P's partners will not recognize any gain or loss upon the transfer of the interests in P to PLLC and upon the liquidation of P, except as provided in section 752.

Adjusted Basis and Method of Accounting

Section 722 of the Code generally provides that the basis of an interest in a partnership acquired by a contribution of property equals the contributing partner's basis in the contributed property.

Section 723 of the Code provides, in part, that the basis of property contributed to a partnership by a partner will be the adjusted basis of such property to the contributing partner at the time of the contribution.

Rev. Rul. 84-52 and Rev. Rul. 95-37 conclude that if the partners' shares of the partnership's liabilities do not change, the adjusted basis of any partner's partnership interest will not change upon the conversion of a partnership into a limited liability company.

The basis of the PLLC assets will equal the basis of those assets in P immediately before the conversion. Additionally, provided the partners' shares of P's liabilities do not change because of the conversion, the adjusted basis of a member's interest in PLLC will equal such member's partnership interest adjusted basis immediately before the conversion.

We further conclude that PLLC must continue to use the cash receipts and disbursements method of accounting used by P, despite entitlement, until PLLC receives permission to change its method or until the Internal Revenue Service challenges that method on examination.

Holding Period

Rev. Rul. 84-52 further holds that, pursuant to section 1223(1), there will be no change to the holding period of any partner's total interest in the partnership upon the conversion of a partnership into a limited liability company.

Therefore, the holding period of the membership interest of each member in PLLC immediately after the conversion will equal the holding period of such member's partnership interest in PLLC immediately before the conversion.

Except as specifically ruled upon above, we express no opinion concerning the federal tax consequences of the facts described under any other provision of the Code or regulations. Specifically, we express no opinion concerning P's entitlement to use the cash method of accounting before or after its conversion into PLLC and whether the conversion of P into PLLC will affect PLLC's entitlement to use the cash method.

PLLC should attach a copy of this letter to its first federal tax return. A copy of this letter is enclosed for that purpose.

This ruling is directed only to the taxpayer who requested it. Section 6110(j)(3) of the Code provides that it may not be used or cited as precedent.

Sincerely yours,

J. THOMAS HINES
Senior Technician Reviewer, Branch 2
Office of the Assistant Chief Counsel
(Passthroughs and Special Industries)

Appendix C

DELAWARE CODE ANNOTATED
TITLE 6. COMMERCE AND TRADE
LIMITED LIABILITY COMPANY ACT

SUBCHAPTER I. GENERAL PROVISIONS

§18-101. Definitions

As used in this chapter unless the context otherwise requires:

(1) "Bankruptcy" means an event that causes a person to cease to be a member as provided in §18-304 of this title.

(2) "Certificate of formation" means the certificate referred to in §18-201 of this title, and the certificate as amended.

(3) "Contribution" means any cash, property, services rendered or a promissory note or other obligation to contribute cash or property or to perform services, which a person contributes to a limited liability company in the person's capacity as a member.

(4) "Foreign limited liability company" means a limited liability company formed under the laws of any state or under the laws of any foreign country or other foreign jurisdiction and denominated as such under the laws of such state or foreign country or other foreign jurisdiction.

(5) "Knowledge" means a person's actual knowledge of a fact, rather than the person's constructive knowledge of the fact.

(6) "Limited liability company" and "domestic limited liability company" means a limited liability company formed under the laws of the State of Delaware and having 1 or more members.

(7) "Limited liability company agreement" means any agreement, written or oral, of the member or members as to the affairs of a limited liability company and the conduct of its business. A limited liability company agreement of a limited liability company having only 1 member

shall not be unenforceable by reason of there being only 1 person who is a party to the limited liability company agreement. A written limited liability company agreement or another written agreement or writing:

a. May provide that a person shall be admitted as a member of a limited liability company, or shall become an assignee of a limited liability company interest or other rights or powers of a member to the extent assigned, and shall become bound by the limited liability company agreement: 1. If such person (or a representative authorized by such person orally, in writing or by other action such as payment for a limited liability company interest) executes the limited liability company agreement or any other writing evidencing the intent of such person to become a member or assignee; or 2.Without such execution, if such person (or a representative authorized by such person orally, in writing or by other action such as payment for a limited liability company interest) complies with the conditions for becoming a member or assignee as set forth in the limited liability company agreement or any other writing; and

b. Shall not be unenforceable by reason of its not having been signed by a person being admitted as a member or becoming an assignee as provided in subparagraph a. of this paragraph, or by reason of its having been signed by a representative as provided in this chapter.

(8) "Limited liability company interest" means a member's share of the profits and losses of a limited liability company and a member's right to receive distributions of the limited liability company's assets.

(9) "Liquidating trustee" means a person carrying out the winding up of a limited liability company.

(10) "Manager" means a person who is named as a manager of a limited liability company in, or designated as a manager of a limited liability company pursuant to, a limited liability company agreement or similar instrument under which the limited liability company is formed.

(11) "Member" means a person who has been admitted to a limited liability company as a member as provided in §18-301 of this title or, in the case of a foreign limited liability company, in accordance with the laws

of the state or foreign country or other foreign jurisdiction under which the foreign limited liability company is organized.

(12) "Person" means a natural person, partnership (whether general or limited and whether domestic or foreign), limited liability company, foreign limited liability company, trust, estate, association, corporation, custodian, nominee or any other individual or entity in its own or any representative capacity.

(13) "Personal representative" means, as to a natural person, the executor, administrator, guardian, conservator or other legal representative thereof and, as to a person other than a natural person, the legal representative or successor thereof.

(14) "State" means the District of Columbia or the Commonwealth of Puerto Rico or any state, territory, possession or other jurisdiction of the United States other than the State of Delaware.

§18-102. Name set forth in certificate

The name of each limited liability company as set forth in its certificate of formation:

(1) Shall contain the words "Limited Liability Company" or the abbreviation "L.L.C." or the designation "LLC";

(2) May contain the name of a member or manager;

(3) Must be such as to distinguish it upon the records in the office of the Secretary of State from the name of any corporation, limited partnership, business trust, registered limited liability partnership or limited liability company reserved, registered, formed or organized under the laws of the State of Delaware or qualified to do business or registered as a foreign corporation, foreign limited partnership or foreign limited liability company in the State of Delaware; provided however, that a limited liability company may register under any name which is not such as to distinguish it upon the records in the office of the Secretary of State from the name of any domestic or foreign corporation, limited partnership, business trust, registered limited liability partnership or limited liability company reserved, registered, formed or organized under the laws of the State of

Delaware with the written consent of the other corporation, limited partnership, business trust, registered limited liability partnership or limited liability company, which written consent shall be filed with the Secretary of State; and

(4) May contain the following words: "Company," "Association," "Club," "Foundation," "Fund," "Institute," "Society," "Union," "Syndicate," "Limited" or "Trust" (or abbreviations of like import).

§18-103. Reservation of name

(a) The exclusive right to the use of a name may be reserved by:

(1) Any person intending to organize a limited liability company under this chapter and to adopt that name;

(2) Any domestic limited liability company or any foreign limited liability company registered in the State of Delaware which, in either case, proposes to change its name;

(3) Any foreign limited liability company intending to register in the State of Delaware and adopt that name; and

(4) Any person intending to organize a foreign limited liability company and intending to have it register in the State of Delaware and adopt that name.

(b) The reservation of a specified name shall be made by filing with the Secretary of State an application, executed by the applicant, specifying the name to be reserved and the name and address of the applicant. If the Secretary of State finds that the name is available for use by a domestic or foreign limited liability company, the Secretary shall reserve the name for the exclusive use of the applicant for a period of 120 days. Once having so reserved a name, the same applicant may again reserve the same name for successive 120-day periods. The right to the exclusive use of a reserved name may be transferred to any other person by filing in the office of the Secretary of State a notice of the transfer, executed by the applicant for whom the name was reserved, specifying the name to be transferred and the name and address of the transferee. The reservation of a specified name may be cancelled by filing with the Secretary of State a notice of cancellation, executed by the applicant or transferee, specifying the name reservation to be cancelled and the name and address of the applicant or transferee. Unless the Secretary of State finds that any application, notice of transfer, or notice of cancellation filed with the Secretary of State as required by this subsection does not conform to law, upon receipt of all filing fees required by law the Secretary shall prepare and return to the person who filed such instrument a copy of the filed instrument with a notation thereon of the action taken by the Secretary of State.

(c) A fee as set forth in §18-1105(a)(1) of this title shall be paid at the time of the initial reservation of any name, at the time of the renewal of any such reservation and at the time of the filing of a notice of the transfer or cancellation of any such reservation.

§18-104. Registered office; registered agent

(a) Each limited liability company shall have and maintain in the State of Delaware:

(1) A registered office, which may but need not be a place of its business in the State of Delaware; and

(2) A registered agent for service of process on the limited liability company, which agent may be either an individual resident of the State of Delaware whose business office is identical with the limited liability company's registered office, or a domestic corporation, or a domestic limited partnership, or a domestic limited liability company, or a domestic business trust, or a foreign corporation, or a foreign limited partnership, or a foreign limited liability company authorized to do business in the State of Delaware having a business office identical with such registered office, which is generally open during normal business hours to accept service of process and otherwise perform the functions of a registered agent, or the limited liability company itself.

(b) A registered agent may change the address of the registered office of the limited liability company(ies) for which such registered agent is registered agent to another address in the State of Delaware by paying a fee as set forth in §18-1105(a)(2) of this title and filing with the Secretary of State a certificate, executed by such registered agent, setting forth the names of all the limited liability companies represented by such registered agent, and the address at which such registered agent has maintained the registered office for each of such limited liability companies, and further certifying to the new address to which each such registered office will be changed on a given day, and at which new address such registered agent will thereafter maintain the registered office for each of the limited liability companies recited in the certificate. Upon the filing of such certificate, the Secretary of State shall furnish to the registered agent a certified copy of the same under the Secretary's hand and seal of office, and thereafter, or until further change of address, as authorized by law, the registered office in the State of Delaware of each of the limited liability companies recited in the certificate shall be located at the new address of the registered agent thereof as given in the certificate. In the event of a change of name of any person acting as a registered agent of a limited liability company, such registered agent shall file with the Secretary of State a certificate, executed by such registered agent, setting forth the new name of such registered agent, the name of such registered agent before it was changed, the names of all the limited liability companies represented by such registered agent, and the address at which such registered agent has maintained the registered office for each of such limited liability companies, and shall pay a fee as set forth in §18-1105(a)(2) of this title. Upon the filing of such certificate, the Secretary of State shall furnish to the registered agent a certified copy of the certificate under the Secretary's hand and seal of office. Filing a certificate under this section shall be deemed to be an amendment of the certificate of formation of each limited liability company affected thereby and each such limited liability company shall not be required to take any further action with respect thereto, company shall not be required to take any further action with respect thereto, to amend its certificate of formation under §18-202 of this title. Any registered agent filing a certificate under this section shall promptly, upon such filing, deliver a copy of any such certificate to each limited liability company affected thereby.

(c) The registered agent of 1 or more limited liability companies may resign and appoint a successor registered agent by paying a fee as set forth in §18-1105(a)(2) of this title and filing a certificate with the Secretary of State, stating that it resigns and the name and address of the successor registered agent.There shall be attached to such certificate a statement executed by each affected limited liability company ratifying and approving such change of registered agent. Upon such filing, the successor registered agent shall become the registered agent of such limited liability companies as have ratified and approved such substitution and the successor registered agent's address, as stated in such certificate, shall become the address of each such limited liability company's registered office in the State of Delaware.The Secretary of State shall furnish to the successor registered agent a certified copy of the certificate of resignation. Filing of such certificate of resignation shall be deemed to be an amendment of the certificate of formation of each limited liability company affected thereby and each such limited liability company shall not be required to take any further action with respect thereto, to amend its certificate of formation under §18-202 of this title.

(d) The registered agent of a limited liability company may resign without appointing a successor registered agent by paying a fee as set forth in §18-1105(a)(2) of this title and filing a certificate with the Secretary of State stating that it resigns as registered agent for the limited liability company identified in the certificate, but such resignation shall not become effective until 120 days after the certificate is filed. There shall be attached to such certificate an affidavit of such registered agent, if an individual, or the president, a vice-president or the secretary thereof if a corporation, that at least 30 days prior to and on or about the date of the filing of said certificate, notices were sent by certified or registered mail to the limited liability company for which such registered agent is resigning as registered agent, at the principal office thereof within or outside the State of Delaware, if known to such registered agent or, if not, to the last known address of the attorney or other individual at whose request such registered agent was appointed for such limited liability company, of the resignation of such registered agent. After receipt of the notice of the resignation of its registered agent, the limited liability company for which such registered agent was acting shall obtain and designate a new registered agent, to take the place of the registered agent so resigning.If such limited liability company fails to obtain and designate a new registered agent as aforesaid prior to the expiration of the period of 120 days after the filing by the registered agent of the certificate of resignation, the certificate of formation of such limited liability company shall be deemed to be cancelled. After the resignation of the registered agent shall have become effective as provided in this section and if no new registered agent shall have been obtained and designated in the time and manner aforesaid, service of legal process against the limited liability company for which the resigned registered agent had been acting shall thereafter be upon the Secretary of State in accordance with §18-105 of this title.

§18-105. Service of process on domestic limited liability companies

(a) Service of legal process upon any domestic limited liability company shall be made by delivering a copy personally to any manager of the limited liability company in the State of Delaware or the registered agent of the limited liability company in the State of Delaware, or by leaving it at the dwelling house or usual place of abode in the State of Delaware of any such manager or registered agent (if the registered agent be an individual), or at the registered office or other place of business of the limited liability company in the State of Delaware. If the registered agent be a corporation, service of process upon it as such may be made by serving, in the State of Delaware, a copy thereof on the president, vice-president, secretary, assistant secretary or any director of the corporate registered agent. Service by copy left at the dwelling house or usual place of abode of a manager or registered agent, or at the registered office or other place of business of the limited liability company in the State of Delaware, to be effective, must be delivered thereat at least 6 days before the return date of the process, and in the presence of an adult person, and the officer serving the process shall distinctly state the manner of service in the officer's return thereto. Process returnable forthwith must be delivered personally to the manager or registered agent.

(b) In case the officer whose duty it is to serve legal process cannot by due diligence serve the process in any manner provided for by subsection (a) of this section, it shall be lawful to serve the process against the limited liability company upon the Secretary of State, and such service shall be as effectual for all intents and purposes as if made in any of the ways provided for in subsection (a) of this section. In the event that service is effected through the Secretary of State in accordance with this subsection, the Secretary of State shall forthwith notify the limited liability company by letter, certified mail, return receipt requested, directed to the limited liability company at its address as it appears on the records relating to such limited liability company on file with the Secretary of State or, if no such address appears, at its last registered office.Such letter shall enclose a copy of the process and any other papers served on the Secretary of State pursuant to this subsection.It shall be the duty of the plaintiff in the event of such service to serve process and any other papers in duplicate, to notify the Secretary of State that service is being effected pursuant to this subsection, and to pay the Secretary of State the sum of $50 for the use of the State of Delaware, which sum shall be taxed as part of the costs in the proceeding if the plaintiff shall prevail therein. The Secretary of State shall maintain an alphabetical record of any such service setting forth the name of the plaintiff and defendant, the title, docket number and nature of the proceeding in which process has been served upon the Secretary, the fact that service has been effected pursuant to this subsection, the return date thereof, and the day and hour when the service was made. The Secretary of State shall not be required to retain such information for a longer than 5 years from the Secretary's receipt of the service of process.

§18-106. Nature of business permitted; powers

(a) A limited liability company may carry on any lawful business, purpose or activity, whether or not for profit, with the exception of the business of granting policies of insurance, or assuming insurance risks or banking as defined in §126 of Title 8.

(b) A limited liability company shall possess and may exercise all the powers and privileges granted by this chapter or by any other law or by its limited liability company agreement, together with any powers incidental thereto, including such powers and privileges as are necessary or convenient to the conduct, promotion or attainment of the business, purposes or activities of the limited liability company.

§18-107. Business transactions of member or manager with the limited liability company

Except as provided in a limited liability company agreement, a member or manager may lend money to, borrow money from, act as a surety, guarantor or endorser for, guarantee or assume 1 or more obligations of, provide collateral for, and transact other business with, a limited liability company and, subject to other applicable law, has the same rights and obligations with respect to any such matter as a person who is not a member or manager.

§18-108. Indemnification

Subject to such standards and restrictions, if any, as are set forth in its limited liability company agreement, a limited liability company may, and shall have the power to, indemnify and hold harmless any member or manager or other person from and against any and all claims and demands whatsoever.

§18-109. Service of process on managers and liquidating trustees

(a) A manager or a liquidating trustee of a limited liability company may be served with process in the manner prescribed in this section in all civil actions or proceedings brought in the State of Delaware involving or relating to the business of the limited liability company or a violation by the manager or the liquidating trustee of a duty to the limited liability company, or any member of the limited liability company, whether or not the manager or the liquidating trustee is a manager or a liquidating trustee at the time suit is commenced.A manager's or a liquidating trustee's serving as such constitutes such person's consent to the appointment of the registered agent of the limited liability company (or, if there is none, the Secretary of State) as such person's agent upon whom service of process may be made as provided in this section.Such service as a manager or a liquidating trustee shall signify the consent of such manager or liquidating trustee that any process when so served shall be of the same legal force and validity as if served upon such manager or liquidating trustee within the State of Delaware and such appointment of the registered agent (or, if there is none, the Secretary of State) shall be irrevocable. As used in this subsection (a) and in subsections (b) and (c) of this section, the term "manager" refers (i) to a person who is a manager as defined in §18-101(10) of this title and (ii) to a person who is a member of a limited liability company and who, although not a manager as defined in §18-101(10) of this title, participates materially in the management of the limited liability company; provided however, that the power to elect or otherwise select or to participate in the election or selection of a person to be a manager as defined in §18-101(10) of this title shall not, by itself, constitute participation in the management of the limited liability company.

(b) Service of process shall be effected by serving the registered agent (or, if there is none, the Secretary of State) with 1 copy of such process in the manner provided by law for service of writs of summons.In the event service is made under this subsection upon the Secretary of State, the plaintiff shall pay to the Secretary of State the sum of $50 for the use of the State of Delaware, which sum shall be taxed as part of the costs of the proceeding if the plaintiff shall prevail therein. In addition, the Prothonotary or the Register in Chancery of the court in which the civil action or proceeding is pending shall, within 7 days of such service, deposit in the United States mails, by registered mail, postage prepaid, true and attested copies of the process, together with a statement that service is being made pursuant to this section, addressed to such manager or liquidating trustee at the registered office of the limited liability company and at the manager's or liquidating trustee's address last known to the party desiring to make such service.

(c) In any action in which any such manager or liquidating trustee has been served with process as hereinabove provided, the time in which a defendant be required to appear and file a responsive pleading shall be computed from the date of mailing by the Prothonotary or the Register in Chancery as provided in subsection (b) of this section; however, the court in which such action has been commenced may order such continuance or continuances as may be necessary to afford such manager or liquidating trustee reasonable opportunity to defend the action.

(d) In a written limited liability company agreement or other writing, a manager or member may consent to be subject to the nonexclusive jurisdiction of the courts of, or arbitration in, a specified jurisdiction, or the exclusive jurisdiction of the courts of the State of Delaware, or the exclusivity of arbitration in a specified jurisdiction or the State of Delaware, and to be served with legal process in the manner prescribed in such limited liability company agreement or other writing.

(e) Nothing herein contained limits or affects the right to serve process in any other manner now or hereafter provided by law. This section is an extension of and not a limitation upon the right otherwise existing of service of legal process upon nonresidents.

(f) The Court of Chancery and the Superior Court may make all necessary rules respecting the form of process, the manner of issuance and return thereof and such other rules which may be necessary to implement this section and are not inconsistent with this section.

§18-110. Contested matters relating to managers; contested votes

(a) Upon application of any member or manager, the Court of Chancery may hear and determine the validity of any admission, election, appointment, removal or resignation of a manager of a limited liability company, and the right of any person to become or continue to be a manager of a limited liability company, and, in case the right to serve as a manager is claimed by more than 1 person, may determine the person or persons entitled to serve as managers; and to that end make such order or decree in any such case as may be just and proper, with power to enforce the production of any books, papers and records of the limited liability company relating to the issue. In any such application, the limited liability company shall be named as a party and service of copies of the application upon the registered agent of the limited liability company shall be deemed to be service upon the limited liability company and upon the person or persons whose right to serve as a manager is contested and upon the person or persons, if any, claiming to be a manager or claiming the right to be a manager; and the registered agent shall forward immediately a copy of the application to the limited liability company and to the person or persons whose right to serve as a manager is contested and to the person or persons, if any, claiming to be a manager or the right to be a manager, in a postpaid, sealed, registered letter addressed to such limited liability company and such person or persons at their post-office addresses last known to the registered agent or furnished to the registered agent by the applicant member or manager. The Court may make such order respecting further or other notice of such application as it deems proper under these circumstances.

(b) Upon application of any member or manager, the Court of Chancery may hear and determine the result of any vote of members or managers upon matters as to which the members or managers of the limited liability company, or any class or group of members or managers, have the right to vote pursuant to the limited liability company agreement or other agreement or this chapter (other than the admission, election, appointment, removal or resignation of managers). In any such application, the limited liability company shall be named as a party and service of the application upon the registered agent of the limited liability company shall be deemed to be service upon the limited liability company, and no other party need be joined in order for the Court to adjudicate the result of the vote.The Court may make such order respecting further or other notice of such application as it deems proper under these circumstances.

(c) Nothing herein contained limits or affects the right to serve process in any other manner now or hereafter provided by law. This section is an extension of and not a limitation upon the right otherwise existing of service of legal process upon nonresidents.

§18-111. Interpretation and enforcement of limited liability company agreement

Any action to interpret, apply or enforce the provisions of a limited liability company agreement, or the duties, obligations or liabilities of a limited liability company to the members or managers of the limited liability company, or the duties, obligations or liabilities among members or managers and of members or managers to the limited liability company, or the rights or powers of, or restrictions on, the limited liability company, members or managers, may be brought in the Court of Chancery.

SUBCHAPTER II. FORMATION; CERTIFICATE OF FORMATION

§18-201. Certificate of formation

(a) In order to form a limited liability company, 1 or more authorized persons must execute a certificate of formation. The certificate of formation shall be filed in the office of the Secretary of State and set forth:

(1) The name of the limited liability company;

(2) The address of the registered office and the name and address of the registered agent for service of process required to be maintained by §18-104 of this title; and

(3) Any other matters the members determine to include therein.

(b) A limited liability company is formed at the time of the filing of the initial certificate of formation in the office of the Secretary of State or at any later date or time specified in the certificate of formation if, in either case, there has been substantial compliance with the requirements of this section.A limited liability company formed under this chapter shall be a separate legal entity, the existence of which as a separate legal entity shall continue until cancellation of the limited liability company's certificate of formation.

(c) The filing of the certificate of formation in the office of the Secretary of State shall make it unnecessary to file any other documents under Chapter 31 of this title.

(d) A limited liability company agreement may be entered into either before, after or at the time of the filing of a certificate of formation and, whether entered into before, after or at the time of such filing, may be made effective as of the formation of the limited liability company or at such other time or date as provided in the limited liability company agreement.

§18-202. Amendment to certificate of formation

(a) A certificate of formation is amended by filing a certificate of amendment thereto in the office of the Secretary of State.The certificate of amendment shall set forth:

(1) The name of the limited liability company; and

(2) The amendment to the certificate of formation.

(b) A manager or, if there is no manager, then any member who becomes aware that any statement in a certificate of formation was false when made, or that any matter described has changed making the certificate of formation false in any material respect, shall promptly amend the certificate of formation.

(c) A certificate of formation may be amended at any time for any other proper purpose.

(d) Unless otherwise provided in this chapter or unless a later effective date or time (which shall be a date or time certain) is provided for in the certificate of amendment, a certificate of amendment shall be effective at the time of its filing with the Secretary of State.

§18-203. Cancellation of certificate

A certificate of formation shall be cancelled upon the dissolution and the completion of winding up of a limited liability company, or as provided in §18-104(d) or §18-1108 of this chapter, or upon the filing of a certificate of merger or consolidation if the limited liability company is not the surviving or resulting entity in a merger or consolidation, or upon the conversion of a domestic limited liability company approved in accordance with §18-216 of this title.A certificate of cancellation shall be filed in the office of the Secretary of State to accomplish the cancellation of a certificate of formation upon the dissolution and the completion of winding up of a limited liability company or upon the conversion of a domestic limited liability company approved approved in accordance with §18-216 of this title and shall set forth:

(1) The name of the limited liability company;

(2) The date of filing of its certificate of formation;

(3) The reason for filing the certificate of cancellation;

(4) The future effective date or time (which shall be a date or time certain) of cancellation if it is not to be effective upon the filing of the certificate;

(5) In the case of the conversion of a domestic limited liability company, the name of the entity to which the domestic limited liability company has been converted; and

(6) Any other information the person filing the certificate of cancellation determines.

§18-204. Execution

(a) Each certificate required by this subchapter to be filed in the office of the Secretary of State shall be executed by 1 or more authorized persons.

(b) Unless otherwise provided in a limited liability company agreement, any person may sign any certificate or amendment thereof or enter into a limited liability company agreement or amendment thereof by an agent, including an attorney-in-fact. An authorization, including a power of attorney, to sign any certificate or amendment thereof or to enter into a limited liability company agreement or amendment thereof need not be in writing, need not be sworn to, verified or acknowledged, and need not be filed in the office of the Secretary of State, but if in writing, must be retained by the limited liability company.

(c) The execution of a certificate by an authorized person constitutes an oath or affirmation, under the penalties of perjury in the third degree, that, to the best of the authorized person's knowledge and belief, the facts stated therein are true.

§18-205. Execution, amendment or cancellation by judicial order

(a) If a person required to execute a certificate required by this subchapter fails or refuses to do so, any other person who is adversely affected by the failure or refusal may petition the Court of Chancery to direct the execution of the certificate. If the Court finds that the execution of the certificate is proper and that any person so designated has failed or refused to execute the certificate, it shall order the Secretary of State to record an appropriate certificate.

(b) If a person required to execute a limited liability company agreement or amendment thereof fails or refuses to do so, any other person who is adversely affected by the failure or refusal may petition the Court of Chancery to direct the execution of the limited liability company agreement or amendment thereof. If the Court finds that the limited liability company agreement or amendment amendment thereof should be executed and that any person required to execute the limited liability company agreement or amendment thereof has failed or refused to do so, it shall enter an order granting appropriate relief.

§18-206. Filing

(a) The original signed copy of the certificate of formation and of any certificates of amendment, correction, amendment of a certificate of merger or consolidation, termination of a merger or consolidation or cancellation (or of any judicial decree of amendment or cancellation), and of any certificate of merger or consolidation, any restated certificate, any certificate of conversion to limited liability company, any certificate of transfer, any certificate of transfer and continuance, any certificate of limited liability company domestication, and of any certificate of revival shall be delivered to the Secretary of State. A person who executes a certificate as an agent or fiduciary need not exhibit evidence of that person's authority as a prerequisite to filing. Any signature on any certificate authorized to be filed with the Secretary of State under any provision of this chapter may be a facsimile, a conformed signature or an electronically transmitted signature. Unless the Secretary of State finds that any certificate does not conform to law, upon receipt of all filing fees required by law the Secretary of State shall:

(1) Certify that the certificate of formation, the certificate of amendment, the certificate of correction, the certificate of amendment of a certificate of merger or consolidation, the certificate of termination of a merger or consolidation, the certificate of cancellation (or of any judicial decree of amendment or cancellation), the certificate of merger or consolidation, the restated certificate, the certificate of conversion to limited liability company, the certificate of transfer, the certificate of transfer and continuance, the certificate of limited liability company domestication or the certificate of revival has been filed in the Secretary of State's office by endorsing upon the original certificate the word "Filed," and the date and hour of the filing.This endorsement is conclusive of the date and time of its filing in the absence of actual fraud;

(2) File and index the endorsed certificate; and

(3) Prepare and return to the person who filed it or that person's representative a copy of the original signed instrument, similarly endorsed, and shall certify such copy as a true copy of the original signed instrument.

(b) Upon the filing of a certificate of amendment (or judicial decree of amendment), certificate of correction or restated certificate in the office of the Secretary of State, or upon the future effective date or time of a certificate of amendment (or judicial decree thereof) or restated certificate, as provided for therein, the certificate of formation shall be amended or restated as set forth therein.Upon the filing of a certificate of cancellation (or a judicial decree thereof), or a certificate of merger or consolidation which acts as a certificate of cancellation or a certificate of transfer, or upon the future effective date or time of a certificate of cancellation (or a judicial decree thereof) or of a certificate of merger or consolidation which acts as a certificate of cancellation or a certificate of transfer, as provided for therein, or as specified in §18-104(d) of this title, the certificate of formation is cancelled.Upon the filing of a certificate of limited liability company domestication or upon the future effective date or time of a certificate of limited liability company domestication, the entity filing the certificate of limited liability company domestication is domesticated as a limited liability company with the effect provided in §18-212 of this title. Upon the filing of a certificate of conversion to limited liability company or upon the future effective date or time of a certificate of conversion to limited liability company, the entity filing the certificate of conversion to limited liability company is converted to a limited liability company with the effect provided in §18-214 of this title.Upon the filing of a certificate of amendment of a certificate of merger or consolidation, the certificate of merger or consolidation identified in the certificate of amendment of a certificate of merger or consolidation is amended. Upon the filing of a certificate of termination of a merger or consolidation, the certificate of merger or consolidation identified in the certificate of termination of a merger or consolidation is terminated. Upon the filing of a certificate of revival, the limited liability company is revived with the effect provided in §18-1109 of this title.Upon the filing of a certificate of transfer and continuance, or upon the future effective date or time of a certificate of transfer and continuance, as provided for therein, the limited liability company filing the certificate of transfer and continuance shall continue to exist as a limited liability company of the State of Delaware with the effect provided in §18-213 of this title.

(c) A fee as set forth in §18-1105(a)(3) of this title shall be paid at the time of the filing of a certificate of formation, a certificate of amendment, a certificate of correction, a certificate of amendment of a certificate of merger or consolidation, a certificate of termination of a merger or consolidation, a certificate of cancellation, a certificate of merger or consolidation, a restated certificate, a certificate of conversion to limited liability company, a certificate of transfer, a certificate of transfer and continuance, a certificate of limited liability company domestication or a certificate of revival.

(d) A fee as set forth in §18-1105(a)(4) of this title shall be paid for a certified copy of any paper on file as provided for by this chapter, and a fee as set forth in §18-1105(a)(5) of this title shall be paid for each page copied.

§18-207. Notice

The fact that a certificate of formation is on file in the office of the Secretary of State is notice that the entity formed in connection with the filing of the certificate of formation is a limited liability company formed under the laws of the State of Delaware and is notice of all other facts set forth therein which are required to be set forth in a certificate of formation by §18-201(a)(1) and (2) of this title and which are permitted to be set forth in a certificate of formation by §18-215(b) of this title.

§18-208. Restated certificate

(a) A limited liability company may, whenever desired, integrate into a single instrument all of the provisions of its certificate of formation which are then in effect and operative as a result of there having theretofore been filed with the Secretary of State 1 or more certificates or other instruments pursuant to any of the sections referred to in this subchapter, and it may at the same time also further amend its certificate of formation by adopting a restated certificate of formation.

(b) If a restated certificate of formation merely restates and integrates but does not further amend the initial certificate of formation, as theretofore amended or supplemented by any instrument that was executed and filed pursuant to any of the sections in this subchapter, it shall be specifically designated in its heading as a "Restated Certificate of Formation" together with such other words as the limited liability company may deem appropriate and shall be executed by an authorized person and filed as provided in § 18-206 of this title in the office of the Secretary of State. If a restated certificate restates and integrates and also further amends in any respect the certificate of formation, as theretofore amended or supplemented, it shall be specifically designated in its heading as an "Amended and Restated Certificate of Formation" together with such other words as the limited liability company may deem appropriate and shall be executed by at least 1 authorized person, and filed as provided in § 18-206 of this title in the office of the Secretary of State.

(c) A restated certificate of formation shall state, either in its heading or in an introductory paragraph, the limited liability company's present name, and, if it has been changed, the name under which it was originally filed, and the date of filing of its original certificate of formation with the Secretary of State, and the future effective date or time (which shall be a date or time certain) of the restated certificate if it is not to be effective upon the filing of the restated certificate. A restated certificate shall also state that it was duly executed and is being filed in accordance with this section. If a restated certificate only restates and integrates and does not further amend a limited liability company's certificate of formation as theretofore amended or supplemented and there is no discrepancy between those provisions and the restated certificate, it shall state that fact as well.

(d) Upon the filing of a restated certificate of formation with the Secretary of State, or upon the future effective date or time of a restated certificate of formation as provided for therein, the initial certificate of formation, as theretofore amended or supplemented, shall be superseded; thenceforth, the restated certificate of formation, including any further amendment or changes made thereby, shall be the certificate of formation of the limited liability company, but the original effective date of formation shall remain unchanged.

(e) Any amendment or change effected in connection with the restatement andintegration of the certificate of formation shall be subject to any other provision of this chapter, not inconsistent with this section, which would apply if a separate certificate of amendment were filed to effect such amendment or change.

§18-209. Merger and consolidation

(a) As used in this section, "other business entity" means a corporation, or a business trust or association, a real estate investment trust, a common-law trust, or any other unincorporated business, including a partnership (whether general (including a registered limited liability partnership) or limited (including a registered limited liability limited partnership)), and a foreign limited liability company, but excluding a domestic limited liability company.

(b) Pursuant to an agreement of merger or consolidation, 1 or more domestic limited liability companies may merge or consolidate with or into 1 or more domestic limited liability companies or 1 or more other business entities formed or organized under the laws of the State of Delaware or any other state or the United States or any foreign country or other foreign jurisdiction, or any combination thereof, with such domestic limited liability companies or other business entity as the agreement shall provide being the surviving or resulting domestic limited liability companies or other business entity.Unless otherwise provided in the limited liability company agreement, a merger or consolidation shall be approved by each domestic limited liability company which is to merge or consolidate by the members or, if there is more than one class or group of members, then by each class or group of members, in either case, by members who own more than 50 percent of the then current percentage or other interest in the profits of the domestic limited liability company owned by all of the members or by the members in each class or group, as appropriate. In connection with a merger or consolidation hereunder, rights or securities of, or interests in, a domestic limited liability company or other business entity which is a constituent party to the merger or consolidation may be exchanged for or converted into cash, property, rights or securities of, or interests in, the surviving or resulting domestic limited liability company or other business entity or, in addition to or in lieu thereof, may be exchanged for or converted into cash, property, rights or securities of, or interests in, a domestic limited liability company or other business entity which is not the surviving or resulting limited liability company or other business entity in the merger or consolidation.Notwithstanding prior approval, an agreement of merger or consolidation may be terminated or amended pursuant to a provision for such termination or amendment contained in the agreement of merger or consolidation.

(c) If a domestic limited liability company is merging or consolidating under this section, the domestic limited liability company or other business entity surviving or resulting in or from the merger or consolidation shall file a certificate of merger or consolidation executed by 1 or more authorized persons on behalf of the domestic limited liability company when it is the surviving or resulting entity in the office of the Secretary of State.The certificate of merger or consolidation shall state:

(1) The name and jurisdiction of formation or organization of each of the domestic limited liability companies and other business entities which is to merge or consolidate;

(2) That an agreement of merger or consolidation has been approved and executed by each of the domestic limited liability companies and other business entities which is to merge or consolidate;

(3) The name of the surviving or resulting domestic limited liability company or other business entity;

(4) The future effective date or time (which shall be a date or time certain) of the merger or consolidation if it is not to be effective upon the filing of the certificate of merger or consolidation;

(5) That the agreement of merger or consolidation is on file at a place of business of the surviving or resulting domestic limited liability company or other business entity, and shall state the address thereof;

(6) That a copy of the agreement of merger or consolidation will be furnished by the surviving or resulting domestic limited liability company or other business entity, on request and without cost, to any member of any domestic limited liability company or any person holding an interest in any other business entity which is to merge or consolidate; and

(7) If the surviving or resulting entity is not a domestic limited liability company, or a corporation or limited partnership organized under the laws of the State of Delaware, or a business trust organized under Chapter 38 of Title 12, a statement that such surviving or resulting other business entity agrees that it may be served with process in the State of Delaware in any action, suit or proceeding for the enforcement of any obligation of any domestic limited liability company which is to merge or consolidate, irrevocably appointing the Secretary of State as its agent to accept service of process in any such action, suit or proceeding and specifying the address to which a copy of such process shall be mailed to it by the Secretary of State.In the event of service hereunder upon the Secretary of State, the procedures set forth in §18-911(c) of this title shall be applicable, except that the plaintiff in any such action, suit or proceeding shall furnish the Secretary of State with the address specified in the certificate of merger or consolidation provided for in this section and any other address which the plaintiff may elect to furnish, together with copies of such process as required by the Secretary of State, and the Secretary of State shall notify such surviving or resulting other business entity at all such addresses furnished by the plaintiff in accordance with the procedures set forth in §18-911(c) of this title.

(d) Unless a future effective date or time is provided in a certificate of merger or consolidation, in which event a merger or consolidation shall be effective at any such future effective date or time, a merger or consolidation shall be effective upon the filing in the office of the Secretary of State of a certificate of merger or consolidation. If a certificate of merger or consolidation provides for a future effective date or time and if an agreement of merger or consolidation is amended to change the future effective date or time, or if an agreement of merger or consolidation permits a certificate of merger or consolidation to be amended to change the future effective date or time without an amendment to the agreement of merger or consolidation, or if an agreement of merger or consolidation is amended to change any other matter described in the certificate of merger or consolidation so as to make the certificate of merger or consolidation false in any material respect, as permitted by subsection (b) of this section prior to the future effective date or time, the certificate of merger or consolidation shall be amended by the filing of a certificate of amendment of a certificate of merger or consolidation which shall identify the certificate of merger or consolidation and the agreement of merger or consolidation, if applicable, which has been amended and shall state that the agreement of merger or consolidation, if applicable, has been amended and shall set forth the amendment to the certificate of merger or consolidation. If a certificate of merger or consolidation provides for a future effective date or time and if an agreement of merger or consolidation is terminated as permitted by subsection (b) of this section prior to the future effective date or time, the certificate of merger or consolidation shall be terminated by the filing of a certificate of termination of a merger or consolidation which shall identify the certificate of merger or consolidation and the agreement of merger or consolidation which has been terminated and shall state that the agreement of merger or consolidation has been terminated.

(e) A certificate of merger or consolidation shall act as a certificate of cancellation for a domestic limited liability company which is not the surviving or resulting entity in the merger or consolidation. Whenever this section requires the filing of a certificate of merger or consolidation, such requirement shall be deemed satisfied by the filing of an agreement of merger or consolidation containing the information required by this section to be set forth in the certificate of merger or consolidation.

(f) An agreement of merger or consolidation approved in accordance with subsection (b) of this section may:

(1) Effect any amendment to the limited liability company agreement; or

(2) Effect the adoption of a new limited liability company agreement, for a limited liability company if it is the surviving or resulting limited liability company in the merger or consolidation. Any amendment to a limited liability company agreement or adoption of a new limited liability company agreement made pursuant to the foregoing sentence shall be effective at the effective time or date of the merger or consolidation. The provisions of this subsection shall not be construed to limit the accomplishment of a merger or of any of the matters referred to herein by any other means provided for in a limited liability company agreement or other agreement or as otherwise permitted by law, including that the limited liability company agreement of any constituent limited liability company to the merger or onsolidation (including a limited liability company formed for the purpose of consummating a merger or consolidation) shall be the limited liability company agreement of the surviving or resulting limited liability company.

(g) When any merger or consolidation shall have become effective under this section, for all purposes of the laws of the State of Delaware, all of the rights, privileges and powers of each of the domestic limited liability companies and other business entities that have merged or consolidated, and all property, real, personal and mixed, and all debts due to any of said domestic limited liability companies and other business entities, as well as all other things and causes of action belonging to each of such domestic limited liability companies and other business entities, shall be vested in the surviving or resulting domestic limited liability company or other business entity, and shall thereafter be the property of the surviving or resulting domestic limited liability company or other business entity as they were of each of the domestic limited liability companies and other business entities that have merged or consolidated, and the title to any real property vested by deed or otherwise, under the laws of the State of Delaware, in any of such domestic limited liability companies and other business entities, shall not revert or be in any way impaired by reason of this chapter; but all rights of creditors and all liens upon any property of any of said domestic limited liability companies and other business entities shall be preserved unimpaired, and all debts, liabilities and duties of each of the said domestic limited liability companies and other business entities that have merged or consolidated shall thenceforth attach to the surviving or resulting domestic limited liability company or other business entity, and may be enforced against it to the same extent as if said debts, liabilities and duties had been incurred or contracted by it.Unless otherwise agreed, a merger or consolidation of a domestic limited liability company, including a domestic limited liability company which is not the surviving or resulting entity in the merger or consolidation, shall not require such domestic limited liability company to wind up its affairs under §18-803 of this title or pay its liabilities and distribute its assets under §18-804 of this title.

§18-210. Contractual appraisal rights

A limited liability company agreement or an agreement of merger or consolidation may provide that contractual appraisal rights with respect to a limited liability company interest or another interest in a limited liability company shall be available for any class or group of members or limited liability company interests in connection with any amendment of a limited liability company agreement, any merger or consolidation in which the limited liability company is a constituent party to the merger or consolidation, or the sale of all or substantially all of the limited liability company's assets. The Court of Chancery shall have jurisdiction to hear and determine any matter relating to any such appraisal rights.

§18-211. Certificate of correction

(a) Whenever any certificate authorized to be filed with the office of the Secretary of State under any provision of this chapter has been so filed and is an inaccurate record of the action therein referred to, or was defectively or erroneously executed, such certificate may be corrected by filing with the office of the Secretary of State a certificate of correction of such certificate.The certificate of correction shall specify the inaccuracy or defect to be corrected, shall set forth the portion of the certificate in corrected form, and shall be executed and filed as required by this chapter. The certificate of correction shall be effective as of the date the original certificate was filed, except as to those persons who are substantially and adversely affected by the correction, and as to those persons the certificate of correction shall be effective from the filing date.

(b) In lieu of filing a certificate of correction, a certificate may be corrected by filing with the Secretary of State a corrected certificate which shall be executed and filed as if the corrected certificate were the certificate being corrected, and a fee equal to the fee payable to the Secretary of State if the certificate being corrected were then being filed shall be paid and collected by the Secretary of State for the use of the State of Delaware in connection with the filing of the corrected certificate.The corrected certificate shall be specifically designated as such in its heading, shall specify the inaccuracy or defect to be corrected and shall set forth the entire certificate in corrected form. A certificate corrected in accordance with this section shall be effective as of the date the original certificate was filed, except as to those persons who are substantially and adversely affected by the correction and as to those persons the certificate as corrected shall be effective from the filing date.

§18-212. Domestication of non-United States entities

(a) As used in this section, "non-United States entity" means a foreign limited liability company (other than one formed under the laws of a state) or a corporation, a business trust or association, a real estate investment trust, a common-law trust or any other unincorporated business, including a partnership (whether general (including a registered limited liability partnership) or limited (including a registered limited liability limited partnership)) formed, incorporated, created or that otherwise came into being under the laws of any foreign country or other foreign jurisdiction (other than any state).

(b) Any non-United States entity may become domesticated as a limited liability company in the State of Delaware by complying with subsection (g) of this section and filing in the office of the Secretary of State in accordance with §18-206 of this title:

(1) A certificate of limited liability company domestication that has been executed by 1 or more authorized persons in accordance with §18-204 of this title; and

(2) A certificate of formation that complies with §18-201 of this title and has been executed by 1 or more authorized persons in accordance with §18-204 of this title.

(c) The certificate of limited liability company domestication shall state:

(1) The date on which and jurisdiction where the non-United States entity was first formed, incorporated, created or otherwise came into being;

(2) The name of the non-United States entity immediately prior to the filing of the certificate of limited liability company domestication;

(3) The name of the limited liability company as set forth in the certificate of formation filed in accordance with subsection (b) of this section;

(4) The future effective date or time (which shall be a date or time certain) of the domestication as a limited liability company if it is not to be effective upon the filing of the certificate of limited liability company domestication and the certificate of formation; and

(5) The jurisdiction that constituted the seat, siege social, or principal place of business or central administration of the non-United States entity, or any other equivalent thereto under applicable law, immediately prior to the filing of the certificate of limited liability company domestication.

(d) Upon the filing in the office of the Secretary of State of the certificate of limited liability company domestication and the certificate of formation or upon the future effective date or time of the certificate of limited liability company domestication and the certificate of formation, the non-United States entity shall be domesticated as a limited liability company in the State of Delaware and the limited liability company shall thereafter be subject to all of the provisions of this chapter, except that notwithstanding §18-201 of this title, the existence of the limited liability company shall be deemed to have commenced on the date the non-United States entity commenced its existence in the jurisdiction in which the non-United States entity was first formed, incorporated, created or otherwise came into being.

(e) The domestication of any non-United States entity as a limited liability company in the State of Delaware shall not be deemed to affect any obligations or liabilities of the non-United States entity incurred prior to its domestication as a limited liability company in the State of Delaware, or the personal liability of any person therefor.

(f) The filing of a certificate of limited liability company domestication shall not affect the choice of law applicable to the non-United States entity, except that from the effective date or time of the domestication, the law of the State of Delaware, including the provisions of this chapter, shall apply to the non-United States entity to the same extent as if the non-United States entity had been formed as a limited liability company on that date.

(g) Prior to filing a certificate of limited liability company domestication with the Office of the Secretary of State, the domestication shall be approved in the manner provided for by the document, instrument, agreement or other writing, as the case may be, governing the internal affairs of the non-United States entity and the conduct of its business or by applicable non-Delaware law, as appropriate, and a limited liability company agreement shall be approved by the same authorization required to approve the domestication.

(h) When any domestication shall have become effective under this section, for all purposes of the laws of the State of Delaware, all of the rights, privileges and powers of the non-United States entity that has been domesticated, and all property, real, personal and mixed, and all debts due to such non-United States entity, as well as all other things and causes of action belonging to such non-United States entity, shall be vested in the domestic limited liability company and shall thereafter be the property of the domestic limited liability company as they were of the non-United States entity immediately prior to its domestication, and the title to any real property vested by deed or otherwise in such non-United States entity shall not revert or be in any way impaired by reason of this chapter, but all rights of creditors and all liens upon any property of such non-United States entity shall be preserved unimpaired, and all debts, liabilities and duties of the non-United States entity that has been domesticated shall thenceforth attach to the domestic limited liability company and may be enforced against it to the same extent as if said debts, liabilities and duties had been incurred or contracted by the domestic limited liability company.

(i) When a non-United States entity has become domesticated as a limited liability company pursuant to this section, the limited liability company shall, for all purposes of the laws of the State of Delaware, be deemed to be the same entity as the domesticating non-United States entity. Unless otherwise agreed, or as required under applicable non-Delaware law, the domesticating non-United States entity shall not be required to wind up its affairs or pay its liabilities and distribute its assets, and the domestication shall not be deemed to constitute a dissolution of such non-United States entity and shall constitute a continuation of the existence of the domesticating non-United States entity in the form of a domestic limited liability company. If, following domestication, a non-United States entity that has become domesticated as a limited liability company continues its existence in the foreign country or other foreign jurisdiction in which it was existing immediately prior to domestication, the limited liability company and such non-United States entity shall, for all purposes of the laws of the State of Delaware, constitute a single entity formed, incorporated, created or otherwise having come into being, as applicable, and existing under the laws of the State of Delaware and the laws of such foreign country or other foreign jurisdiction.

§18-213. Transfer or continuance of domestic limited liability companies

(a) Upon compliance with this section, any limited liability company may transfer to or domesticate in any jurisdiction, other than any state, that permits the transfer to or domestication in such jurisdiction of a limited liability company and, in connection therewith, may elect to continue its existence as a limited liability company in the State of Delaware.

(b) Unless otherwise provided in a limited liability company agreement, a transfer or domestication or continuance described in subsection (a) of this section shall be approved in writing by all of the managers and all of the members.If all of the managers and all of the members of the limited liability company or such other vote as may be stated in a limited liability company agreement shall approve the transfer or domestication described in subsection (a) of this section, a certificate of transfer if the limited liability company's existence as a limited liability company of the State of Delaware is to cease, or a certificate of transfer and continuance if the limited liability company's existence as a limited liability company in the State of Delaware is to continue, executed in accordance with §18-

204 of this title, shall be filed in the office of the Secretary of State in accordance with §18-206 of this title. The certificate of transfer or the certificate of transfer and continuance shall state:

(1) The name of the limited liability company and, if it has been changed, the name under which its certificate of formation was originally filed;

(2) The date of the filing of its original certificate of formation with the Secretary of State;

(3) The jurisdiction to which the limited liability company shall be transferred or in which it shall be domesticated;

(4) The future effective date or time (which shall be a date or time certain) of the transfer or domestication to the jurisdiction specified in subsection (b)(3) of this section if it is not to be effective upon the filing of the certificate of transfer or the certificate of transfer and continuance;

(5) That the transfer or domestication or continuance of the limited liability company has been approved in accordance with this section;

(6) In the case of a certificate of transfer, (i) that the existence of the limited liability company as a limited liability company of the State of Delaware shall cease when the certificate of transfer becomes effective, and (ii) the agreement of the limited liability company that it may be served with process in the State of Delaware in any action, suit or proceeding for enforcement of any obligation of the limited liability company arising while it was a limited liability company of the State of Delaware, and that it irrevocably appoints the Secretary of State as its agent to accept service of process in any such action, suit or proceeding;

(7) The address to which a copy of the process referred to in subsection (b)(6) of this section shall be mailed to it by the Secretary of State. In the event of service hereunder upon the Secretary of State, the procedures set forth in §18-911(c) of this title shall be applicable, except that the plaintiff in any such action, suit or proceeding shall

furnish the Secretary of State with the address specified in this subsection and any other address that the plaintiff may elect to furnish, together with copies of such process as required by the Secretary of State, and the Secretary of State shall notify the limited liability company that has transferred or domesticated out of the State of Delaware at all such addresses furnished by the plaintiff in accordance with the procedures set forth in §18-911(c) of this title; and

(8) In the case of a certificate of transfer and continuance, that the limited liability company will continue to exist as a limited liability company of the State of Delaware after the certificate of transfer and continuance becomes effective.

(c) Upon the filing in the office of the Secretary of State of the certificate of transfer or upon the future effective date or time of the certificate of transfer and payment to the Secretary of State of all fees prescribed in this chapter, the Secretary of State shall certify that the limited liability company has filed all documents and paid all fees required by this chapter, and thereupon the limited liability company shall cease to exist as a limited liability company of the State of Delaware. Such certificate of the Secretary of State shall be prima facie evidence of the transfer or domestication by such limited liability company out of the State of Delaware.

(d) The transfer or domestication of a limited liability company out of the State of Delaware in accordance with this section and the resulting cessation of its existence as a limited liability company of the State of Delaware pursuant to a certificate of transfer shall not be deemed to affect any obligations or liabilities of the limited liability company incurred prior to such transfer or domestication or the personal liability of any person incurred prior to such transfer or domestication, nor shall it be deemed to affect the choice of law applicable to the limited liability company with respect to matters arising prior to such transfer or domestication.

(e) If a limited liability company files a certificate of transfer and continuance, after the time the certificate of transfer and continuance becomes effective, the limited liability company shall continue to exist as a limited liability company of the State of Delaware, and the laws of the State of Delaware, including this chapter, shall apply to the limited liability company to the same extent as prior to such time. So long as a limited liability company continues to exist as a limited liability company of the State of Delaware following the filing of a certificate of transfer and continuance, the continuing domestic limited liability company and the entity formed, incorporated, created or that otherwise came into being as a consequence of the transfer of the limited liability company to, or its domestication in, a foreign country or other foreign jurisdiction shall, for all purposes of the laws of the State of Delaware, constitute a single entity formed, incorporated, created or otherwise having come into being, as applicable, and existing under the laws of the State of Delaware and the laws of such foreign country or other foreign jurisdiction.

§18-214. Conversion of certain entities to a limited liability company

(a) As used in this section, the term "other entity" means a corporation, business trust or association, a real estate investment trust, a common-law trust or any other unincorporated business, including a partnership (whether general (including a registered limited liability partnership) or limited (including a registered limited liability limited partnership)) or a foreign limited liability company.

(b) Any other entity may convert to a domestic limited liability company by complying with subsection (h) of this section and filing in the office of the Secretary of State in accordance with §18-206 of this title:

(1) A certificate of conversion to limited liability company that has been executed by 1 or more authorized persons in accordance with §18-204 of this title; and

(2) A certificate of formation that complies with §18-201 of this title and has been executed by 1 or more authorized persons in accordance with §18-204 of this title.

(c) The certificate of conversion to limited liability company shall state:

(1) The date on which and jurisdiction where the other entity was first created, incorporated, formed or otherwise came into being and, if it has changed, its jurisdiction immediately prior to its conversion to a domestic limited liability company;

(2) The name of the other entity immediately prior to the filing of the certificate of conversion to limited liability company;

(3) The name of the limited liability company as set forth in its certificate of formation filed in accordance with subsection (b) of this section; and

(4) The future effective date or time (which shall be a date or time certain) of the conversion to a limited liability company if it is not to be effective upon the filing of the certificate of conversion to limited liability company and the certificate of formation.

(d) Upon the filing in the office of the Secretary of State of the certificate of conversion to limited liability company and the certificate of formation or upon the future effective date or time of the certificate of conversion to limited liability company and the certificate of formation, the other entity shall be converted into a domestic limited liability company and the limited liability company shall thereafter be subject to all of the provisions of this chapter, except that notwithstanding §18-201 of this title, the existence of the limited liability company shall be deemed to have on the date the other entity commenced its existence in the jurisdiction in which the other entity was first created, formed, incorporated or otherwise came into being.

(e) The conversion of any other entity into a domestic limited liability company shall not be deemed to affect any obligations or liabilities of the other entity incurred prior to its conversion to a domestic limited liability company or the personal liability of any person incurred prior to such conversion.

(f) When any conversion shall have become effective under this section, for all purposes of the laws of the State of Delaware, all of the rights, privileges and powers of the other entity that has converted, and all property, real, personal and mixed, and all debts due to such other entity, as well as all other things and causes of action belonging to such other entity, shall be vested in the domestic limited liability company and shall thereafter be the property of the domestic limited liability company as they were of the other entity that has converted, and the title to any real property vested by deed or otherwise in such other entity shall not revert or be in any way impaired by reason of this chapter, but all rights of creditors and all liens upon any property of such other entity shall be preserved unimpaired, and all debts, liabilities and duties of the other entity that has converted shall thenceforth attach to the domestic limited liability company and may be enforced against it to the same extent as if said debts, liabilities and duties had been incurred or contracted by it.

(g) Unless otherwise agreed, or as required under applicable non-Delaware law, the converting other entity shall not be required to wind up its affairs or pay its liabilities and distribute its assets, and the conversion shall not be deemed to constitute a dissolution of such other entity and shall constitute a continuation of the existence of the converting other entity in the form of a domestic limited liability company. When an other entity has been converted to a limited liability company pursuant to this section, the limited liability company shall, for all purposes of the laws of the State of Delaware, be deemed to be the same entity as the converting other entity.

(h) Prior to filing a certificate of conversion to limited liability company with the office of the Secretary of State, the conversion shall be approved in the manner provided for by the document, instrument, agreement or other writing, as the case may be, governing the internal affairs of the other entity and the conduct of its business or by applicable law, as appropriate and a limited liability company agreement shall be approved by the same authorization required to approve the conversion.

(i) The provisions of this section shall not be construed to limit the accomplishment of a change in the law governing, or the domicile of, an other entity to the State of Delaware by any other means provided for in a limited liability company agreement or other agreement or as otherwise permitted by law, including by the amendment of a limited liability company agreement or other agreement.

§18-215. Series of members, managers or limited liability company interests

(a) A limited liability company agreement may establish or provide for the establishment of designated series of members, managers or limited liability company interests having separate rights, powers or duties with respect to specified property or obligations of the limited liability company or profits and losses associated with specified property or obligations, and, to the extent provided in the limited liability company agreement, any such series may have a separate business purpose or investment objective.

(b) Notwithstanding anything to the contrary set forth in this chapter or under other applicable law, in the event that a limited liability company agreement creates 1 or more series, and if separate and distinct records are maintained for any such series and the assets associated with any such series are held and accounted for separately from the other assets of the limited liability company, or any other series thereof, and if the limited liability company agreement so provides, and notice of the limitation on liabilities of a series as referenced in this subsection is set forth in the certificate of formation of the limited liability company, then the debts, liabilities and obligations incurred, contracted for or otherwise existing with respect to a particular series shall be enforceable against the assets of such series only, and not against the assets of the limited liability company generally or any other series thereof, and, unless otherwise provided in the limited liability company agreement, none of the debts, liabilities, obligations and expenses incurred, contracted for or otherwise existing with respect to the limited liability company generally or any other series thereof shall be enforceable against the assets of such series. The fact that a certificate of formation that contains the foregoing notice of the limitation on liabilities of a series is on file in the office of the Secretary of State shall constitute notice of such limitation on liabilities of a series.

(c) Notwithstanding §18-303(a) of this title, under a limited liability company agreement or under another agreement, a member or manager may agree to be obligated personally for any or all of the debts, obligations and liabilities of one or more series.

(d) A limited liability company agreement may provide for classes or groups of members or managers associated with a series having such relative rights, powers and duties as the limited liability company agreement may provide, and may make provision for the future creation in the manner provided in the limited liability company agreement of additional classes or groups of members or managers associated with the series having such relative rights, powers and duties as may from time to time be established, including rights, powers and duties senior to existing classes and groups of members or managers associated with the series. A limited liability company agreement may provide for the taking of an action, including the amendment of the limited liability company agreement, without the vote or approval of any member or manager or class or group of members or managers, including an action to create under the provisions of the limited liability company agreement a class or group of the series of limited liability company interests that was not previously outstanding. A limited liability company agreement may provide that any member or class or group of members associated with a series shall have no voting rights.

(e) A limited liability company agreement may grant to all or certain identified members or managers or a specified class or group of the members or managers associated with a series the right to vote separately or with all or any class or group of the members or managers associated with the series, on any matter. Voting by members or managers associated with a series may be on a per capita, number, financial interest, class, group or any other basis.

(f) Unless otherwise provided in a limited liability company agreement, the management of a series shall be vested in the members associated with such series in proportion to the then current percentage or other interest of members in the profits of the series owned by all of the members associated with such series, the decision of members owning more than 50 percent of the said percentage or other interest in the profits controlling; provided, however, that if a limited liability company agreement provides for the management of the series, in whole or in part, by a manager, the management of the series, to the extent so provided, shall be vested in the manager who shall be chosen in the manner provided in the limited liability company agreement. The manager of the series shall also hold the offices and have the responsibilities accorded to the manager as set forth in a limited liability company agreement. A series may have more than 1 manager. Subject to §18-602 of this title, a manager shall cease to be a manager with respect to a series as provided in a limited liability company agreement. Except as otherwise provided in a limited liability company agreement, any event under this chapter or in a limited liability company agreement that causes a manager to cease to be a manager with respect to a series shall not, in itself, cause such manager to cease to be a manager of the limited liability company or with respect to any other series thereof.

(g) Notwithstanding §18-606 of this title, but subject to subsections (h) and (k) of this section, and unless otherwise provided in a limited liability company agreement, at the time a member associated with a series that has been established in accordance with subsection (b) of this section becomes entitled to receive a distribution with respect to such series, the member has the status of, and is entitled to all remedies available to, a creditor of the series, with respect to the distribution. A limited liability company agreement may provide for the establishment of a record date with respect to allocations and distributions with respect to a series.

(h) Notwithstanding §18-607(a) of this title, a limited liability company may make a distribution with respect to a series that has been established in accordance with subsection (b) of this section; provided, that a limited liability company shall not make a distribution with respect to a series that has been established in accordance with subsection (b) of this section to a member to the extent that at the time of the distribution, after giving effect to the distribution, all liabilities of such series, other than liabilities to members on account of their limited liability company interests with respect to such series and liabilities for which the recourse of creditors is limited to specified property of such series, exceed the fair value of the assets associated with such series, except that the fair value of property of the series that is subject to a liability for which the recourse of creditors is limited shall be included in the assets associated with such series only to the extent that the fair value of that property exceeds that liability. A member who receives a distribution in violation of this subsection, and who knew at the time of the distribution that the distribution violated this subsection, shall be liable to a series for the amount of the distribution. A member who receives a distribution in violation of this subsection, and who did not know at the time of the distribution that the distribution violated this subsection, shall not be liable for the amount of the distribution. Subject to §18-607(c) of this title, which shall apply to any distribution made with respect to a series under this subsection, this subsection shall not affect any obligation or liability of a member under an agreement or other applicable law for the amount of a distribution.

(i) Unless otherwise provided in the limited liability company agreement, a member shall cease to be associated with a series and to have the power to exercise any rights or powers of a member with respect to such series upon the assignment of all of the member's limited liability company interest with respect to such series. Except as otherwise provided in a limited liability company agreement, any event under this chapter or a limited liability company agreement that causes a member to cease to be associated with a series shall not, in itself, cause such member to cease to be associated with any other series or terminate the continued membership of a member in the limited liability company or cause the termination of the series, regardless of whether such member was the last remaining member associated with such series.

(j) Subject to §18-801 of this title, except to the extent otherwise provided in the limited liability company agreement, a series may be terminated and its affairs wound up without causing the dissolution of the limited liability company. The termination of a series established in accordance with subsection (b) of this section shall not affect the limitation on liabilities of such series provided by subsection (b) of this section. A series is terminated and its affairs shall be wound up upon the dissolution of the limited liability company under §18-801 of this title or otherwise upon the first to occur of the following:

(1) At the time specified in the limited liability company agreement;

(2) Upon the happening of events specified in the limited liability company agreement;

(3) Unless otherwise provided in the limited liability company agreement, upon the written consent of the members of the limited liability company associated with such series or, if there is more than 1 class or group of members associated with such series, then by each class or group of members associated with such series, in either case, by members associated with such series who own more than two-thirds of the then-current percentage or other interest in the profits of the series of the limited liability company owned by all of the members associated with such series or by the members in each class or group of such series, as appropriate;

(4) At any time there are no members associated with the series; provided, that, unless otherwise provided in the limited liability company agreement, the series is not terminated and is not required to be wound up if, within 90 days or such other period as is provided for in the limited liability company agreement after the occurrence of the event that terminated the continued membership of the last remaining member associated with the series, the personal represen-

tative of the last member associated with the series agrees in writing to continue the business of the series and to the admission of a personal representative of such member or its nominee or designee to the limited liability company as a member associated with the series, effective as of the occurrence of the event that terminated the continued membership of the last remaining member associated with the series; or

(5) The termination of such series under subsection (l) of this section.

(k) Notwithstanding §18-803(a) of this title, unless otherwise provided in the limited liability company agreement, a manager associated with a series who has not wrongfully terminated the series or, if none, the members associated with the series or a person approved by the members associated with the series or, if there is more than 1 class or group of members associated with the series, then by each class or group of members associated with the series, in either case, by members who own more than 50 percent of the then current percentage or other interest in the profits of the series owned by all of the members associated with the series or by the members in each class or group associated with the series, as appropriate, may wind up the affairs of the series; but, if the series has been established in accordance with subsection (b) of this section, the Court of Chancery, upon cause shown, may wind up the affairs of the series upon application of any member associated with the series, the member's personal representative or assignee, and in connection therewith, may appoint a liquidating trustee. The persons winding up the affairs of a series may, in the name of the limited liability company and for and on behalf of the limited liability company and such series, take all actions with respect to the series as are permitted under §18-803(b) of this title. The persons winding up the affairs of a series shall provide for the claims and obligations of the series as provided in §18-804(b) of this title and distribute the assets of the series as provided in §18-804(a) of this title. Actions taken in accordance with this subsection shall not affect the liability of members and shall not impose liability on a liquidating trustee.

(l) On application by or for a member or manager associated with a series established in accordance with subsection (b) of this section, the Court of Chancery may decree termination of such series whenever it is not reasonably practicable to carry on the business of the series in conformity with a limited liability company agreement.

(m) If a foreign limited liability company that is registering to do business in the State of Delaware in accordance with §18-902 of this title is governed by a limited liability company agreement that establishes or provides for the establishment of designated series of members, managers or limited liability company interests having separate rights, powers or duties with respect to specified property or obligations of the foreign limited liability company or profits and losses associated with specified property or obligations, that fact shall be so stated on the application for registration as a foreign limited liability company. In addition, the foreign limited liability company shall state on such application whether the debts, liabilities and obligations incurred, contracted for or otherwise existing with respect to a particular series, if any, shall be enforceable against the assets of such series only, and not against the assets of the foreign limited liability company generally or any other series thereof, and, unless otherwise provided in the limited liability company agreement, none of the debts, liabilities, obligations and expenses incurred, contracted for or otherwise existing with respect to the foreign limited liability company generally or any other series thereof shall be enforceable against the assets of such series.

§18-216. Approval of conversion of a limited liability company

A domestic limited liability company may convert to a corporation, business trust or association, a real estate investment trust, a common-law trust, a general partnership (including a registered limited liability partnership) or a limited partnership (including a registered limited liability limited partnership), organized, formed or created under the laws of the State of Delaware, upon the authorization of such conversion in accordance with this section. If the limited liability company agreement specifies the manner of authorizing a conversion of the limited liability company, the conversion shall be authorized as specified in the limited liability company agreement. If the limited liability company agreement does not specify the manner of authorizing a authorizing a conversion of the limited liability company and does not prohibit a conversion of the limited liability company, the conversion shall be authorized in the same manner as is specified in the limited liability company agreement for authorizing a merger or consolidation that involves the limited liability company as a constituent party to the merger or consolidation. If the limited liability company agreement does not specify the manner of authorizing a conversion of the limited liability company or a merger or consolidation that involves the limited liability company as a constituent party and does not prohibit a conversion of the limited liability company, the conversion shall be authorized by the approval by the members or, if there is more than 1 class or group of members, then by each class or group of members, in either case, by members who own more than 50 percent of the then current percentage or other interest in the profits of the domestic limited liability company owned by all of the members or by the members in each class or group, as appropriate.

SUBCHAPTER III. MEMBERS

§18-301. Admission of members

(a) In connection with the formation of a limited liability company, a person is admitted as a member of the limited liability company upon the later to occur of:

(1) The formation of the limited liability company; or

(2) The time provided in and upon compliance with the limited liability company agreement or, if the limited liability company agreement does not so provide, when the person's admission is reflected in the records of the limited liability company.

(b) After the formation of a limited liability company, a person is admitted as a member of the limited liability company:

(1) In the case of a person who is not an assignee of a limited liability company interest, including a person acquiring a limited liability company interest directly from the limited liability company and a person to be admitted as a member of the limited liability company without acquiring a limited liability company interest in the limited liability company at the time provided in and upon compliance with the limited liability company agreement or, if the limited liability company agreement does not so provide, upon the consent of all members and when the person's admission is reflected in the records of the limited liability company;

(2) In the case of an assignee of a limited liability company interest, as provided in §18-704(a) of this title and at the time provided in and upon compliance with the limited liability company agreement or, if the limited liability company agreement does not so provide, when any such person's permitted admission is reflected in the records of the limited liability company; or

(3) Unless otherwise provided in an agreement of merger or consolidation, in the case of a person acquiring a limited liability company interest in a surviving or resulting limited liability company pursuant to a merger or consolidation approved in accordance with §18-209(b) of this title, at the time provided in and upon compliance with the limited liability company agreement of the surviving or resulting limited liability company.

(c) In connection with the domestication of a non-United States entity (as defined in §18-212 of this title) as a limited liability company in the State of Delaware in accordance with §18-212 of this title or the conversion of an other entity (as defined in §18-214 of this title) to a domestic limited liability company in accordance with §18-214 of this title, a person is admitted as a member of the limited liability company at the time provided in and upon compliance with the limited liability company agreement.

(d) A person may be admitted to a limited liability company as a member of the limited liability company and may receive a limited liability company interest in the limited liability company without making a contribution or obligated to make a contribution to the limited liability company. Unless otherwise provided in a limited liability company agreement, a person may be admitted to a limited liability company as a member of the limited liability company without acquiring a limited liability company interest in the limited liability company. Unless otherwise provided in a limited liability company agreement, a person may be admitted as the sole member of a limited liability company without making a contribution or being obligated to make a contribution to the limited liability company or without acquiring a limited liability company interest in the limited liability company.

§18-302. Classes and voting

(a) A limited liability company agreement may provide for classes or groups of members having such relative rights, powers and duties as the limited liability company agreement may provide, and may make provision for the future creation in the manner provided in the limited liability company agreement of additional classes or groups of members having such relative rights, powers and duties as may from time to time be established, including rights, powers and duties senior to existing classes and groups of members. A limited liability company agreement may provide for the taking of an action, including the amendment of the limited liability company agreement, without the vote or approval of any member or class or group of members, including an action to create under the provisions of the limited liability company agreement a class or group of limited liability company interests that was not previously outstanding. A limited liability company agreement may provide that any member or class or group of members shall have no voting rights.

(b) A limited liability company agreement may grant to all or certain identified members or a specified class or group of the members the right to vote separately or with all or any class or group of the members or managers, on any matter. Voting by members may be on a per capita, number, financial interest, class, group or any other basis.

(c) A limited liability company agreement may set forth provisions relating to notice of the time, place or purpose of any meeting at which any matter is to be voted on by any members, waiver of any such notice, action by consent without a meeting, the establishment of a record date, quorum requirements, voting in person or by proxy, or any other matter with respect to the exercise of any such right to vote.

(d) Unless otherwise provided in a limited liability company agreement, on any matter that is to be voted on by members, the members may take such action without a meeting, without prior notice and without a vote if a consent or consents in writing, setting forth the action so taken, shall be signed by the members having not less than the minimum number of votes that would be necessary to authorize or take such action at a meeting at which all interests in the limited liability company entitled to vote thereon were present and voted. Unless otherwise provided in a limited liability company agreement, on any matter that is to be voted on by members, the members may vote in person or by proxy.

§18-303. Liability to 3rd parties

(a) Except as otherwise provided by this chapter, the debts, obligations and liabilities of a limited liability company, whether arising in contract, tort or otherwise, shall be solely the debts, obligations and liabilities of the limited liability company, and no member or manager of a limited liability company shall be obligated personally for any such debt, obligation or liability of the limited liability company solely by reason of being a member or acting as a manager of the limited liability company.

(b) Notwithstanding the provisions of subsection (a) of this section, under a limited liability company agreement or under another agreement, a member or manager may agree to be obligated personally for any or all of the debts, obligations and liabilities of the limited liability company.

§18-303. Liability to 3rd parties

(a) Except as otherwise provided by this chapter, the debts, obligations and liabilities of a limited liability company, whether arising in contract, tort or otherwise, shall be solely the debts, obligations and liabilities of the limited liability company, and no member or manager of a limited liability company shall be obligated personally for any such debt, obligation or liability of the limited liability company solely by reason of being a member or acting as a manager of the limited liability company.

(b) Notwithstanding the provisions of subsection (a) of this section, under a limited liability company agreement or under another agreement, a member or manager may agree to be obligated personally for any or all of the debts, obligations and liabilities of the limited liability company.

§18-304. Events of bankruptcy

A person ceases to be a member of a limited liability company upon the happening of any of the following events:

(1) Unless otherwise provided in a limited liability company agreement, or with the written consent of all members, a member:

a. Makes an assignment for the benefit of creditors;

b. Files a voluntary petition in bankruptcy;

c. Is adjudged a bankrupt or insolvent, or has entered against the member an order for relief, in any bankruptcy or insolvency proceeding;

d. Files a petition or answer seeking for the member any reorganization, arrangement, composition, readjustment, liquidation, dissolution or similar relief under any statute, law or regulation;

e. Files an answer or other pleading admitting or failing to contest the material allegations of a petition filed against the member in any proceeding of this nature;

f. Seeks, consents to or acquiesces in the appointment of a trustee, receiver or liquidator of the member or of all or any substantial part of the member's properties; or

(2) Unless otherwise provided in a limited liability company agreement, or with the written consent of all members, 120 days after the commencement of any proceeding against the member seeking reorganization, arrangement, composition, readjustment, liquidation, dissolution or similar relief under any statute, law or regulation, if the proceeding has not been dismissed, or if within 90 days after the appointment without the member's consent or acquiescence of a trustee, receiver or liquidator of the member or of all or any substantial part of the member's properties, the appointment is not vacated or stayed, or within 90 days after the expiration of any such stay, the appointment is not vacated.

§18-305. Access to and confidentiality of information; records

(a) Each member of a limited liability company has the right, subject to such reasonable standards (including standards governing what information and documents are to be furnished at what time and location and at whose expense) as may be set forth in a limited liability company agreement or otherwise established by the manager or, if there is no manager, then by the members, to obtain from the limited liability company from time to time upon reasonable demand for any purpose reasonably related to the member's interest as a member of the limited liability company:

(1) True and full information regarding the status of the business and financial condition of the limited liability company;

(2) Promptly after becoming available, a copy of the limited liability company's federal, state and local income tax returns for each year;

(3) A current list of the name and last known business, residence or mailing address of each member and manager;

(4) A copy of any written limited liability company agreement and certificate of formation and all amendments thereto, together with executed copies of any written powers of attorney pursuant to which the limited liability company agreement and any certificate and all amendments thereto have been executed;

(5) True and full information regarding the amount of cash and a description and statement of the agreed value of any other property or services contributed by each member and which each member has agreed to contribute in the future, and the date on which each became a member; and

(6) Other information regarding the affairs of the limited liability company as is just and reasonable.

(b) Each manager shall have the right to examine all of the information described in subsection (a) of this section for a purpose reasonably related to the position of manager.

(c) The manager of a limited liability company shall have the right to keep confidential from the members, for such period of time as the manager deems reasonable, any information which the manager reasonably believes to be in the nature of trade secrets or other information the disclosure of which the manager in good faith believes is not in the best interest of the limited liability company or could damage the limited liability company or its business or which the limited liability company is required by law or by agreement with a 3rd party to keep confidential.

(d) A limited liability company may maintain its records in other than a written form if such form is capable of conversion into written form within a reasonable time.

(e) Any demand by a member under this section shall be in writing and shall state the purpose of such demand.

(f) Any action to enforce any right arising under this section shall be brought in the Court of Chancery. If the limited liability company refuses to permit a member to obtain or a manager to examine the information described in subsection (a)(3) of this section or does not reply to the demand that has been made within 5 business days after the demand has been made, the demanding member or manager may apply to the Court of Chancery for an order to compel such disclosure. The Court of Chancery is hereby vested with exclusive jurisdiction to determine whether or not the person seeking such information is entitled to the information sought. The Court of Chancery may summarily order the limited liability company to permit the demanding member to obtain or manager to examine the information described in subsection (a)(3) of this section and to make copies or abstracts therefrom, or the Court of Chancery may summarily order the limited liability company to furnish to the demanding member or manager the information described in subsection (a)(3) of this section on the condition that the demanding member or manager first pay to the limited liability company the reasonable cost of obtaining and furnishing such information and on such other conditions as the Court of Chancery deems appropriate. When a demanding member seeks to obtain or a manager seeks to examine the information described in subsection (a)(3) of this section, the demanding member or manager shall first establish (1) that the demanding member or manager has complied with the provisions of this section respecting the form and manner of making demand for obtaining or examining of such information, and (2) that the information the demanding member or manager seeks is reasonably related to the member's interest as a member or the manager's position as a manager, as the case may be. The Court of Chancery may, in its discretion, prescribe any limitations or conditions with reference to the obtaining or examining of information, or award such other or further relief as the Court of Chancery may deem just and proper. The Court of Chancery may order books, documents and records, pertinent extracts therefrom, or duly authenticated copies thereof, to be brought within the State of Delaware and kept in the State of Delaware upon such terms and conditions as the order may prescribe.

§18-306. Remedies for breach of limited liability company agreement by member

A limited liability company agreement may provide that:

(1) A member who fails to perform in accordance with, or to comply with the terms and conditions of, the limited liability company agreement shall be subject to specified penalties or specified consequences; and

(2) At the time or upon the happening of events specified in the limited liability company agreement, a member shall be subject to specified penalties or specified consequences.

SUBCHAPTER IV. MANAGERS

§18-401. Admission of managers

A person may be named or designated as a manager of the limited liability company as provided in §18-101(10) of this title.

§18-402. Management of limited liability company

Unless otherwise provided in a limited liability company agreement, the management of a limited liability company shall be vested in its members in proportion to the then current percentage or other interest of members in the profits of the limited liability company owned by all of the members, the decision of members owning more than 50 percent of the said percentage or other interest in the profits controlling; provided however, that if a limited liability company agreement provides for the management, in whole or in part, of a limited liability company by a manager, the management of the limited liability company, to the extent so provided, shall be vested in the manager who shall be chosen in the manner provided in the limited liability company agreement. The manager shall also hold the offices and have the responsibilities responsibilities accorded to the manager by or in the manner provided in a limited liability company agreement. Subject to §18-602 of this title, a manager shall cease to be a manager as provided in a limited liability company agreement. A limited liability company may have more than 1 manager. Unless otherwise provided in a limited liability company agreement, each member and manager has the authority to bind the limited liability company.

§18-403. Contributions by a manager

A manager of a limited liability company may make contributions to the limited liability company and share in the profits and losses of, and in distributions from, the limited liability company as a member. A person who is both a manager and a member has the rights and powers, and is subject to the restrictions and liabilities, of a manager and, except as provided in a limited liability company agreement, also has the rights and powers, and is subject to the restrictions and liabilities, of a member to the extent of the manager's participation in the limited liability company as a member.

§18-404. Classes and voting

(a) A limited liability company agreement may provide for classes or groups of managers having such relative rights, powers and duties as the limited liability company agreement may provide, and may make provision for the future creation in the manner provided in the limited liability company agreement of additional classes or groups of managers having such relative rights, powers and duties as may from time to time be established, including rights, powers and duties senior to existing classes and groups of managers. A limited liability company agreement may provide for the taking of an action, including the amendment of the limited liability company agreement, without the vote or approval of any manager or class or group of managers, including an action to create under the provisions of the limited liability company agreement a class or group of limited liability company interests that was not previously outstanding.

(b) A limited liability company agreement may grant to all or certain identified managers or a specified class or group of the managers the right to vote, separately or with all or any class or group of managers or members, on any matter. Voting by managers may be on a per capita, number, financial interest, class, group or any other basis.

(c) A limited liability company agreement may set forth provisions relating to notice of the time, place or purpose of any meeting at which any matter is to be voted on by any manager or class or group of managers, waiver of any such notice, action by consent without a meeting, the establishment of a record date, quorum requirements, voting in person or by proxy, or any other matter with respect to the exercise of any such right to vote.

(d) Unless otherwise provided in a limited liability company agreement, on any matter that is to be voted on by managers, the managers may take such action without a meeting, without prior notice and without a vote if a consent or consents in writing, setting forth the action so taken, shall be signed by the managers having not less than the minimum number of votes that would be necessary to authorize or take such action at a meeting. Unless otherwise provided in a limited liability company agreement, on any matter that is to be voted on by managers, the managers may vote in person or by proxy.

§18-405. Remedies for breach of limited liability company agreement by manager

A limited liability company agreement may provide that:

(1) A manager who fails to perform in accordance with, or to comply with the terms and conditions of, the limited liability company agreement shall be subject to specified penalties or specified consequences; and

(2) At the time or upon the happening of events specified in the limited liability company agreement, a manager shall be subject to specified penalties or specified consequences.

§18-406. Reliance on reports and information by member or manager

A member or manager of a limited liability company shall be fully protected in relying in good faith upon the records of the limited liability company and upon such information, opinions, reports or statements presented to the limited liability company by any of its other managers, members, officers, employees or committees of the limited liability company, or by any other person, as to matters the member or manager reasonably believes are within such other person's professional or expert competence and who has been selected with reasonable care by or on behalf of the limited liability company, including information, opinions, reports or statements as to the value and amount of the assets, liabilities, profits or losses of the limited liability company or any other facts pertinent to the existence and amount of assets from which distributions to members might properly be paid.

§18-407. Delegation of rights and powers to manage

Unless otherwise provided in the limited liability company agreement, a member or manager of a limited liability company has the power and authority to delegate to 1 or more other persons the member's or manager's, as the case may be, rights and powers to manage and control the business and affairs of the limited liability company, including to delegate to agents, officers and employees of a member or manager or the limited liability company, and to delegate by a management agreement or another agreement with, or otherwise to, other persons. Unless otherwise provided in the limited liability company agreement, such delegation by a member or manager of a limited liability company shall not cause the member or manager to cease to be a member or manager, as the case may be, of the limited liability company.

SUBCHAPTER V. FINANCE

§18-501. Form of contribution

The contribution of a member to a limited liability company may be in cash, property or services rendered, or a promissory note or other obligation to contribute cash or property or to perform services.

§18-502. Liability for contribution

(a) Except as provided in a limited liability company agreement, a member is obligated to a limited liability company to perform any promise to contribute cash or property or to perform services, even if the member is unable to perform because of death, disability or any other reason. If a member does not make the required contribution of property or services, the member is obligated at the option of the limited liability company to contribute cash equal to that portion of the agreed value (as stated in the records of the limited liability company) of the contribution that has not been made. The foregoing option shall be in addition to, and not in lieu of, any other rights, including the right to specific performance, that the limited liability company may have against such member under the limited liability company agreement or applicable law.

(b) Unless otherwise provided in a limited liability company agreement, the obligation of a member to make a contribution or return money or other property paid or distributed in violation of this chapter may be compromised only by consent of all the members.Notwithstanding the compromise, a creditor of a limited liability company who extends credit, after the entering into of a limited liability company agreement or an amendment thereto which, in either case, reflects the obligation, and before the amendment thereof to reflect the compromise, may enforce the original obligation to the extent that, in extending credit, the creditor reasonably relied on the obligation of a member to make a contribution or return. A conditional obligation of a member to make a contribution or return money or other property to a limited liability company may not be enforced unless the conditions of the obligation have been satisfied or waived as to or by such member. Conditional obligations include contributions payable upon a discretionary call of a limited liability company prior to the time the call occurs.

(c) A limited liability company agreement may provide that the interest of any member who fails to make any contribution that the member is obligated to make shall be subject to specified penalties for, or specified consequences of, such failure. Such penalty or consequence may take the form of reducing or eliminating the defaulting member's proportionate interest in a limited liability company, subordinating the member's limited liability company interest to that of nondefaulting members, a forced sale of that limited liability company interest, forfeiture of his or her limited liability company interest, the lending by other members of the amount necessary to meet the defaulting member's commitment, a fixing of the value of his or her limited liability company interest by appraisal or by formula and redemption or sale of the limited liability company interest at such value, or other penalty or consequence.

§18-503. Allocation of profits and losses

The profits and losses of a limited liability company shall be allocated among the members, and among classes or groups of members, in the manner provided in a limited liability company agreement. If the limited liability company agreement does not so provide, profits and losses shall be allocated on the basis of the agreed value (as stated in the records of the limited liability company) of the contributions made by each member to the extent they have been received by the limited liability company and have not been returned.

§18-504. Allocation of distributions

Distributions of cash or other assets of a limited liability company shall be allocated among the members, and among classes or groups of members, in the manner provided in a limited liability company agreement. If the limited liability company agreement does not so provide, distributions shall be made on the basis of the agreed value (as stated in the records of the limited liability company) of the contributions made by each member to the extent they have been received by the limited liability company and have not been returned.

§18-505. Defense of usury not available

No obligation of a member or manager of a limited liability company to the limited liability company arising under the limited liability company agreement or a separate agreement or writing, and no note, instrument or other writing evidencing any such obligation of a member or manager, shall be subject to the defense of usury, and no member or manager shall interpose the defense of usury with respect to any such obligation in any action.

SUBCHAPTER VI. DISTRIBUTIONS AND RESIGNATION

§18-601. Interim distributions

Except as provided in this subchapter, to the extent and at the times or upon the happening of the events specified in a limited liability company agreement, a member is entitled to receive from a limited liability company distributions before the member's resignation from the limited liability company and before the dissolution and winding up thereof.

§18-602. Resignation of manager

A manager may resign as a manager of a limited liability company at the time or upon the happening of events specified in a limited liability company agreement and in accordance with the limited liability company agreement. A limited liability company agreement may provide that a manager shall not have the right to resign as a manager of a limited liability company. Notwithstanding that a limited liability company agreement provides that a manager does not have the right to resign as a manager of a limited liability company, a manager may resign as a manager of a limited liability company at any time by giving written notice to the members and other managers. If the resignation of a manager violates a limited liability company agreement, in addition to any remedies otherwise available under applicable law, a limited liability company may recover from the resigning manager damages for breach of the limited liability company agreement and offset the damages against the amount otherwise distributable to the resigning manager.

§18-603. Resignation of member

A member may resign from a limited liability company only at the time or upon the happening of events specified in a limited liability company agreement and in accordance with the limited liability company agreement. Notwithstanding anything to the contrary under applicable law, unless a limited liability company agreement provides otherwise, a member may not resign from a limited liability company prior to the dissolution and winding up of the limited liability company. Notwithstanding anything to the contrary under applicable law, a limited liability company agreement may provide that a limited liability company interest may not be assigned prior to the dissolution and winding up of the limited liability company. Unless otherwise provided in a limited liability company agreement, a limited liability company whose original certificate of formation was filed with the Secretary of State and effective on or prior to July 31, 1996, shall continue to continue to be governed by this section as in effect on July 31, 1996, and shall not be governed by this section.

§18-604. Distribution upon resignation

Except as provided in this subchapter, upon resignation any resigning member is entitled to receive any distribution to which such member is entitled under a limited liability company agreement and, if not otherwise provided in a limited liability company agreement, such member is entitled to receive, within a reasonable time after resignation, the fair value of such member's limited liability company interest as of the date of resignation based upon such member's right to share in distributions from the limited liability company.

§18-605. Distribution in kind

Except as provided in a limited liability company agreement, a member, regardless of the nature of the member's contribution, has no right to demand and receive any distribution from a limited liability company in any form other than cash. Except as provided in a limited liability company agreement, a member may not be compelled to accept a distribution of any asset in kind from a limited liability company to the extent that the percentage of the asset distributed exceeds a percentage of that asset which is equal to the percentage in which the member shares in distributions from the limited liability company. Except as provided in the limited liability company agreement, a member may be compelled to accept a distribution of any asset in kind from a limited liability company to the extent that the percentage of the asset distributed is equal to a percentage of that asset which is equal to the percentage in which the member shares in distributions from the limited liability company.

§18-606. Right to distribution

Subject to §§18-607 and 18-804 of this title, and unless otherwise provided in a limited liability company agreement, at the time a member becomes entitled to receive a distribution, the member has the status of, and is entitled to all remedies available to, a creditor of a limited liability company with respect to the distribution. A limited liability company agreement may provide for the establishment of a record date with respect to allocations and distributions by a limited liability company.

§18-607. Limitations on distribution

(a) A limited liability company shall not make a distribution to a member to the extent that at the time of the distribution, after giving effect to the distribution, all liabilities of the limited liability company, other than liabilities to members on account of their limited liability company interests and liabilities for which the recourse of creditors is limited to specified property of the limited liability company, exceed the fair value of the assets of the limited liability company, except that the fair value of property that is subject to a liability for which the recourse of creditors is limited shall be included in the assets of the limited liability company only to the extent that the fair value of that property exceeds that liability.

(b) A member who receives a distribution in violation of subsection (a) of this section, and who knew at the time of the distribution that the distribution violated subsection (a) of this section, shall be liable to a limited liability company for the amount of the distribution. A member who receives a distribution in violation of subsection (a) of this section, and who did not know at the time of the distribution that the distribution violated subsection (a) of this section, shall not be liable for the amount of the distribution. Subject to subsection (c) of this section, this subsection shall not affect any obligation or liability of a member under an agreement or other applicable law for the amount of a distribution.

(c) Unless otherwise agreed, a member who receives a distribution from a limited liability company shall have no liability under this chapter or other applicable law for the amount of the distribution after the expiration of 3 years from the date of the distribution unless an action to recover the distribution from such member is commenced prior to the expiration of the said 3-year period and an adjudication of liability against such member is made in the said action.

SUBCHAPTER VII. ASSIGNMENT OF LIMITED LIABILITY COMPANY INTERESTS

§18-701. Nature of limited liability company interest

A limited liability company interest is personal property. A member has no interest in specific limited liability company property.

§18-702. Assignment of limited liability company interest

(a) A limited liability company interest is assignable in whole or in part except as provided in a limited liability company agreement. The assignee of a member's limited liability company interest shall have no right to participate in the management of the business and affairs of a limited liability company except as provided in a limited liability company agreement and upon:

(1) The approval of all of the members of the limited liability company other than the member assigning the limited liability company interest; or

(2) Compliance with any procedure provided for in the limited liability company agreement.

(b) Unless otherwise provided in a limited liability company agreement:

(1) An assignment of a limited liability company interest does not entitle the assignee to become or to exercise any rights or powers of a member;

(2) An assignment of a limited liability company interest entitles the assignee to share in such profits and losses, to receive such distribution or distributions, and to receive such allocation of income, gain, loss, deduction, or credit or similar item to which the assignor was entitled, to the extent assigned; and

(3) A member ceases to be a member and to have the power to exercise any rights or powers of a member upon assignment of all of the member's limited liability company interest. Unless otherwise provided in a limited liability company agreement, the pledge of, or granting of a security interest, lien or other encumbrance in or against, any or all of the limited liability company interest of a member shall not cause the member to cease to be a member or to have the power to exercise any rights or powers of a member.

(c) A limited liability company agreement may provide that a member's interest in a limited liability company may be evidenced by a certificate of limited liability company interest issued by the limited liability company.

(d) Unless otherwise provided in a limited liability company agreement and except to the extent assumed by agreement, until an assignee of a limited liability company interest becomes a member, the assignee shall have no liability as a member solely as a result of the assignment.

(e) Unless otherwise provided in the limited liability company agreement, a limited liability company may acquire, by purchase, redemption or otherwise, any limited liability company interest or other interest of a member or manager in the limited liability company. Unless otherwise provided in the limited liability company agreement, any such interest so acquired by the limited liability company shall be deemed canceled.

§18-703. Rights of judgment creditor

On application to a court of competent jurisdiction by any judgment creditor of a member, the court may charge the limited liability company interest of the member with payment of the unsatisfied amount of the judgment with interest. To the extent so charged, the judgment creditor has only the rights of an assignee of the limited liability company interest. This chapter does not deprive any member of the benefit of any exemption laws applicable to the member's limited liability company interest.

§18-704. Right of assignee to become member

(a) An assignee of a limited liability company interest may become a member as provided in a limited liability company agreement and upon:

(1) The approval of all of the members of the limited liability company other than the member assigning limited liability company interest; or

(2) Compliance with any procedure provided for in the limited liability company agreement.

(b) An assignee who has become a member has, to the extent assigned, the rights and powers, and is subject to the restrictions and liabilities, of a member under a limited liability company agreement and this chapter. Notwithstanding the foregoing, unless otherwise provided in a limited liability company agreement, an assignee who becomes a member is liable for the obligations of the assignor to make contributions as provided in §18-502 of this title, but shall not be liable for the obligations of the assignor under subchapter VI of this chapter. However, the assignee is not obligated for liabilities, including the obligations of the assignor to make contributions as provided in §18-502 of this title, unknown to the assignee at the time the assignee became a member and which could not be ascertained from a limited liability company agreement.

(c) Whether or not an assignee of a limited liability company interest becomes a member, the assignor is not released from liability to a limited liability company under subchapters V and VI of this chapter.

§18-705. Powers of estate of deceased or incompetent member

If a member who is an individual dies or a court of competent jurisdiction adjudges the member to be incompetent to manage the member's person or property, the member's personal representative may exercise all of the member's rights for the purpose of settling the member's estate or administering the member's property, including any power under a limited liability company agreement of an assignee to become a member. If a member is a corporation, trust or other entity and is dissolved or terminated, the powers of that member may be exercised by its personal representative.

SUBCHAPTER VIII. DISSOLUTION

§18-801. Dissolution

(a) A limited liability company is dissolved and its affairs shall be wound up upon the first to occur of the following:

(1) At the time specified in a limited liability company agreement, but if no such time is set forth in the limited liability company agreement, then the limited liability company shall have a perpetual existence;

(2) Upon the happening of events specified in a limited liability company agreement;

(3) Unless otherwise provided in a limited liability company agreement, upon the affirmative vote or written consent of the members of the limited liability company or, if there is more than 1 class or group of members, then by each class or group of members, in either case, by members who own more than two-thirds of the then-current percentage or other interest in the profits of the limited liability company owned by all of the members or by the members in each class or group, as appropriate;

(4) At any time there are no members; provided, that the limited liability company is not dissolved and is not required to be wound up if:

a. Unless otherwise provided in a limited liability company agreement, within 90 days or such other period as is provided for in the limited liability company agreement after the occurrence of the event that terminated the continued membership of the last remaining member, the personal representative of the last remaining member agrees in writing to continue the limited liability company and to the admission of the personal representative of such member or its nominee or designee to the limited liability company as a member, effective as of the occurrence of the event that terminated the continued membership of the last remaining member; provided, that a limited liability company agreement may provide that the personal representative of the last remaining member shall be obligated to agree in writing to continue the limited liability company and to the admission of the personal representative of such member or its nominee or designee to the limited liability company as a member, effective as of the occurrence of the event that terminated the continued membership of the last remaining member, or

b. A member is admitted to the limited liability company in the manner provided for in the limited liability company agreement, effective as of the occurrence of the event that terminated the continued membership of the last remaining member, within 90 days or such other period as is provided for in the limited liability company agreement after the occurrence of the event that terminated the continued membership of the last remaining member, pursuant to a provision of the limited liability company agreement that specifically provides for the admission of a member to the limited liability company after there is no longer a remaining member of the limited liability company.

(5) The entry of a decree of judicial dissolution under §18-802 of this title.

(b) Unless otherwise provided in a limited liability company agreement, the death, retirement, resignation, expulsion, bankruptcy or dissolution of any member or the occurrence of any other event that terminates the continued membership of any member shall not cause the limited liability company to be dissolved or its affairs to be wound up, and upon the occurrence of any such event, the limited liability company shall be continued without dissolution.

§18-802. Judicial dissolution

On application by or for a member or manager the Court of Chancery may decree dissolution of a limited liability company whenever it is not reasonably practicable to carry on the business in conformity with a limited liability company agreement.

§18-803. Winding up

(a) Unless otherwise provided in a limited liability company agreement, a manager who has not wrongfully dissolved a limited liability company or, if none, the members or a person approved by the members or, if there is more than 1 class or group of members, then by each class or group of members, in either case, by members who own more than 50 percent of the then current percentage or other interest in the profits of the limited liability company owned by all of the members or by the members in each class or group, as appropriate, may wind up the limited liability company's affairs; but the Court of Chancery, upon cause shown, may wind up the limited liability company's affairs upon application of any member or manager, the member's or manager's personal representative or assignee, and in connection therewith, may appoint a liquidating trustee.

(b) Upon dissolution of a limited liability company and until the filing of a certificate of cancellation as provided in §18-203 of this title, the persons winding up the limited liability company's affairs may, in the name of, and for and on behalf of, the limited liability company, prosecute and defend suits, whether civil, criminal or administrative, gradually settle and close the limited liability company's business, dispose of and convey the limited liability company's property, discharge or make reasonable provision for the limited liability company's liabilities, and distribute to the members any remaining assets of the limited liability company, all without affecting the liability of members and managers and without imposing liability on a liquidating trustee.

§18-804. Distribution of assets

(a) Upon the winding up of a limited liability company, the assets shall be distributed as follows:

(1) To creditors, including members and managers who are creditors, to the extent otherwise permitted by law, in satisfaction of liabilities of the limited liability company (whether by payment or the making of reasonable provision for payment thereof) other than liabilities for which reasonable provision for payment has been made and liabilities for distributions to members and former members under §18-601 or §18-604 of this title;

(2) Unless otherwise provided in a limited liability company agreement, to members and former members in satisfaction of liabilities for distributions under §18-601 or §18-604 of this title; and

(3) Unless otherwise provided in a limited liability company agreement, to members first for the return of their contributions and second respecting their limited liability company interests, in the proportions in which the members share in distributions.

(b) A limited liability company which has dissolved:

(1) Shall pay or make reasonable provision to pay all claims and obligations, including all contingent, conditional or unmatured contractual claims, known to the limited liability company;

(2) Shall make such provision as will be reasonably likely to be sufficient to provide compensation for any claim against the limited liability company which is the subject of a pending action, suit or proceeding to which the limited liability company is a party; and

(3) Shall make such provision as will be reasonably likely to be sufficient to provide compensation for claims that have not been made known to the limited liability company or that have not arisen but that, based on facts known to the limited liability company, are likely to arise or to become known to the limited liability company

within 10 years after the date of dissolution. If there are sufficient assets, such claims and obligations shall be paid in full and any such provision for payment made shall be made in full. If there are insufficient assets, such claims and obligations shall be paid or provided for according to their priority and, among claims of equal priority, ratably to the extent of assets available therefor. Unless otherwise provided in the limited liability company agreement, any remaining assets shall be distributed as provided in this chapter. Any liquidating trustee winding up a limited liability company's affairs who has complied with this section shall not be personally liable to the claimants of the dissolved limited liability company by reason of such person's actions in winding up the limited liability company.

(c) A member who receives a distribution in violation of subsection (a) of this section, and who knew at the time of the distribution that the distribution violated subsection (a) of this section, shall be liable to the limited liability company for the amount of the distribution. A member who receives a distribution in violation of subsection (a) of this section, and who did not know at the time of the distribution that the distribution violated subsection (a) of this section, shall not be liable for the amount of the distribution. Subject to subsection (d) of this section, this subsection shall not affect any obligation or liability of a member under an agreement or other applicable law for the amount of a distribution.

(d) Unless otherwise agreed, a member who receives a distribution from a limited liability company to which this section applies shall have no liability under this chapter or other applicable law for the amount of the distribution after the expiration of 3 years from the date of the distribution unless an action to recover the distribution from such member is commenced prior to the expiration of the said 3-year period and an adjudication of liability against such member is made in the said action.

(e) Section 18-607 of this title shall not apply to a distribution to which this section applies.

SUBCHAPTER IX. FOREIGN LIMITED LIABILITY COMPANIES

§18-901. Law governing

(a) Subject to the Constitution of the State of Delaware:

(1) The laws of the state, territory, possession, or other jurisdiction or country under which a foreign limited liability company is organized govern its organization and internal affairs and the liability of its members and managers; and

(2) A foreign limited liability company may not be denied registration by reason of any difference between those laws and the laws of the State of Delaware.

(b) A foreign limited liability company shall be subject to §18-106 of this title.

§18-902. Registration required; application

(a) Before doing business in the State of Delaware, a foreign limited liability company shall register with the Secretary of State. In order to register, a foreign limited liability company shall submit to the Secretary of State:

(1) A copy executed by an authorized person of an application for registration as a foreign limited liability company, setting forth:

a. The name of the foreign limited liability company and, if different, the name under which it proposes to register and do business in the State of Delaware;

b. The state, territory, possession or other jurisdiction or country where formed, the date of its formation and a statement from an authorized person that, as of the date of filing, the foreign limited liability company validly exists as a limited liability company under the laws of the jurisdiction of its formation;

c. The nature of the business or purposes to be conducted or promoted in the State of Delaware;

d. The address of the registered office and the name and address of the registered agent for service of process required to be maintained by §18-904(b) of this title;

e. A statement that the Secretary of State is appointed the agent of the foreign limited liability company for service of process under the circumstances set forth in §18-910(b) of this title; and

f. The date on which the foreign limited liability company first did, or intends to do, business in the State of Delaware.

(2) A fee as set forth in §18-1105(a)(6) of this title shall be paid.

(b) A person shall not be deemed to be doing business in the State of Delaware solely by reason of being a member or manager of a domestic limited liability company or a foreign limited liability company.

§18-903. Issuance of registration

(a) If the Secretary of State finds that an application for registration conforms to law and all requisite fees have been paid, the Secretary shall:

(1) Certify that the application has been filed by endorsing upon the original application the word "Filed", and the date and hour of the filing. This endorsement is conclusive of the date and time of its filing in the absence of actual fraud;

(2) File and index the endorsed application.

(b) The Secretary of State shall prepare and return to the person who filed the application or the person's representative a copy of the original signed application, similarly endorsed, and shall certify such copy as a true copy of the original signed application.

(c) The filing of the application with the Secretary of State shall make it unnecessary to file any other documents under Chapter 31 of this title.

§18-904. Name; registered office; registered agent

(a) A foreign limited liability company may register with the Secretary of State under any name (whether or not it is the name under which it is registered in the jurisdiction of its formation) that includes the words "Limited Liability Company" or the abbreviation "L.L.C." or the designation "LLC" and that could be registered by a domestic limited liability company; provided however, that a foreign limited liability company may register under any name which is not such as to distinguish it upon the records in the office of the Secretary of State from the name of any domestic or foreign corporation, business trust, limited liability company or limited partnership reserved, registered or organized under the laws of the State of Delaware with the written consent of the other corporation, business trust, limited liability company or limited partnership, which written consent shall be filed with the Secretary of State.

(b) Each foreign limited liability company shall have and maintain in the State of Delaware:

(1) A registered office which may but need not be a place of its business in the State of Delaware; and

(2) A registered agent for service of process on the foreign limited liability company, which agent may be either an individual resident of the State of Delaware whose business office is identical with the foreign limited liability company's registered office, or a domestic corporation, or a domestic limited partnership, or a domestic limited liability company, or a domestic business trust, or a foreign corporation, or a foreign limited partnership, or a foreign limited liability company authorized to do business in the State of Delaware having a business office identical with such registered office, which is generally open during normal business hours to accept service of process and otherwise perform the functions of a registered agent.

(c) A registered agent may change the address of the registered office of the foreign limited liability company(s) for which he or she is registered agent to another address in the State of Delaware by paying a fee as set forth in §18-1105(a)(7) of this title and filing with the Secretary of State a certificate, executed by such registered agent, setting forth the names of all the foreign limited liability companies represented by such registered agent, and the address at which such registered agent has maintained the registered office for each of such foreign limited liability companies, and further certifying to the new address to which each such registered office will be changed on a given day, and at which new address such registered agent will thereafter maintain the registered office for each of the foreign limited liability companies recited in the certificate. Upon the filing of such certificate, the Secretary of State shall furnish to the registered agent a certified copy of the same under the Secretary's hand and seal of office, and thereafter, or until further change of address, as authorized by law, the registered office in the State of Delaware of each of the foreign limited liability companies recited in he certificate shall be located at the new address of the registered agent thereof as given in the certificate. In the event of a change of name of any person acting as a registered agent of a foreign limited liability company, such registered agent shall file with the Secretary of State a certificate, executed by such registered agent, setting forth the new name of such registered agent, the name of such registered agent before it was changed, the names of all the foreign limited liability companies represented by such registered agent, and the address at which such registered agent has maintained the registered office for each of such foreign limited liability companies, and shall pay a fee as set forth in §18-1105(a)(7) of this title. Upon the filing of such certificate, the Secretary of State shall furnish to the registered agent a certified copy of the same under the Secretary's hand and seal of office. Filing a certificate under this section shall be deemed to be an amendment of the application of each foreign limited liability company affected thereby and each foreign limited liability company shall not be required to take any further action with respect thereto, to amend its application under §18-905 of this title. Any registered agent filing a certificate under this section shall promptly, upon such filing, deliver a copy of any such certificate to each foreign limited liability company affected thereby.

(d) The registered agent of 1 or more foreign limited liability companies may resign and appoint a successor registered agent by paying a fee as set forth in §18-1105(a)(7) of this title and filing a certificate with the Secretary of State, stating that it resigns and the name and address of the successor registered agent. There shall be attached to such certificate a statement executed by each affected foreign limited liability company ratifying and approving such change of registered agent.Upon such filing, the successor registered agent shall become the registered agent of such foreign limited liability company as has ratified and approved such substitution and the successor registered agent's address, as stated in such certificate, shall become the address of each such foreign limited liability company's registered office in the State of Delaware. The Secretary of State shall furnish to the successor registered agent a certified copy of the certificate of resignation. Filing of such certificate of resignation shall be deemed to be an amendment of the application of each foreign limited liability company affected thereby and each such foreign limited liability company shall not be required to take any further action with respect thereto, to amend its application under §18-905 of this title.

(e) The registered agent of a foreign limited liability company may resign without appointing a successor registered agent by paying a fee as set forth in §18-1105(a)(7) of this title and filing a certificate with the Secretary of State stating that it resigns as registered agent for the foreign limited liability company identified in the certificate, but such resignation shall not become effective until 120 days after the certificate is filed. There shall be attached to such certificate an affidavit of such registered agent, if an individual, or of the president, a vice-president or the secretary thereof if a corporation, that at least 30 days prior to and on or about the date of the filing of said certificate, notices were sent by certified or registered mail to the foreign limited liability companies for which such registered agent is resigning as registered agent, at the principal office thereof within or outside the State of Delaware, if known to such registered agent or, if not, to the last known address of the attorney or other individual at whose request such registered agent was appointed for such foreign limited liability company, of the resignation of such registered agent. After receipt of the notice of the resignation of its registered agent, the foreign limited liability company for which such registered agent was acting shall obtain and designate a new registered agent, to take the place of the registered agent so resigning.If such foreign limited liability company fails to obtain and designate a new registered agent as aforesaid prior to the expiration of the period of 120 days after the filing by the registered agent of the certificate of resignation, such foreign limited liability company shall not be permitted to do business in the State of Delaware and its registration shall be deemed to be cancelled.After the resignation of the registered agent shall have become effective as provided in this section and if no new registered agent shall have been obtained and designated in the time and manner aforesaid, service of legal process against the foreign limited liability company for which the resigned registered agent had been acting shall thereafter be upon the Secretary of State in accordance with §18-911 of this title.

§18-905. Amendments to application

If any statement in the application for registration of a foreign limited liability company was false when made or any arrangements or other facts described have changed, making the application false in any respect, the foreign limited liability company shall promptly file in the office of the Secretary of State a certificate, executed by an authorized person, correcting such statement, together with a fee as set forth in §18-1105(a)(6) of this title.

§18-906. Cancellation of registration

A foreign limited liability company may cancel its registration by filing with the Secretary of State a certificate of cancellation, executed by an authorized person, together with a fee as set forth in §18-1105(a)(6) of this title. A cancellation does not terminate the authority of the Secretary of State to accept service of process on the foreign limited liability company with respect to causes of action arising out of the doing of business in the State of Delaware.

§18-907. Doing business without registration

(a) A foreign limited liability company doing business in the State of Delaware may not maintain any action, suit or proceeding in the State of Delaware until it has registered in the State of Delaware, and has paid to the State of Delaware all fees and penalties for the years or parts thereof, during which it did business in the State of Delaware without having registered.

(b) The failure of a foreign limited liability company to register in the State of Delaware does not impair:

(1) The validity of any contract or act of the foreign limited liability company;

(2) The right of any other party to the contract to maintain any action, suit or proceeding on the contract; or

(3) Prevent the foreign limited liability company from defending any action, suit or proceeding in any court of the State of Delaware.

(c) A member or a manager of a foreign limited liability company is not liable for the obligations of the foreign limited liability company solely by reason of the limited liability company's having done business in the State of Delaware without registration.

(d) Any foreign limited liability company doing business in the State of Delaware without first having registered shall be fined and shall pay to the Secretary of State $200 for each year or part thereof during which the foreign limited liability company failed to register in the State of Delaware.

§18-908. Foreign limited liability companies doing business without having qualified; injunctions

The Court of Chancery shall have jurisdiction to enjoin any foreign limited liability company, or any agent thereof, from doing any business in the State of Delaware if such foreign limited liability company has failed to register under this subchapter or if such foreign limited liability company has secured a certificate of the Secretary of State under §18-903 of this title on the basis of false or misleading representations. Upon the motion of the Attorney General or upon the relation of proper parties, the Attorney General shall proceed for this purpose by complaint in any county in which such foreign limited liability company is doing or has done business.

§18-909. Execution; liability

Section 18-204 (c) of this title shall be applicable to foreign limited liability companies as if they were domestic limited liability companies.

§18-910. Service of process on registered foreign limited liability companies

(a) Service of legal process upon any foreign limited liability company shall be made by delivering a copy personally to any managing or general agent or manager of the foreign limited liability company in the State of Delaware or the registered agent of the foreign limited liability company in the State of Delaware, or by leaving it at the dwelling house or usual place of abode in the State of Delaware of any such managing or general agent, manager or registered agent (if the registered agent be an individual), or at the registered office or other place of business of the foreign limited liability company in the State of Delaware. If the registered agent be a corporation, service of process upon it as such may be made by serving, in the State of Delaware, a copy thereof on the president, vice-president, secretary, assistant secretary or any director of the the corporate registered agent.Service by copy left at the dwelling house or usual place of abode of any managing or general agent, manager or registered agent, or at the registered office or other place of business of the foreign limited liability company in the State of Delaware, to be effective must be delivered thereat at least 6 days before the return date of the process, and in the presence of an adult person, and the officer serving the process shall distinctly state the manner of service in the officer's return thereto. Process returnable forthwith must be delivered personally to the managing or general agent, manager or registered agent.

(b) In case the officer whose duty it is to serve legal process cannot by due diligence serve the process in any manner provided for by subsection (a) of this section, it shall be lawful to serve the process against the foreign limited liability company upon the Secretary of State, and such service shall be as effectual for all intents and purposes as if made in any of the ways provided for in subsection (a) of this section.In the event service is effected through the Secretary of State in accordance with this subsection, the Secretary of State shall forthwith notify the foreign limited liability company by letter, certified mail, return receipt requested, directed to the foreign limited liability company at its last registered office. Such letter shall enclose a copy of the process and any other papers served on the Secretary of State pursuant to this subsection.It shall be the duty of the plaintiff in the event of such service to serve process and any other papers in duplicate, to notify the Secretary of State that service is being effected pursuant to this subsection, and to pay to the Secretary of State the sum of $50 for the use of the State of Delaware, which sum shall be taxed as a part of the costs in the proceeding if the plaintiff shall prevail therein.The Secretary of State shall maintain an alphabetical record of any such service setting forth the name of the plaintiff and defendant, the title, docket number and nature of the proceeding in which process has been served upon the Secretary, the fact that service has been effected pursuant to this subsection, the return date thereof and the day and hour when the service was made. The Secretary of State shall not be required to retain such information for a period longer than 5 years from the Secretary's receipt of the service of process.

§18-911. Service of process on unregistered foreign limited liability companies

(a) Any foreign limited liability company which shall do business in the State of Delaware without having registered under §18-902 of this title shall be deemed to have thereby appointed and constituted the Secretary of State of the State of Delaware its agent for the acceptance of legal process in any civil action, suit or proceeding against it in any state or federal court in the State of Delaware arising or growing out of any business done by it within the State of Delaware.The doing of business in the State of Delaware by such foreign limited liability company shall be a signification of the agreement of such foreign limited liability company that any such process when so served shall be of the same legal force and validity as if served upon an authorized manager or agent personally within the State of Delaware.

(b) Whenever the words "doing business," "the doing of business" or "business done in this State," by any such foreign limited liability company are used in this section, they shall mean the course or practice of carrying on any business activities in the State of Delaware, including, without limiting the generality of the foregoing, the solicitation of business or orders in the State of Delaware.

(c) In the event of service upon the Secretary of State in accordance with subsection (a) of this section, the Secretary of State shall forthwith notify the foreign limited liability company thereof by letter, certified mail, return receipt requested, directed to the foreign limited liability company at the address furnished to the Secretary of State by the plaintiff in such action, suit or proceeding. Such letter shall enclose a copy of the process and any other papers served upon the Secretary of State. It shall be the duty of the plaintiff in the event of such service to serve process and any other papers in duplicate, to notify the Secretary of State that service is being made pursuant to this subsection, and to pay to the Secretary of State the sum of $50 for the use of the State of Delaware, which sum shall be taxed as part of the costs in the proceeding, if the plaintiff shall prevail therein.The Secretary of State shall maintain an alphabetical record of any such process setting forth the name of the plaintiff and defendant, the title, docket number and nature of the proceeding in which process has been served upon the Secretary, the return date thereof, and the day and hour when the service was made. The Secretary of State shall not be required to retain such information for a period longer than 5 years from the receipt of the service of process.

SUBCHAPTER X. DERIVATIVE ACTIONS

§18-1001. Right to bring action

A member or an assignee of a limited liability company interest may bring an action in the Court of Chancery in the right of a limited liability company to recover a judgment in its favor if managers or members with authority to do so have refused to bring the action or if an effort to cause those managers or members to bring the action is not likely to succeed.

§18-1002. Proper plaintiff

In a derivative action, the plaintiff must be a member or an assignee of a limited liability company interest at the time of bringing the action and:

(1) At the time of the transaction of which the plaintiff complains; or

(2) The plaintiff's status as a member or an assignee of a limited liability company interest had devolved upon the plaintiff by operation of law or pursuant to the terms of a limited liability company agreement from a person who was a member or an assignee of a limited liability company interest at the time of the transaction.

§18-1003. Complaint

In a derivative action, the complaint shall set forth with particularity the effort, if any, of the plaintiff to secure initiation of the action by a manager or member or the reasons for not making the effort.

§18-1004. Expenses

If a derivative action is successful, in whole or in part, as a result of a judgment, compromise or settlement of any such action, the court may award the plaintiff reasonable expenses, including reasonable attorney's fees, from any recovery in any such action or from a limited liability company.

SUBCHAPTER XI. MISCELLANEOUS

§18-1101. Construction and application of chapter and limited liability company agreement

(a) The rule that statutes in derogation of the common law are to be strictly construed shall have no application to this chapter.

(b) It is the policy of this chapter to give the maximum effect to the principle of freedom of contract and to the enforceability of limited liability company agreements.

(c) To the extent that, at law or in equity, a member or manager or other person has duties (including fiduciary duties) and liabilities relating thereto to a limited liability company or to another member or manager:

(1) Any such member or manager or other person acting under a limited liability company agreement shall not be liable to the limited liability company or to any such other member or manager for the member's or manager's or other person's good faith reliance on the provisions of the limited liability company agreement; and

(2) The member's or manager's or other person's duties and liabilities may be expanded or restricted by provisions in a limited liability company agreement.

(d) Unless the context otherwise requires, as used herein, the singular shall include the plural and the plural may refer to only the singular. The use of any gender shall be applicable to all genders. The captions contained herein are for purposes of convenience only and shall not control or affect the construction of this chapter.

§18-1102. Short title

This chapter may be cited as the "Delaware Limited Liability Company Act."

§18-1103. Severability

If any provision of this chapter or its application to any person or circumstances is held invalid, the invalidity does not affect other provisions or applications of the chapter which can be given effect without the invalid provision or application, and to this end, the provisions of this chapter are severable.

§18-1104. Cases not provided for in this chapter

In any case not provided for in this chapter, the rules of law and equity, including the law merchant, shall govern.

§18-1105. Fees

(a) No document required to be filed under this chapter shall be effective until the applicable fee required by this section is paid. The following fees shall be paid to and collected by the Secretary of State for the use of the State of Delaware:

(1) Upon the receipt for filing of an application for reservation of name, an application for renewal of reservation or a notice of transfer or cancellation of reservation pursuant to §18-103(b) of this title, a fee in the amount of $75.

(2) Upon the receipt for filing of a certificate under §18-104(b) of this title, a fee in the amount of $50, upon the receipt for filing of a certificate under §18-104(c) of this title, a fee in the amount of $50 and a further fee of $2 for each limited liability company affected by such certificate, and upon the receipt for filing of a certificate under §18-104(d) of this title, a fee in the amount of $2.50.

(3) Upon the receipt for filing of a certificate of limited liability company domestication under §18-212 of this title, a certificate of transfer or a certificate of transfer and continuance under §18-213 of this title, a certificate of conversion to limited liability company under §18-214 of this title, a certificate of formation under §18-201 of this title, a certificate of amendment under §18-202 of this title, a certificate of cancellation under §18-203 of this title, a certificate of merger or consolidation under §18-209 of this title, a restated certificate of formation under §18-208 of this title, a certificate of amendment of a certificate of merger or consolidation under §18-209(d) of this title, a certificate of termination of a merger or consolidation under §18-209(d) of this title, a certificate of correction under §18-

211 of this title, or a certificate of revival under §18-1109 of this title, and upon the restoration of a domestic limited liability company or a foreign limited liability company under §18-1107(i) of this title, a fee in the amount of $50.

(4) For certifying copies of any paper on file as provided for by this chapter, a fee in the amount of $20 for each copy certified.

(5) The Secretary of State may issue photocopies or electronic image copies of instruments on file, as well as instruments, documents and other papers not on file, and for all such photocopies or electronic image copies, whether certified or not, a fee of $5 shall be paid for the 1st page and $1 for each additional page. The Secretary of State may also issue microfiche copies of instruments on file as well as instruments, documents and other papers not on file, and for each such microfiche a fee of $2 shall be paid therefor. Notwithstanding the State of Delaware's Freedom of Information Act or other provision of this Code granting access to public records, the Secretary of shall issue only photocopies, microfiche or electronic image copies of records in exchange for the fees described above.

(6) Upon the receipt for filing of an application for registration as a foreign limited liability company under §18-902 of this title, a certificate under §18-905 of this title or a certificate of cancellation under §18-906 of this title, a fee in the amount of $50.

(7) Upon the receipt for filing of a certificate under §18-904(c) of this title, a fee in the amount of $50, upon the receipt for filing of a certificate under §18-904(d) of this title, a fee in the amount of $50 and a further fee of $2 for each foreign limited liability company affected by such certificate, and upon the receipt for filing of a certificate under §18-904(e) of this title, a fee in the amount of $2.50.

(8) For preclearance of any document for filing, a fee in the amount of $250.

(9) For preparing and providing a written report of a record search, a fee in the amount of $30.

(10) For issuing any certificate of the Secretary of State, including but not limited to a certificate of good standing, other than a certification of a copy under paragraph (4) of this subsection, a fee in the amount of $20, except that for issuing any certificate of the Secretary of State that recites all of a limited liability company's filings with the Secretary of State, a fee of $100 shall be paid for each such certificate.

(11) For receiving and filing and/or indexing any certificate, affidavit, agreement or any other paper provided for by this chapter, for which no different fee is specifically prescribed, a fee in the amount of $25.

(12) The Secretary of State may in his or her discretion charge a fee of $25 for each check received for payment of any fee that is returned due to insufficient funds or the result of a stop payment order.

(b) In addition to those fees charged under subsection (a) of this section, there shall be collected by and paid to the Secretary of State the following:

(1) For all services described in subsection (a) of this section that are requested to be completed within 2 hours on the same day as the day of the request, an additional sum of up to $500;

(2) For all services described in subsection (a) of this section that are requested to be completed within the same day as the day of the request, an additional sum of up to $200; and

(3) For all services described in subsection (a) of this section that are requested to be completed within a 24-hour period from the time of the request, an additional sum of up to $100.The Secretary of State shall establish (and may from time to time amend) a schedule of specific fees payable pursuant to this subsection.

(c) The Secretary of State may in his or her discretion permit the extension of credit for the fees required by this section upon such terms as the secretary shall deem to be appropriate.

(d) The Secretary of State shall retain from the revenue collected from the fees required by this section a sum sufficient to provide at all times a fund of at least $500, but not more than $1,500, from which the secretary may refund any payment made pursuant to this section to the extent that it exceeds the fees required by this section.The funds shall be deposited in a financial institution which is a legal depository of State of Delaware moneys to the credit of the Secretary of State and shall be disbursable on order of the Secretary of State.

(e) Except as provided in this section, the fees of the Secretary of State shall be as provided in §2315 of Chapter 29.

§18-1106. Reserved power of State of Delaware to alter or repeal chapter

All provisions of this chapter may be altered from time to time or repealed and all rights of members and managers are subject to this reservation. Unless expressly stated to the contrary in this chapter, all amendments of this chapter shall apply to limited liability companies and members and managers whether or not existing as such at the time of the enactment of any such amendment.

§18-1107. Taxation of limited liability companies

(a) For purposes of any tax imposed by the State of Delaware or any instrumentality, agency or political subdivision of the State of Delaware, a limited liability company formed under this chapter or qualified to do business in the State of Delaware as a foreign limited liability company shall be classified as a partnership unless classified otherwise for federal income tax purposes, in which case the limited liability company shall be classified in the same manner as it is classified for federal income tax purposes. For purposes of any tax imposed by the State of Delaware or any instrumentality, agency or political subdivision of the State of Delaware, a member or an assignee of a member of a limited liability company formed under this chapter or qualified to do business in the State of Delaware as a foreign limited liability company shall be treated as either a resident or nonresident partner unless classified otherwise for federal income tax purposes, in which case the member or assignee of a member shall have the same status as such member or assignee of a member has for federal income tax purposes.

(b) Every domestic limited liability company and every foreign limited liability company registered to do business in the State of Delaware shall pay an annual tax, for the use of the State of Delaware, in the amount of $100.

(c) The annual tax shall be due and payable on the first day of June following the close of the calendar year or upon the cancellation of a certificate of formation. The Secretary of State shall receive the annual tax and pay over all taxes collected to the Department of Finance of the State of Delaware. If the annual tax remains unpaid after the due date, the tax shall bear interest at the rate of 1 and one-half percent for each month or portion thereof until fully paid.

(d) The Secretary of State shall, at least 60 days prior to the first day of June of each year, cause to be mailed to each domestic limited liability company and each foreign limited liability company required to comply with the provisions of this section in care of its registered agent in the State of Delaware an annual statement for the tax to be paid hereunder.

(e) In the event of neglect, refusal or failure on the part of any domestic limited liability company or foreign limited liability company to pay the annual tax to be paid hereunder on or before the 1st day of June in any year, such domestic limited liability company or foreign limited liability company shall pay the sum of $100 to be recovered by adding that amount to the annual tax and such additional sum shall become a part of the tax and shall be collected in the same manner and subject to the same penalties.

(f) In case any domestic limited liability company or foreign limited liability company shall fail to pay the annual tax due within the time required by this section, and in case the agent in charge of the registered office of any domestic limited liability company or foreign limited liability company upon whom process against such domestic limited liability company or foreign limited liability company may be served shall die, resign, refuse to act as such, from the State of Delaware or cannot with due diligence be found, it shall be lawful while default continues to serve process against such domestic limited liability company or foreign limited liability company upon the Secretary of State.Such service upon the Secretary of State shall be made in the manner and shall have the effect stated in §18-105 of this title in the case of a domestic limited liability company and §18-910 of this title in the case of a foreign limited liability company and shall be governed in all respects by said sections.

(g) The annual tax shall be a debt due from a domestic limited liability company or foreign limited liability company to the State of Delaware, for which an action at law may be maintained after the same shall have been in arrears for a period of 1 month. The tax shall also be a preferred debt in the case of insolvency.

(h) A domestic limited liability company or foreign limited liability company that neglects, refuses or fails to pay the annual tax when due shall cease to be in good standing as a domestic limited liability company or registered as a foreign limited liability company in the State of Delaware.

(i) A domestic limited liability company that has ceased to be in good standing or a foreign limited liability company that has ceased to be registered by reason of the failure to pay an annual tax shall be restored to and have the status of a domestic limited liability company in good standing or a foreign limited liability company that is registered in the State of Delaware upon the payment of the annual tax and all penalties and interest thereon for each year for which such domestic limited liability company or foreign limited liability company neglected, refused or failed to pay an annual tax. A fee as set forth in §18-1105(a)(3) of this title shall be paid at the time of restoration.

(j) On the motion of the Attorney General or upon request of the Secretary of State, whenever any annual tax due under this chapter from any domestic limited liability company or foreign limited liability company shall have remained in arrears for a period of 3 months after the tax shall have become payable, the Attorney General may apply to the Court of Chancery, by petition in the name of the State of Delaware, on 5 days' notice to such domestic limited liability company or foreign limited liability company, which notice may be served in such manner as the Court may direct, for an injunction to restrain such domestic limited liability company or foreign limited liability company from the transaction of any business within the State of Delaware or elsewhere, until the payment of the annual tax, and all penalties and interest due thereon and the cost of the application which shall be fixed by the Court.The Court of Chancery may grant the injunction, if a proper case appears, and upon ranting and service of the injunction, such domestic limited liability company or foreign limited liability company thereafter shall not transact any business until the injunction shall be dissolved.

(k) A domestic limited liability company that has ceased to be in good standing by reason of its neglect, refusal or failure to pay an annual tax shall remain a domestic limited liability company formed under this chapter. The Secretary of State shall not accept for filing any certificate (except a certificate of resignation of a registered agent when a successor registered agent is not being appointed) required or permitted by this chapter to be filed in respect of any domestic limited liability company or foreign limited liability company which has neglected, refused or failed to pay an annual tax, and shall not issue any certificate of good standing with respect to such domestic limited liability company or foreign limited liability company, unless or until such domestic limited liability company or foreign limited liability company shall have been restored to and have the status of a domestic limited liability company in good standing or a foreign limited liability company duly registered in the State of Delaware.

(l) A domestic limited liability company that has ceased to be in good standing or a foreign limited liability company that has ceased to be registered in the State of Delaware by reason of its neglect, refusal or failure to pay an annual tax may not maintain any action, suit or proceeding in any court of the State of Delaware until such domestic limited liability company or foreign limited liability company has been restored to and has the status of a domestic limited liability company or foreign limited liability company in good standing or duly registered in the State of Delaware. An action, suit or proceeding may not be maintained in any court of the State of Delaware by any successor or assignee of such domestic limited liability company or foreign limited liability company on any right, claim or demand arising out the transaction of business by such domestic limited liability company after it has ceased to be in good standing or a foreign limited liability company that has ceased to be registered in the State of Delaware until such domestic limited liability company or foreign limited liability company, or any person that has acquired all or substantially all of its assets, has paid any annual tax then due and payable, together with penalties and interest thereon.

(m) The neglect, refusal or failure of a domestic limited liability company or foreign limited liability company to pay an annual tax shall not impair the validity on any contract, deed, mortgage, security interest, lien or act or such domestic limited liability company or foreign limited liability company or prevent such domestic limited liability company or foreign limited liability company from defending any action, suit or proceeding with any court of the State of Delaware.

(n) A member or manager of a domestic limited liability company or foreign limited liability company is not liable for the debts, obligations or liabilities of such domestic limited liability company or foreign limited liability company solely by reason of the neglect, refusal or failure of such domestic limited liability company or foreign limited liability company to pay an annual tax or by reason of such domestic limited liability company or foreign limited liability company ceasing to be in good standing or duly registered.

§18-1108. Cancellation of certificate of formation for failure to pay taxes

(a) The certificate of formation of a domestic limited liability company shall be deemed to be canceled if the domestic limited liability company shall fail to pay the annual tax due under §18-1107 of this title for a period of 3 years from the date it is due, such cancellation to be effective on the third anniversary of such due date.

(b) On or before October 31 of each calendar year, the Secretary of State shall publish once in at least 1 newspaper of general circulation in the State of Delaware a list of those domestic limited liability companies whose certificates of formation were canceled on June 1 of such calendar year pursuant to §18-1108(a) of this title.

§18-1109. Revival of domestic limited liability company

(a) A domestic limited liability company whose certificate of formation has been canceled pursuant to §18-104(d) or §18-1108(a) of this title may be revived by filing in the office of the Secretary of State a certificate of revival accompanied by the payment of the fee required by §18-1105(a)(3) of this title and payment of the annual tax due under §18-1107 of this title and all penalties and interest thereon for each year for which such domestic limited liability company neglected, refused or failed to pay such annual tax, including each year between the cancellation of its certificate of formation and its revival. The certificate of revival shall set forth:

(1) The name of the limited liability company at the time its certificate of formation was canceled and, if such name is not available at the time of revival, the name under which the limited liability company is to be revived;

(2) The date of filing of the original certificate of formation of the limited liability company;

(3) The address of the limited liability company's registered office in the State of Delaware and the name and address of the limited liability company's registered agent in the State of Delaware;

(4) A statement that the certificate of revival is filed by 1 or more persons authorized to execute and file the certificate of revival to revive the limited liability company; and

(5) Any other matters the persons executing the certificate of revival determine to include therein.

(b) The certificate of revival shall be deemed to be an amendment to the certificate of formation of the limited liability company, and the limited liability company shall not be required to take any further action to amend its certificate of formation under §18-202 of this title with respect to the matters set forth in the certificate of revival.

(c) Upon the filing of a certificate of revival, a limited liability company shall be revived with the same force and effect as if its certificate of formation had not been canceled pursuant to §18-104(d) or §18-1108(a) of this title.Such revival shall validate all contracts, acts, matters and things made, done and performed by the limited liability company, its members, managers, employees and agents during the time when its certificate of formation was canceled pursuant to §18-104(d) or §18-1108(a) of this title, with the same force and effect and to all intents and purposes as if the certificate of formation had remained in full force and effect. All real and personal property, and all rights and interests, which belonged to the limited liability company at the time its certificate of formation was canceled pursuant to §18-104(d) or §18-1108(a) of this title or which were acquired by the limited liability company following the cancellation of its certificate of formation pursuant to §18-104(d) or §18-1108(a) of this title, and which were not disposed of prior to the time of its revival, shall be vested in the limited liability company its revival as fully as they were held by the limited liability company at, and after, as the case may be, the time its certificate of formation was canceled pursuant to §18-104(d) or §18-1108(a) of this title.After its revival, the limited liability company shall be as exclusively liable for all contracts, acts, matters and things made, done or performed in its name and on its behalf by its members, managers, employees and agents prior to its revival as if its certificate of formation had at all times remained in full force and effect.

Appendix D

SAMPLE OPERATING AGREEMENT

OPERATING AGREEMENT
OF
XYZ LIMITED LIABILITY COMPANY

This Operating Agreement made and entered into this ____________ day of ______________, 19__, by and between ______________________ and ____________________, whereby the parties hereto agree to form a limited liability company (hereinafter "Company") upon the following terms and conditions:

Article I.
Formation

1. Organization — On ____________, 19__, the Members organized the Company as a limited liability company pursuant to the State X Limited Liability Company Act contained in (statute or act reference here) and delivered Articles of Organization to (the Secretary of State or other appropriate state agency).

2. Agreement — For and in consideration of the mutual covenants herein contained and for other good and valuable consideration, the receipt and sufficiency of which is hereby acknowledged, the Members executing this Agreement hereby agree to its terms and conditions, as it may from time to time be amended according to its terms. It is the express intention of the Members that this Agreement shall be the sole source of agreement of the parties and shall not be amended except in accordance with its terms.

3. Name and Office — The name of the Company is XYZ Limited Liability Company, and all business of the Company shall be conducted under that name. The principal office and place of business of the Company shall be located at ______________________________________.
The principal office may be moved to any location in the United States

upon agreement of the parties and filing the appropriate documents under the Act.

4. Term — The Company shall commence on the ___________ day of _______________, 19__ and shall continue until the Company is dissolved and terminated in accordance with the Act or this Agreement.

5. Registered Office and Registered Agent — The Company's initial registered office shall be located at ___________________________ and its initial registered agent for service of process shall be ____________________________, located at the registered office. The registered office and/or registered agent may be changed from time to time through appropriate filings with the Secretary of State (or other appropriate state agency).

6. Purpose — The purpose of this Company shall be to (state general purpose of business here), and to engage in any lawful act or activity related thereto for which limited liability companies may be formed pursuant to the Act.

Article II.
Definitions

For purposes of this Operating Agreement, unless the context clearly indicates otherwise, the following terms shall have the following meanings:

1. Act — The Limited Liability Company Act of the State of X and all amendments thereto.

2. Agreement — This Operating Agreement and all of its terms and amendments.

3. Articles — The Articles of Organization of the Company as properly adopted and amended from time to time by the Members and filed with the Secretary of State (or appropriate state agency).

4. Capital Account — The account maintained for a Member as determined in accordance with this Agreement.

5. Company — The XYZ Limited Liability Company, a limited liability company formed under the laws of State X, and any successor limited liability company.

6. Company Liability — Any enforceable debt or obligation for which the Company is liable or which is secured by any property owned by the Company.

7. Contribution — Any contribution of property made by or on behalf of a new or existing Member as consideration for a membership interest.

8. Distribution — A transfer of property to a member on account of a membership interest as described herein.

9. Dissociation — Any action which causes a person to cease to be a member as described herein.

10. Initial Contribution — The contribution agreed to be made by the initial members as described herein.

11. Initial Members — Those persons identified in Exhibit A, which is attached hereto and incorporated herein by reference, who have executed this Agreement.

12. Member-Manager — A member selected to manage the affairs of the Company in accordance with the provisions contained herein.

13. Member — An initial member, substituted member or additional member, including, unless the context expressly indicates to the contrary, a member-manager or assignee.

14. Membership Interest — The rights of a member and allocations of the profits, losses, gains, deductions, and credits of the Company.

15. Property — Any property, real or personal, tangible or intangible, including goodwill, money and any legal or equitable interest in such property. Property, for these purposes, will not include services performed or promises to perform services in the future.

16. Taxable Year — The taxable year of the Company shall be the calendar year. The term "fiscal year" shall have the same meaning.

Article III.
Capital Contributions and Capital Accounts

1. Initial Capital Contribution — Each Member shall contribute such amount as is set forth in Exhibit A attached hereto to the capital of the Company. The value of the contributions shall be as set forth in Exhibit A. No interest shall accrue on any contribution and no Member shall have the right to withdraw or be repaid any contribution except as provided in this Agreement.

2. Additional Capital — In addition to the initial contributions, the Managers may determine from time to time that additional contributions are needed to enable the Company to conduct its business. In this event and upon notification to the Members, the Members may contribute a proportionate share of any additional capital that is necessary for the operation of the Company.

3. Company Borrowings — Upon unanimous consent of the Members, the Company may borrow sums for Company purposes from any source, including any Member, provided that the amount of money so advanced shall be as a loan to the Company and shall not be considered an increase in the Member's capital account nor increase the Member's share in the profits or losses of the company. No Member shall be required to guarantee any note, mortgage or other evidence of indebtedness in connection with the operation of the Company, unless all Members are required to guarantee such indebtedness.

4. Maintenance of Capital Accounts — The Company shall establish and maintain a Capital Account for each Member and Assignee.

5. Distribution of Assets — If the Company at any time distributes any property (other than money) in-kind to any Member, the Capital Account of each Member shall be adjusted to account for that Member's allocable share of the net profits or net losses that would have been realized by the Company had it sold the assets that were distributed at their respective fair market values immediately prior to their distribution.

Article IV.
Names and Addresses of Members and Member-Managers

The names and addresses of the initial Members and the designation of Member-Managers are set out in Exhibit A, which is attached hereto and incorporated herein by reference.

Article V.
Rights and Duties of Members

1. Voting — All Members shall be entitled to vote on any matter submitted to a vote of the Members.

2. Management Restrictions — No Member shall assume any liability in the name of the Company for the account or benefit of any other firm, person or corporation, or use the name, credit or assets of the Company for its personal benefit or that of any other person, firm, or corporation, without the written consent of all other members.

(a) No member shall, without the written consent of all other Members, compromise or release any claim of or debt due the Company except upon payment in full.

(b) No member shall, without the written consent of all other members, borrow money in the name of the Company.

(c) No member shall, without the written consent of all other Members, sell, lease or mortgage any Company real estate or interest therein or any personal property of the Company, or enter into any contract for such purpose.

3. Liability of Members — No Member shall be liable as either a Member or as a Manager for any debt, obligation or liability of the Company, whether arising in contract, tort, or otherwise, or for the acts or omissions of any other Member, Manager, agent or employee of the Company.

4. Indemnification — The Company shall indemnify the Members and agents for all costs, losses, liabilities, and damages paid or accrued by such Member (either as a Member or as a Manager) or agent in connection with the business of the Company, to the fullest extent provided or allowed by the laws of (insert state here).

Article VI.
Rights and Duties of Managers

1. Management of Company Business — The ordinary and usual decisions concerning the business affairs of the Company shall be made by the Managers, each of whom shall be a Member. Except for situations where the approval of the Members is required by this Agreement or applicable law, the Managers shall have full and complete authority and power to manage and control the business, affairs and properties of the Company and do any and all acts necessary and incident thereto. At any time when there is more than one Manager, any action taken shall require the approval of a majority of the Managers. Each Manager has the power, on behalf of the Company, to do all things necessary to carry out the business and affairs of the Company, including, but not limited to, the following:

a. hiring and appointing employees and agents of the Company, structuring their duties, and determining compensation therefor;

b. compensating Members and employees for services rendered to the Company;

c. instituting, prosecuting and defending any proceeding in the Company's name;

d. purchasing, receiving, leasing or otherwise acquiring, the ownership, holding, improvement, use and otherwise dealing with Property, wherever located;

e. selling, conveying, mortgaging, pledging, leasing, exchanging, and other disposition of Property;

f. entering into contracts and guaranties; incurring liabilities; borrowing money, issuing notes, bonds, and other obligations; and the securing of any of its obligations by mortgage or pledge of any of its Property or income;

g. lending money, investing Company funds, and receiving and holding Property as security for repayment:

h. paying out pensions and establishing pension plans, pension trusts, profit sharing plans, and benefit and incentive plans for Members, employees, and agents of the Company;

i. purchasing life insurance on the life of any of its Members or employees for the benefit of the Company;

j. participating in partnership agreements, joint ventures, or other associations of any kind with any person or persons;

k. indemnifying Members in accordance with the terms of this Agreement or under law.

2. Number, Election and Term of Manager — There shall be (x number of) Managers who must be Members of the Company. This number shall be fixed from time to time by the unanimous vote of the Members. Managers shall be elected by the affirmative vote of a majority of the Members. No Member-Manager shall have any contractual right to such position. The initial Managers and number of votes allocated to each are set out in Exhibit A.

3. Resignation — Any Manager may resign at any time by giving (x number of days) written notice to the Members. Said resignation shall not affect the Manager's rights as a Member and shall not constitute a withdrawal of the Member.

4. Removal — Any Manager may be removed for gross negligence, self-dealing, embezzlement, fraud or any other act that is deemed by the Members to be harmful to the Company, by an affirmative vote of a majority of the Members.

5. Vacancies — Any vacancy in the number of Managers shall be filled as soon as practicable by a majority vote of the Members.

6. Compensation — The compensation, if any, of the Managers shall be fixed from time to time by an affirmative vote of a majority of the Members. Each Manager shall be reimbursed all reasonable expenses incurred in managing the Company.

Article VII.
Allocations and Distributions

1. Allocation of Profits, Losses and Equity —

(a) Except as may be required by Code section 704(c), net profits, net losses, and other items of income, gain, loss, deduction and credit shall be apportioned among the Members in proportion to their Capital Accounts. The respective equity interests of the Members in the Company shall be allocated equally among the Members.

(b) All profits and losses of the Company shall be determined in accordance with the accounting methods followed by the Company for federal income tax purposes.

(c) The profits and losses of the Company arising from the sale or other disposition of all or substantially all of the assets of the Company shall be apportioned among the Members in proportion to their Capital Accounts.

2. Net Company Receipts (Cash Flow) —

(a) Net Company receipts shall be determined for each fiscal year as soon as possible after the end of such fiscal year and shall be distributed in accordance with this Article.

(b) Net Company receipts for a particular fiscal year shall include all profits and losses of the Company for such fiscal year, except profits and losses for such fiscal year arising from the sale of all or substantially all of the assets of the Company, and shall be determined by adjusting such profits and losses as follows:

(i) depreciation of buildings, improvements and personal property shall not be considered as a deduction.

(ii) amortization of any financing fee shall not be considered as a deduction.

(iii) amortization of any loan shall be considered as a deduction.

(iv) if the members unanimously agree, a reasonable reserve shall be deducted to provide for working capital needs, funds for improvements or replacements or for any other contingencies of the Company.

(v) any amounts paid by the Company for capital expenditures or replacements shall be considered as a deduction, except that amounts withdrawn from any reserve fund for capital expenditures or replacements shall not be considered as a deduction.

(vi) capital contributions to the Company, the proceeds of any mortgage financing or other loans, the profits and losses of any sale, exchange, condemnation, damage or destruction by fire or other casualty, whether insured or uninsured, or other disposition of all or any part of the Company's assets shall not be included in net Company receipts.

(c) The foregoing provisions shall not be construed to prohibit distributions of net Company receipts for any fiscal year more often than annually and in anticipation of the year end determination thereof. If net Company receipts for any fiscal year are distributed in anticipation of the year end determination thereof, such distribution shall be subject to year end adjustment.

(d) The Members shall contribute in equal shares the negative amount of net Company receipts calculated pursuant to this Article.

Article VIII.
Fiscal Matters

1. Books and Records — At the Company's expense, the Managers shall maintain full and accurate books and records of the Company, at its principal office, necessary for recording the Company's business and affairs. At a minimum, the Company shall keep and maintain the following records:

(a) A current list of the full name and last known business address of each current Member and former Member;

(b) A copy of the Articles of Organization and all amendments thereto, together with executed copies of any powers of attorney pursuant to which any amendment has been executed;

(c) Copies of the Company's federal, state, and local income tax returns and reports, if any, for the three most recent years;

(d) Any financial statements of the Company for the three most recent years;

(e) Copies of this Agreement including all amendments thereto.

2. Inspection — Each Member, Manager and their duly authorized representatives shall, at reasonable times during regular business hours, have access to and may inspect and copy Company books and records.

3. Fiscal Year — The fiscal year of the Company shall be the calendar year.

4. Accounting Principles — The records of the Company shall be maintained on a cash receipts and disbursements method of accounting.

5. Reports — Annual statements showing the income and expenses of the Company for the fiscal year and the balance thereof as of the end of such year shall be prepared by any firm of independent certified public accountants selected by the Managers. The Company shall have an annual audit of its books by such accountants. Within 90 days after the end of each fiscal year of the Company, each Member shall be furnished copies of such statements of income and expenses and of such balance sheet, together with a certificate from the Company's accountants covering the results of such audit.

6. Tax Matters — All decisions as to accounting and tax matters shall be made in accordance with generally accepted accounting principles consistently applied. The Managers shall prepare or cause to be prepared a federal and state income tax return for each fiscal year of the Company. In connection therewith, the Managers may make any tax elections for the Company allowed under the Internal Revenue Code or the tax laws of any state or other jurisdiction having taxing jurisdiction over the Company.

7. Accounting Between Members — Each Member shall, upon reasonable request, give to the other Members a true accounting of all transactions relating to the business of the Company and full information of all letters, accounts, writings and other things which shall come into its hands or to its knowledge concerning the business of the Company.

Article IX.
Dissociation of a Member

1. Dissociation — A person shall cease to be a Member upon the happening of any of the following events:

a. The Member becomes bankrupt, meaning he has filed a petition in bankruptcy, voluntarily taken advantage of any bankruptcy or insolvency laws, an adjudication of bankruptcy has been entered, or 60 days after the filing of a petition or answer proposing the adjudication of such Member as bankrupt, unless such pleading is discharged or denied and continues to be challenged by such Member; or,

b. The death of the Member or the entry of an order by a court of competent jurisdiction adjudicating the Member incompetent to manage his estate; or

c. In the case of a Member that is a corporation, the filing of a certificate of dissolution, or its equivalent, for the corporation or the revocation of its charter; or

d. In the case of an estate, the distribution by the fiduciary of the estate's entire interest in the limited liability company.

2. Expulsion — Expulsion of a Member from the Company may occur if a Member is economically unable to perform his duties and obligations to the Company as contained in this Agreement, or fails for any other reason to fulfill such obligations, for a period of (x amount of time) and other Members unanimously vote to expel such Member from the Company. Such expulsion shall be effective (x number of days) from the date that written notice is delivered to the expelled Member.

3. Sale of Membership Interest to Remaining Members — Upon retirement or expulsion of a Member, the remaining Members shall have an equal right to purchase such Member's interest in the Company. The purchase price of such Member's interest shall be the fair market value of such interest on the date of retirement or expulsion.

4. Sale of Membership Interest to Third Party — Upon the retirement or expulsion of a Member and the failure of the remaining

Members to exercise their right to purchase same, the retired or expelled Member may sell or otherwise dispose of his interest to a third party, but first must give notice to the remaining Members of any such sale or disposition, which notice shall set forth the name of the party to whom such interest is to be sold and the price and other terms of sale. The remaining Members shall have (x number of days) from the date of such notice to purchase said interest at the price and upon the terms offered by or to the third party. In the alternative, the remaining Members may elect within (x number of days) to terminate this Agreement, dissolve the Company and distribute its assets.

5. Transferee Not Member in Absence of Consent — Notwithstanding anything contained herein to the contrary, if a majority of the remaining members holding a majority interest of capital and profits interests in the Company do not approve in writing to the proposed sale or transfer of the transferring Member's interest in the Company, or any portion thereof, to a transferee who is not a Member immediately prior to the sale or transfer, then the proposed transferee shall have no rights to become a Member of the Company.

Article X.
Admission of Assignees and Additional Members

1. Additional Members — From the date of this Agreement, any person or entity acceptable to the Members may become a Member in this Company either by the issuance by the Company of Membership Interests for such consideration as the Members by their unanimous votes shall determine, or as a transferee of a Member's interest in the Company or any portion thereof, subject to the terms and conditions of this agreement. No new Members shall be entitled to any retroactive allocation of gains, losses, income, deductions, or credits incurred by the Company.

2. Rights of Assignees — The Assignee of a Membership Interest has no right to participate in the management of the business and affairs of the Company or to become a Member. The Assignee is only entitled to receive the distributions and return of capital and to be allocated the net profits and net losses attributable the Membership Interest.

Article XI.
Dissolution and Winding Up

1. Dissolution — The Company shall be dissolved and its affairs wound up, upon the occurrence of any of the following events:

a. Upon unanimous written agreement of all of the Members;

b. Upon the dissolution, retirement, expulsion, bankruptcy or other occurrence creating a disassociation of the Company, unless the business of the Company is continued by the consent of other Members holding a majority of capital and profits interests in the Company within (x number of days) of the occurrence of the event and there are (x number of members) remaining.

2. Winding Up and Certificate of Dissolution — The winding up of the Company shall be completed when all debts, liabilities, and obligations of the limited liability company have been paid and discharged or reasonably adequate provision therefor has been made and all of the remaining property and assets of the Company have been distributed to the members. Upon the completion of winding up of the Company, a certificate of dissolution shall be delivered to the Secretary of State for filing. The certificate of dissolution shall set forth the information required by the Act.

Article XII.
Miscellaneous Provisions

1. Amendment — This Agreement may be amended at any time by the unanimous vote of the Members. No such amendment or variation of the terms of this Agreement shall be valid unless made in writing and signed by all Members.

2. Integration — This Agreement embodies the entire agreement and understanding among the parties relating to the subject matter hereof, and supersedes all prior agreements and understandings relating to such subject matter.

3. Separability — In case any one or more of the provisions contained in this Agreement or an application thereof shall be invalid, illegal or unenforceable in any respect, the validity, legality and enforceability of any remaining provisions contained herein and any other application thereof shall in no way be affected or impaired thereby.

4. Applicable Law — This Agreement and the rights of the parties hereto shall be governed by and construed and enforced in accordance with the laws of (insert state here).

IN WITNESS WHEREOF, we have hereunto set our hands and seals on the date set forth beside our names.

XYZ Limited Liability Company.

(Signatures of Members).

Appendix E

CHECK-THE-BOX REGULATIONS

DEPARTMENT OF THE TREASURY

Title 26–Internal Revenue Service

[Reg.] Sec. 301.7701-1 Classification of organizations for federal tax purposes.

(a) Organizations for federal tax purposes–(1) In general. The Internal Revenue Code prescribes the classification of various organizations for federal tax purposes. Whether an organization is an entity separate from its owners for federal tax purposes is a matter of federal tax law and does not depend on whether the organization is recognized as an entity under local law.

(2) Certain joint undertakings give rise to entities for federal tax purposes. A joint venture or other contractual arrangement may create a separate entity for federal tax purposes if the participants carry on a trade, business, financial operation, or venture and divide the profits therefrom. For example, a separate entity exists for federal tax purposes if co-owners of an apartment building lease space and in addition provide services to the occupants either directly or through an agent. Nevertheless, a joint undertaking merely to share expenses does not create a separate entity for federal tax purposes. For example, if two or more persons jointly construct a ditch merely to drain surface water from their properties, they have not created a separate entity for federal tax purposes. Similarly, mere co-ownership of property that is maintained, kept in repair, and rented or leased does not constitute a separate entity for federal tax purposes. For example, if an individual owner, or tenants in common, of farm property lease it to a farmer for a cash rental or a share of the crops, they do not necessarily create a separate entity for federal tax purposes.

(3) Certain local law entities not recognized. An entity formed under local law is not always recognized as a separate entity for federal tax purposes. For example, an organization wholly owned by

a State is not recognized as a separate entity for federal tax purposes if it is an integral part of the State. Similarly, tribes incorporated under section 17 of the Indian Reorganization Act of 1934, as amended, 25 U.S.C. 477, or under section 3 of the Oklahoma Indian Welfare Act, as amended, 25 U.S.C. 503, are not recognized as separate entities for federal tax purposes.

(4) Single owner organizations. Under Secs. 301.7701-2 and 301.7701-3, certain organizations that have a single owner can choose to be recognized or disregarded as entities separate from their owners.

(b) Classification of organizations. The classification of organizations that are recognized as separate entities is determined under Secs. 301.7701-2, 301.7701-3, and 301.7701-4 unless a provision of the Internal Revenue Code (such as section 860A addressing Real Estate Mortgage Investment Conduits (REMICs)) provides for special treatment of that organization. For the classification of organizations as trusts, see Sec. 301.7701-4. That section provides that trusts generally do not have associates or an objective to carry on business for profit. Sections 301.7701-2 and 301.7701-3 provide rules for classifying organizations that are not classified as trusts.

(c) Qualified cost sharing arrangements. A qualified cost sharing arrangement that is described in Sec. 1.482-7 of this chapter and any arrangement that is treated by the Commissioner as a qualified cost sharing arrangement under Sec. 1.482-7 of this chapter is not recognized as a separate entity for purposes of the Internal Revenue Code. See Sec. 1.482-7 of this chapter for the proper treatment of qualified cost sharing arrangements.

(d) Domestic and foreign entities. For purposes of this section and Secs. 301.7701-2 and 301.7701-3, an entity is a domestic entity if it is created or organized in the United States or under the law of the United States or of any State; an entity is foreign if it is not domestic. See sections 7701(a)(4) and (a)(5).

(e) State. For purposes of this section and Sec. 301.7701-2, the term State includes the District of Columbia.

(f) Effective date. The rules of this section are effective as of January 1, 1997.

[T.D. 8697, 61 FR 66588, Dec. 18, 1996]

[Reg.] Sec. 301.7701-2 Business entities; definitions.

(a) Business entities. For purposes of this section and Sec. 301.7701-3, a business entity is any entity recognized for federal tax purposes (including an entity with a single owner that may be disregarded as an entity separate from its owner under Sec. 301.7701-3) that is not properly classified as a trust under Sec. 301.7701-4 or otherwise subject to special treatment under the Internal Revenue Code. A business entity with two or more members is classified for federal tax purposes as either a corporation or a partnership. A business entity with only one owner is classified as a corporation or is disregarded; if the entity is disregarded, its activities are treated in the same manner as a sole proprietorship, branch, or division of the owner.

(b) Corporations. For federal tax purposes, the term corporation means–

(1) A business entity organized under a Federal or State statute, or under a statute of a federally recognized Indian tribe, if the statute describes or refers to the entity as incorporated or as a corporation, body corporate, or body politic;

(2) An association (as determined under Sec. 301.7701-3);

(3) A business entity organized under a State statute, if the statute describes or refers to the entity as a joint-stock company or joint-stock association;

(4) An insurance company;

(5) A State-chartered business entity conducting banking activities, if any of its deposits are insured under the Federal Deposit Insurance Act, as amended, 12 U.S.C. 1811 et seq., or a similar federal statute;

(6) A business entity wholly owned by a State or any political subdivision thereof;

(7) A business entity that is taxable as a corporation under a provision of the Internal Revenue Code other than section 7701(a)(3); and

(8) Certain foreign entities–(i) In general. Except as provided in paragraphs (b)(8)(ii) and (d) of this section, the following business entities formed in the following jurisdictions:

American Samoa, Corporation
Argentina, Sociedad Anonima
Australia, Public Limited Company
Austria, Aktiengesellschaft
Barbados, Limited Company
Belgium, Societe Anonyme
Belize, Public Limited Company
Bolivia, Sociedad Anonima
Brazil, Sociedade Anonima
Canada, Corporation and Company
Chile, Sociedad Anonima
People's Republic of China, Gufen Youxian Gongsi
Republic of China (Taiwan), Ku-fen Yu-hsien Kung-szu
Colombia, Sociedad Anonima
Costa Rica, Sociedad Anonima
Cyprus, Public Limited Company
Czech Republic, Akciova Spolecnost
Denmark, Aktieselskab
Ecuador, Sociedad Anonima or Compania Anonima
Egypt, Sharikat Al-Mossahamah
El Salvador, Sociedad Anonima
Finland, Julkinen Osakeyhtio/Publikt Aktiebolag
France, Societe Anonyme
Germany, Aktiengesellschaft
Greece, Anonymos Etairia
Guam, Corporation
Guatemala, Sociedad Anonima
Guyana, Public Limited Company
Honduras, Sociedad Anonima
Hong Kong, Public Limited Company
Hungary, Reszvenytarsasag
Iceland, Hlutafelag

India, Public Limited Company
Indonesia, Perseroan Terbuka
Ireland, Public Limited Company
Israel, Public Limited Company
Italy, Societa per Azioni
Jamaica, Public Limited Company
Japan, Kabushiki Kaisha
Kazakstan, Ashyk Aktsionerlik Kogham
Republic of Korea, Chusik Hoesa
Liberia, Corporation
Luxembourg, Societe Anonyme
Malaysia, Berhad
Malta, Public Limited Company
Mexico, Sociedad Anonima
Morocco, Societe Anonyme
Netherlands, Naamloze Vennootschap
New Zealand, Limited Company
Nicaragua, Compania Anonima
Nigeria, Public Limited Company
Northern Mariana Islands, Corporation
Norway, Allment Aksjeselskap
Pakistan, Public Limited Company
Panama, Sociedad Anonima
Paraguay, Sociedad Anonima
Peru, Sociedad Anonima
Philippines, Stock Corporation
Poland, Spolka Akcyjna
Portugal, Sociedade Anonima
Puerto Rico, Corporation
Romania, Societe pe Actiuni
Russia, Otkrytoye Aktsionernoy Obshchestvo
Saudi Arabia, Sharikat Al-Mossahamah
Singapore, Public Limited Company
Slovak Republic, Akciova Spolocnost
South Africa, Public Limited Company
Spain, Sociedad Anonima
Surinam, Naamloze Vennootschap
Sweden, Publika Aktiebolag
Switzerland, Aktiengesellschaft
Thailand, Borisat Chamkad (Mahachon)

Trinidad and Tobago, Limited Company
Tunisia, Societe Anonyme
Turkey, Anonim Sirket
Ukraine, Aktsionerne Tovaristvo Vidkritogo Tipu
United Kingdom, Public Limited Company
United States Virgin Islands, Corporation
Uruguay, Sociedad Anonima
Venezuela, Sociedad Anonima or Compania Anonima

(ii) Clarification of list of corporations in paragraph (b)(8)(i) of this section–(A) Exceptions in certain cases. The following entities will not be treated as corporations under paragraph (b)(8)(i) of this section:

(1) With regard to Canada, a Nova Scotia Unlimited Liability Company (or any other company or corporation all of whose owners have unlimited liability pursuant to federal or provincial law).

(2) With regard to India, a company deemed to be a public limited company solely by operation of section 43A(1) (relating to corporate ownership of the company), section 43A(1A) (relating to annual average turnover), or section 43A(1B) (relating to ownership interests in other companies) of the Companies Act, 1956 (or any combination of these), provided that the organizational documents of such deemed public limited company continue to meet the requirements of section 3(1)(iii) of the Companies Act, 1956.

(3) With regard to Malaysia, a Sendirian Berhad.

(B) Inclusions in certain cases. With regard to Mexico, the term Sociedad Anonima includes a Sociedad Anonima that chooses to apply the variable capital provision of Mexican corporate law (Sociedad Anonima de Capital Variable).

(iii) Public companies. For purposes of paragraph (b)(8)(i) of this section, with regard to Cyprus, Hong Kong, and Jamaica, the term Public Limited Company includes any Limited Company that is not defined as a private company under the corporate laws of those jurisdictions. In all other cases, where the term Public Limited Company is not defined, that term shall include any Limited Company defined as a public company under the corporate laws of the relevant jurisdiction.

(iv) Limited companies. For purposes of this paragraph (b)(8), any reference to a Limited Company includes, as the case may be, companies limited by shares and companies limited by guarantee.

(v) Multilingual countries. Different linguistic renderings of the name of an entity listed in paragraph (b)(8)(i) of this section shall be disregarded. For example, an entity formed under the laws of Switzerland as a Societe Anonyme will be a corporation and treated in the same manner as an Aktiengesellschaft.

(c) Other business entities. For federal tax purposes–

(1) The term partnership means a business entity that is not a corporation under paragraph (b) of this section and that has at least two members.

(2) Wholly owned entities–(i) In general. A business entity that has a single owner and is not a corporation under paragraph (b) of this section is disregarded as an entity separate from its owner.

(ii) Special rule for certain business entities. If the single owner of a business entity is a bank (as defined in section 581), then the special rules applicable to banks will continue to apply to the single owner as if the wholly owned entity were a separate entity.

(d) Special rule for certain foreign business entities–(1) In general. Except as provided in paragraph (d)(3) of this section, a foreign business entity described in paragraph (b)(8)(i) of this section will not be treated as a corporation under paragraph (b)(8)(i) of this section if–

(i) The entity was in existence on May 8, 1996;

(ii) The entity's classification was relevant (as defined in Sec. 301.7701-3(d)) on May 8, 1996;

(iii) No person (including the entity) for whom the entity's classification was relevant on May 8, 1996, treats the entity as a corporation for purposes of filing such person's federal income tax returns, information returns, and withholding documents for the taxable year including May 8, 1996;

(iv) Any change in the entity's claimed classification within the sixty months prior to May 8, 1996, occurred solely as a result of a change in the organizational documents of the entity, and the entity and all members of the entity recognized the federal tax consequences of any change in the entity's classification within the sixty months prior to May 8, 1996;

(v) A reasonable basis (within the meaning of section 6662) existed on May 8, 1996, for treating the entity as other than a corporation; and

(vi) Neither the entity nor any member was notified in writing on or before May 8, 1996, that the classification of the entity was under examination (in which case the entity's classification will be determined in the examination).

(2) Binding contract rule. If a foreign business entity described in paragraph (b)(8)(i) of this section is formed after May 8, 1996, pursuant to a written binding contract (including an accepted bid to develop a project) in effect on May 8, 1996, and all times thereafter, in which the parties agreed to engage (directly or indirectly) in an active and substantial business operation in the jurisdiction in which the entity is formed, paragraph (d)(1) of this section will be applied to that entity by substituting the date of the entity's formation for May 8, 1996.

(3) Termination of grandfather status–(i) In general. An entity that is not treated as a corporation under paragraph (b)(8)(i) of this section by reason of paragraph (d)(1) or (d)(2) of this section will be treated permanently as a corporation under paragraph (b)(8)(i) of this section from the earliest of:

(A) The effective date of an election to be treated as an association under Sec. 301.7701-3;

(B) A termination of the partnership under section 708(b)(1)(B) (regarding sale or exchange of 50 percent or more of the total interest in an entity's capital or profits within a twelve month period); or

(C) A division of the partnership under section 708(b)(2)(B).

(ii) Special rule for certain entities. For purposes of paragraph (d)(2) of this section, paragraph (d)(3)(i)(B) of this section shall not apply if the sale or exchange of interests in the entity is to a related person (within the meaning of sections 267(b) and 707(b)) and occurs no later than twelve months after the date of the formation of the entity.

(e) Effective date. Except as otherwise provided in this paragraph (e), the rules of this section apply as of January 1, 1997. The reference to the Finnish, Maltese, and Norwegian entities in paragraph (b)(8)(i) of this section is applicable on November 29, 1999. The reference to the Trinidadian entity in paragraph (b)(8)(i) of this section applies to entities formed on or after November 29, 1999. Any Maltese or Norwegian entity that becomes an eligible entity as a result of paragraph (b)(8)(i) of this section in effect on November 29, 1999 may elect by February 14, 2000 to be classified for federal tax purposes as an entity other than a corporation retroactive to any period from and including January 1, 1997. Any Finnish entity that becomes an eligible entity as a result of paragraph (b)(8)(i) of this section in effect on November 29, 1999 may elect by February 14, 2000 to be classified for federal tax purposes as an entity other than a corporation retroactive to any period from and including September 1, 1997.

[T.D. 8697, 61 FR 66589, Dec. 18, 1996, as amended by T.D. 8844, 64 FR 66583, Nov. 29, 1999]

[Reg.] Sec. 301.7701-3 Classification of certain business entities.

(a) In general. A business entity that is not classified as a corporation under Sec. 301.7701-2(b) (1), (3), (4), (5), (6), (7), or (8) (an eligible entity) can elect its classification for federal tax purposes as provided in this section. An eligible entity with at least two members can elect to be classified as either an association (and thus a corporation under Sec. 301.7701-2(b)(2)) or a partnership, and an eligible entity with a single owner can elect to be classified as an association or to be disregarded as an entity separate from its owner. Paragraph (b) of this section provides a default classification for an eligible entity that does not make an election. Thus, elections are necessary only when an eligible entity chooses to be classified initially as other than the default classification or when an eligible entity chooses to change its classification. An entity whose classification is determined under the default classification retains that classification (regardless of any changes in the members' liability that occurs at any time during the time that the entity's classification is relevant as defined in paragraph (d) of this section) until the entity makes an election to change that classification under paragraph (c)(1) of this section. Paragraph (c) of this section provides rules for making express elections. Paragraph (d) of this section provides special rules for foreign eligible entities. Paragraph (e) of this section provides special rules for classifying entities resulting from partnership terminations and divisions under section 708(b). Paragraph (f) of this section sets forth the effective date of this section and a special rule relating to prior periods.

(b) Classification of eligible entities that do not file an election– (1) Domestic eligible entities. Except as provided in paragraph (b)(3) of this section, unless the entity elects otherwise, a domestic eligible entity is–

(i) A partnership if it has two or more members; or

(ii) Disregarded as an entity separate from its owner if it has a single owner.

(2) Foreign eligible entities–(i) In general. Except as provided in paragraph (b) (3) of this section, unless the entity elects otherwise, a foreign eligible entity is–

(A) A partnership if it has two or more members and at least one member does not have limited liability;

(B) An association if all members have limited liability; or

(C) Disregarded as an entity separate from its owner if it has a single owner that does not have limited liability.

(ii) Definition of limited liability. For purposes of paragraph (b)(2)(i) of this section, a member of a foreign eligible entity has limited liability if the member has no personal liability for the debts of or claims against the entity by reason of being a member. This determination is based solely on the statute or law pursuant to which the entity is organized, except that if the underlying statute or law allows the entity to specify in its organizational documents whether the members will have limited liability, the organizational documents may also be relevant. For purposes of this section, a member has personal liability if the creditors of the entity may seek satisfaction of all or any portion of the debts or claims against the entity from the member as such. A member has personal liability for purposes of this paragraph even if the member makes an agreement under which another person (whether or not a member of the entity) assumes such liability or agrees to indemnify that member for any such liability.

(3) Existing eligible entities–(i) In general. Unless the entity elects otherwise, an eligible entity in existence prior to the effective date of this section will have the same classification that the entity claimed under Secs. 301.7701-1 through 301.7701-3 as in effect on the date prior to the effective date of this section; except that if an eligible entity with a single owner claimed to be a partnership under those regulations, the entity will be disregarded as an entity separate from its owner under this paragraph (b)(3)(i). For special rules regarding the classification of such entities for periods prior to the effective date of this section, see paragraph (f)(2) of this section.

(ii) Special rules. For purposes of paragraph (b)(3)(i) of this section, a foreign eligible entity is treated as being in existence prior to the effective date of this section only if the entity's classification was relevant (as defined in paragraph (d) of this section) at any time during the sixty months prior to the effective date of this section. If an entity claimed different classifications prior to the effective date of this section, the entity's classification for purposes of paragraph (b)(3)(i) of this section is the last classification claimed by the entity. If a foreign eligible entity's classification is relevant prior to the effective date of this section, but no federal tax or information return is filed or the federal tax or information return does not indicate the classification of the entity, the entity's classification for the period prior to the effective date of this section is determined under the regulations in effect on the date prior to the effective date of this section.

(c) Elections–(1) Time and place for filing–(i) In general. Except as provided in paragraphs (c)(1) (iv) and (v) of this section, an eligible entity may elect to be classified other than as provided under paragraph (b) of this section, or to change its classification, by filing Form 8832, Entity Classification Election, with the service center designated on Form 8832. An election will not be accepted unless all of the information required by the form and instructions, including the taxpayer identifying number of the entity, is provided on Form 8832. See Sec. 301.6109-1 for rules on applying for and displaying Employer Identification Numbers.

(ii) Further notification of elections. An eligible entity required to file a federal tax or information return for the taxable year for which an election is made under paragraph (c)(1)(i) of this section must attach a copy of its Form 8832 to its federal tax or information return for that year. If the entity is not required to file a return for that year, a copy of its Form 8832 must be attached to the federal income tax or information return of any direct or indirect owner of the entity for the taxable year of the owner that includes the date on which the election was effective. An indirect owner of the entity does not have to attach a copy of the Form 8832 to its return if an entity in which it has an interest is already filing a copy of the Form 8832 with its return. If an entity, or one of its direct or indirect owners, fails to attach a copy of a Form 8832 to its return as directed in this section, an otherwise valid election under paragraph (c)(1)(i) of this section will not be invalidated, but the non-filing party may be subject to penalties, including any applicable penalties if the federal tax or information returns are inconsistent with the entity's election under paragraph (c)(1)(i) of this section.

(iii) Effective date of election. An election made under paragraph (c)(1)(i) of this section will be effective on the date specified by the entity on Form 8832 or on the date filed if no such date is specified on the election form. The effective date specified on Form 8832 can not be more than 75 days prior to the date on which the election is filed and can not be more than 12 months after the date on which the election is filed. If an election specifies an effective date more than 75 days prior to the date on which the election is filed, it will be effective 75 days prior to the date it was filed. If an election specifies an effective date more than 12 months from the date on which the election is filed, it will be effective 12 months after the date it was filed. If an election specifies an effective date before January 1, 1997, it will be effective as of January 1, 1997. If a purchasing corporation makes an election under section 338 regarding an acquired subsidiary, an election under paragraph (c)(1)(i) of this section for the acquired subsidiary can be effective no earlier than the day after the acquisition date (within the meaning of section 338(h)(2)).

(iv) Limitation. If an eligible entity makes an election under paragraph (c)(1)(i) of this section to change its classification (other than an election made by an existing entity to change its classification as of the effective date of this section), the entity cannot change its classification by election again during the sixty months succeeding the effective date of the election. However, the Commissioner may permit the entity to change its classification by election within the sixty months if more than fifty percent of the ownership interests in the entity as of the effective date of the subsequent election are owned by persons that did not own any interests in the entity on the filing date or on the effective date of the entity's prior election. An election by a newly formed eligible entity that is effective on the date of formation is not considered a change for purposes of this paragraph (c)(1)(iv).

(v) Deemed elections–(A) Exempt organizations. An eligible entity that has been determined to be, or claims to be, exempt from taxation under section 501(a) is treated as having made an election under this section to be classified as an association. Such election will be effective as of the first day for which exemption is claimed or determined to apply, regardless of when the claim or determination is made, and will remain in effect unless an election is made under paragraph (c)(1)(i) of this section after the date the claim for exempt status is withdrawn or rejected or the date the determination of exempt status is revoked.

(B) Real estate investment trusts. An eligible entity that files an election under section 856(c)(1) to be treated as a real estate investment trust is treated as having made an election under this section to be classified as an association. Such election will be effective as of the first day the entity is treated as a real estate investment trust.

(vi) Examples. The following examples illustrate the rules of this paragraph (c)(1):

Example 1. On July 1, 1998, X, a domestic corporation, purchases a 10% interest in Y, an eligible entity formed under Country A law in 1990. The entity's classification was not relevant to any person for federal tax or information purposes prior to X's acquisition of an interest in Y. Thus, Y is not considered to be in existence on the effective date of this section for purposes of paragraph (b)(3) of this section. Under the applicable Country A statute, all members of Y have limited liability as defined in paragraph (b)(2)(ii) of this section. Accordingly, Y is classified as an association under paragraph (b)(2)(i)(B) of this section unless it elects under this paragraph (c) to be classified as a partnership. To be classified as a partnership as of July 1, 1998, Y must file a Form 8832 by September 14, 1998. See paragraph (c)(1)(i) of this section. Because an election cannot be effective more than 75 days prior to the date on which it is filed, if Y files its Form 8832 after September 14, 1998, it will be classified as an association from July 1, 1998, until the effective date of the election. In that case, it could not change its classification by election under this paragraph (c) during the sixty months succeeding the effective date of the election.

Example 2. (i) Z is an eligible entity formed under Country B law and is in existence on the effective date of this section within the meaning of paragraph (b)(3) of this section. Prior to the effective date of this section, Z claimed to be classified as an association. Unless Z files an election under this paragraph (c), it will continue to be classified as an association under paragraph (b)(3) of this section.

(ii) Z files a Form 8832 pursuant to this paragraph (c) to be classified as a partnership, effective as of the effective date of this section. Z can file an election to be classified as an association at any time thereafter, but then would not be permitted to change its classification by election during the sixty months succeeding the effective date of that subsequent election.

(2) Authorized signatures–(i) In general. An election made under paragraph (c)(1)(i) of this section must be signed by–

(A) Each member of the electing entity who is an owner at the time the election is filed; or

(B) Any officer, manager, or member of the electing entity who is authorized (under local law or the entity's organizational documents) to make the election and who represents to having such authorization under penalties of perjury.

(ii) Retroactive elections. For purposes of paragraph (c)(2)(i) of this section, if an election under paragraph (c)(1)(i) of this section is to be effective for any period prior to the time that it is filed, each person who was an owner between the date the election is to be effective and the date the election is filed, and who is not an owner at the time the election is filed, must also sign the election.

(iii) Changes in classification. For paragraph (c)(2)(i) of this section, if an election under paragraph (c)(1)(i) of this section is made to change the classification of an entity, each person who was an owner on the date that any transactions under paragraph (g) of this section are deemed to occur, and who is not an owner at the time the election is filed, must also sign the election. This paragraph (c)(2)(iii) applies to elections filed on or after November 29, 1999.

(d) Special rules for foreign eligible entities–(1) Definition of relevance. For purposes of this section, a foreign eligible entity's classification is relevant when its classification affects the liability of any person for federal tax or information purposes. For example, a foreign entity's classification would be relevant if U.S. income was paid to the entity and the determination by the withholding agent of the amount to be withheld under chapter 3 of the Internal Revenue Code (if any) would vary depending upon whether the entity is classified as a partnership or as an association. Thus, the classification might affect the documentation that the withholding agent must receive from the entity, the type of tax or information return to file, or how the return must be prepared. The date that the classification of a foreign eligible entity is relevant is the date an event occurs that creates an obligation to file a federal tax return, information return, or statement for which the classification of the entity must be determined. Thus, the classification of a foreign entity is relevant, for example, on the date that an interest in the entity is acquired which will require a U.S. person to file an information return on Form 5471.

(2) Special rule when classification is no longer relevant. If the classification of a foreign eligible entity which was previously relevant for federal tax purposes ceases to be relevant for sixty consecutive months, the entity's classification will initially be determined under the default classification when the classification of the foreign eligible entity again becomes relevant. The date that the classification of a foreign entity ceases to be relevant is the date an event occurs that causes the classification to no longer be relevant, or, if no event occurs in a taxable year that causes the classification to be relevant, then the date is the first day of that taxable year.

(e) Coordination with section 708(b). Except as provided in Sec. 301.7701-2(d)(3) (regarding termination of grandfather status for certain foreign business entities), an entity resulting from a transaction described in section 708(b)(1)(B) (partnership termination due to sales or exchanges) or section 708(b)(2)(B) (partnership division) is a partnership.

(f) Changes in number of members of an entity–(1) Associations. The classification of an eligible entity as an association is not affected by any change in the number of members of the entity.

(2) Partnerships and single member entities. An eligible entity classified as a partnership becomes disregarded as an entity separate from its owner when the entity's membership is reduced to one member. A single member entity disregarded as an entity separate from its owner is classified as a partnership when the entity has more than one member. If an elective classification change under paragraph (c) of this section is effective at the same time as a membership change described in this paragraph (f)(2), the deemed transactions in paragraph (g) of this section resulting from the elective change preempt the transactions that would result from the change in membership.

(3) Effect on sixty month limitation. A change in the number of members of an entity does not result in the creation of a new entity for purposes of the sixty month limitation on elections under paragraph (c)(1)(iv) of this section.

(4) Examples. The following examples illustrate the application of this paragraph (f):

Example 1. A, a U.S. person, owns a domestic eligible entity that is disregarded as an entity separate from its owner. On January 1, 1998, B, a U.S. person, buys a 50 percent interest in the entity from A. Under this paragraph (f), the entity is classified as a partnership when B acquires an interest in the entity. However, A and B elect to have the entity classified as an association effective on January 1, 1998. Thus, B is treated as buying shares of stock on January 1, 1998. (Under paragraph (c)(1)(iv) of this section, this election is treated as a change in classification so that the entity generally cannot change its classification by election again during the sixty months succeeding the effective date of the election.) Under paragraph (g)(1) of this section, A is treated as contributing the assets and liabilities of the entity to the newly formed association immediately before the close of December 31, 1997. Because A does not retain control of the association as required by section 351, A's contribution will be a taxable event. Therefore, under section 1012, the association will take a fair market value basis in the assets contributed by A, and A will have a fair market value basis in the stock received. A will have no additional gain upon the sale of stock to B, and B will have a cost basis in the stock purchased from A.

Example 2. (i) On April 1, 1998, A and B, U.S. persons, form X, a foreign eligible entity. X is treated as an association under the default provisions of paragraph (b)(2)(i) of this section, and X does not make an election to be classified as a partnership. A subsequently purchases all of B's interest in X.

(ii) Under paragraph (f)(1) of this section, X continues to be classified as an association. X, however, can subsequently elect to be disregarded as an entity separate from A. The sixty month limitation of paragraph (c)(1)(iv) of this section does not prevent X from making an election because X has not made a prior election under paragraph (c)(1)(i) of this section.

Example 3. (i) On April 1, 1998, A and B, U.S. persons, form X, a foreign eligible entity. X is treated as an association under the default provisions of paragraph (b)(2)(i) of this section, and X does not make an election to be classified as a partnership. On January 1, 1999, X elects to be classified as a partnership effective on that date. Under the sixty month limitation of paragraph (c)(1)(iv) of this section, X cannot elect to be classified as an association until January 1, 2004 (i.e., sixty months after the effective date of the election to be classified as a partnership).

(ii) On June 1, 2000, A purchases all of B's interest in X. After A's purchase of B's interest, X can no longer be classified as a partnership because X has only one member. Under paragraph (f)(2) of this section, X is disregarded as an entity separate from A when A becomes the only member of X. X, however, is not treated as a new entity for purposes of paragraph (c)(1)(iv) of this section. As a result, the sixty month limitation of paragraph (c)(1)(iv) of this section continues to apply to X, and X cannot elect to be classified as an association until January 1, 2004 (i.e., sixty months after January 1, 1999, the effective date of the election by X to be classified as a partnership).

(5) Effective date. This paragraph (f) applies as of November 29, 1999.

(g) Elective changes in classification–(1) Deemed treatment of elective change–(i) Partnership to association. If an eligible entity classified as a partnership elects under paragraph (c)(1)(i) of this section to be classified as an association, the following is deemed to occur: The partnership contributes all of its assets and liabilities to the association in exchange for stock in the association, and immediately thereafter, the partnership liquidates by distributing the stock of the association to its partners.

(ii) Association to partnership. If an eligible entity classified as an association elects under paragraph (c)(1)(i) of this section to be classified as a partnership, the following is deemed to occur: The association distributes all of its assets and liabilities to its shareholders in liquidation of the association, and immediately thereafter, the shareholders contribute all of the distributed assets and liabilities to a newly formed partnership.

(iii) Association to disregarded entity. If an eligible entity classified as an association elects under paragraph (c)(1)(i) of this section to be disregarded as an entity separate from its owner, the following is deemed to occur: The association distributes all of its assets and liabilities to its single owner in liquidation of the association.

(iv) Disregarded entity to an association. If an eligible entity that is disregarded as an entity separate from its owner elects under paragraph (c)(1)(i) of this section to be classified as an association, the following is deemed to occur: The owner of the eligible entity contributes all of the assets and liabilities of the entity to the association in exchange for stock of the association.

(2) Effect of elective changes. The tax treatment of a change in the classification of an entity for federal tax purposes by election under paragraph (c)(1)(i) of this section is determined under all relevant provisions of the Internal Revenue Code and general principles of tax law, including the step transaction doctrine.

(3) Timing of election–(i) In general. An election under paragraph (c)(1)(i) of this section that changes the classification of an eligible entity for federal tax purposes is treated as occurring at the start of the day for which the election is effective. Any transactions that are deemed to occur under this paragraph (g) as a result of a change in classification are treated as occurring immediately before the close of the day before the election is effective. For example, if an election is made to change the classification of an entity from an association to a partnership effective on January 1, the deemed transactions specified in paragraph (g)(1)(ii) of this section (including the liquidation of the association) are treated as occurring immediately before the close of December 31 and must be reported by the owners of the entity on December 31. Thus, the last day of the

association's taxable year will be December 31 and the first day of the partnership's taxable year will be January 1.

(ii) Coordination with section 338 election. A purchasing corporation that makes a qualified stock purchase of an eligible entity taxed as a corporation may make an election under section 338 regarding the acquisition if it satisfies the requirements for the election, and may also make an election to change the classification of the target corporation. If a taxpayer makes an election under section 338 regarding its acquisition of another entity taxable as a corporation and makes an election under paragraph (c) of this section for the acquired corporation (effective at the earliest possible date as provided by paragraph (c)(1)(iii) of this section), the transactions under paragraph (g) of this section are deemed to occur immediately after the deemed asset purchase by the new target corporation under section 338.

(iii) Application to successive elections in tiered situations. When elections under paragraph (c)(1)(i) of this section for a series of tiered entities are effective on the same date, the eligible entities may specify the order of the elections on Form 8832. If no order is specified for the elections, any transactions that are deemed to occur in this paragraph (g) as a result of the classification change will be treated as occurring first for the highest tier entity's classification change, then for the next highest tier entity's classification change, and so forth down the chain of entities until all the transactions under this paragraph (g) have occurred. For example, Parent, a corporation, wholly owns all of the interest of an eligible entity classified as an association (S1), which wholly owns another eligible entity classified as an association (S2), which wholly owns another eligible entity classified as an association (S3). Elections under paragraph (c)(1)(i) of this section are filed to classify S1, S2, and S3 each as disregarded as an entity separate from its owner effective on the same day. If no order is specified for the elections, the following transactions are deemed to occur under this paragraph (g) as a result of the elections, with each successive transaction occurring on the same day immediately after the preceding transaction S1 is treated as liquidating into Parent, then S2 is treated as liquidating into Parent, and finally S3 is treated as liquidating into Parent.

(4) Effective date. This paragraph (g) applies to elections that are filed on or after November 29, 1999. Taxpayers may apply this paragraph (g) retroactively to elections filed before November 29, 1999 if all taxpayers affected by the deemed transactions file consistently with this paragraph (g).

(h) Effective date–(1) In general. Except as otherwise provided in this section, the rules of this section are applicable as of January 1, 1997.

(2) Prior treatment of existing entities. In the case of a business entity that is not described in Sec. 301.7701-2(b) (1), (3), (4), (5), (6), or (7), and that was in existence prior to January 1, 1997, the entity's claimed classification(s) will be respected for all periods prior to January 1, 1997, if–

(i) The entity had a reasonable basis (within the meaning of section 6662) for its claimed classification;

(ii) The entity and all members of the entity recognized the federal tax consequences of any change in the entity's classification within the sixty months prior to January 1, 1997; and

(iii) Neither the entity nor any member was notified in writing on or before May 8, 1996, that the classification of the entity was under examination (in which case the entity's classification will be determined in the examination).

[T.D. 8697, 61 FR 66590, Dec. 18, 1996; 62 FR 11769, Mar. 13, 1997, as amended by T.D. 8767, 63 FR 14619, Mar. 26, 1998; T.D. 8827, 64 FR 37678, July 13, 1999; 64 FR 58782, Nov. 1, 1999; T.D. 8844, 64 FR 66583, Nov. 29, 1999]

Appendix F

COMPARISON OF BUSINESS ENTITIES

	S CORPORATION	C CORPORATION	PARTNERSHIP	LIMITED LIABILITY COMPANY ("LLC")
Limited Liability	Yes, for all shareholders	Yes, for all shareholders	Generally no; however *limited* partners have protection from the partnership's debts	Yes, for all members
Participation In Management	No restrictions	No restrictions	Generally no restrictions, except participation by limited partners must be restricted in order to preserve limited liability	No restrictions
Qualification	Various eligibility requirements including a restrictions on the number and type of shareholders, classes of stock and on the ownership of banks and subsidiaries	No restrictions	A limited partnership usually needs a general partner	No restrictions
Number of Owners	Maximum of 75	No restrictions	Must have at least 2	No restrictions

	S CORPORATION	C CORPORATION	PARTNERSHIP	LIMITED LIABILITY COMPANY ("LLC")
Classes of Ownership Interests	Only one, but voting and non-voting are permitted	Multiple classes are permitted	Multiple classes are permitted	Multiple classes are permitted
Check the Box Regulations Effect on Classification	If incorporated under State, Federal or Indian Tribal law it's a corporation	If incorporated under State, Federal or Indian Tribal law it's a corporation	Taxed as partnership, but may elect corporation treatment	Taxed as partnership, but may elect corporation treatment
Levels of Income Tax	Generally only one, but some states will tax S corporations as corporations (i.e. double tax will result)	Two	One	One
Special Allocations of Income and Loss	No, all allocations are pro rata of stock	Yes, if different classes of stock	Yes	Yes
Deductibility of Losses	Shareholders may deduct the corporation's losses only to the extent of their tax basis in their stock which does not include any portion of the corporation's debt	Shareholders may not deduct any of the corporation's losses	Partners may deduct the partnership's losses only to the extent of their tax bases in their partnership interest which includes their allocable share of debt for which they are liable	Members may deduct the LLC's losses only to the extent of their tax bases in their LLC interest which includes their allocable share of LLC debt
Liquidation	Generally, nontaxable at corporate level and taxable at shareholder level through passthrough of corporate tax items	Taxable to both corporation and shareholders	Nontaxable to the extent of a partner's tax basis in his partnership interest	Nontaxable to the extent of a member's tax basis in his LLC interest

INDEX

V

W

Call **1-800-543-0874** to order and ask for operator BB, fax your order to **1-800-874-1916** or visit our website at www.nuco.com to see our complete line of products.

PAYMENT INFORMATION

**Add shipping & handling charges to all orders as indicated. If your order exceeds total amount listed in chart, call 1-800-543-0874 for shipping & handling charge. Any order of 10 or more items or $250.00 and over will be billed for shipping by actual weight, plus a handling fee. Unconditional 30 day guarantee.

Shipping & Handling (Additional)

Order Total		Shipping & Handling
$20.00 to	$39.95	$6.00
40.00 to	59.99	7.00
60.00 to	79.99	9.00
80.00 to	109.99	10.00
110.00 to	149.99	12.00
150.00 to	199.99	13.00
200.00 to	249.99	15.50

Any order of 10 or more items or $250.00 and over will be billed by actual weight, plus handling fee.

SALES TAX (Additional)
Sales tax is required for residents of the following states; CA, DC, FL, GA, IL, KY, NJ, NY, OH, PA, WA.

The NATIONAL UNDERWRITER Company

The National Underwriter Company
Customer Orders Department #2-BB
P.O. Box 14448/Cincinnati, OH 45250-9786

2-BB

________Copies of *Working with LLCs & FLPs,* 2nd Edition ❑ (#241) $39.95
________Copies of *Working with S Corporations,* 3rd Edition ❑ (#147) $34.95

❑ Check enclosed* Charge my: ❑ VISA/MC/AmEx (circle one)
* Make check payable to The National Underwriter Company.
** Please include the appropriate shipping & handling charges and any applicable sales tax. (see charts above)

Card # ________________ *Exp. Date* ________________
Signature ________________
Name ________________ *Title* ________________
Company ________________
Street Address ________________
City ________ *State* ________ *Zip* ________
Business Phone (   ) ________________ *Business Fax* (   ) ________________
e-mail ________________

The NATIONAL UNDERWRITER Company

The National Underwriter Company
Customer Orders Department #2-BB
P.O. Box 14448/Cincinnati, OH 45250-9786

2-BB

________Copies of *Working with LLCs & FLPs,* 2nd Edition ❑ (#241) $39.95
________Copies of *Working with S Corporations,* 3rd Edition ❑ (#147) $34.95

❑ Check enclosed* Charge my: ❑ VISA/MC/AmEx (circle one)
* Make check payable to The National Underwriter Company.
** Please include the appropriate shipping & handling charges and any applicable sales tax. (see charts above)

Card # ________________ *Exp. Date* ________________
Signature ________________
Name ________________ *Title* ________________
Company ________________
Street Address ________________
City ________ *State* ________ *Zip* ________
Business Phone (   ) ________________ *Business Fax* (   ) ________________
e-mail ________________

NO POSTAGE
NECESSARY
IF MAILED
IN THE
UNITED STATES
BUSINESS REPLY MAIL
FIRST CLASS MAIL
PERMIT NO. 68
CINCINNATI OH
POSTAGE WILL BE PAID BY ADDRESSEE
The National Underwriter Company
Orders Department #2-BB
P. O. Box 14448
Cincinnati, OH 45250-9786
NO POSTAGE
NECESSARY
IF MAILED
IN THE
UNITED STATES
BUSINESS REPLY MAIL
FIRST CLASS MAIL
PERMIT NO. 68
CINCINNATI OH
POSTAGE WILL BE PAID BY ADDRESSEE
The National Underwriter Company
Orders Department #2-BB
P. O. Box 14448
Cincinnati, OH 45250-9786